Koch + Partner

1970 – 2000

Koch + Partner

Architekten
und Stadtplaner
Architects
and Urban Planners

Norbert Koch, Reg.-Baumeister, Architekt BDA
Wolf-Dieter Drohn, Dipl.-Ing., Architekt
Michael Schneider, Dipl.-Ing., Architekt
Wolfgang Voigt, Dipl.-Ing., Architekt BDA

Mit einer Einführung von
Wolfgang Jean Stock

With an introduction by
Wolfgang Jean Stock

Birkhäuser – Verlag für Architektur
Birkhäuser – Publishers for Architecture
Basel · Boston · Berlin

Einführung:	6	1 Flughafen München	14	5 Innere Neustadt Dresden –	58	8 Neue Terrasse – Ostra-Allee,	86
Wolfgang Jean Stock:		Munich Airport		Regierungsviertel		Dresden	
Architektur für die Stadt				Innere Neustadt, Dresden –		New Terrace – Ostra-Allee,	
Introduction:		2 Stadtwerkszentrale München	30	Government District		Dresden	
Wolfgang Jean Stock:		Municipal Department of					
Architecture for an urban		Works, Munich		6 Universität Leipzig –	64	9 Klärwerk München I	90
context				Chemische Institute		Gut Großlappen	
		3 Universität Erfurt	38	University of Leipzig –		Sewage Treatment Plant	
		University of Erfurt		Institutes for Chemistry		Munich I,	
						Grosslappen Estate	
		4 Messestadt Riem, München	48	7 Frankona Rückversicherungs	78		
		Messestadt Riem, Munich		AG München		10 Büro- und Wohnhaus	96
				Frankona Reinsurance		Wittstockstraße Leipzig	
		Bauen im städtischen	56	Building, Munich		Office and Housing Block in	
		Kontext				Wittstockstrasse, Leipzig	
		Building in an urban context		*Aufträge aus Wettbewerben*	84		
				Commissions resulting from		*Kreativität*	98
				competitions		*Creativity*	

Inhalt

Contents

11 Postbank Leipzig 100 Post Office Bank, Leipzig	14 Postsparkassenamt 114 München Post Office Savings Bank, Munich	17 BMW Forschungs- und 130 Ingenieurzentrum München BMW Research and Engineering Centre, Munich
12 Großes Ostragehege – 108 IGA Dresden 2003 Grosses Ostragehege – International Horticultural Show (IGA), Dresden, 2003	15 Arbeitsamt Augsburg 120 Jobcentre, Augsburg	18 Salzachhalle Laufen 134 Salzach Hall, Laufen
13 Deutscher Bundestag Berlin, 110 Alsenblock German Bundestag, Berlin: Alsen Block	16 Siemens AG Augsburg 126 Siemens Building, Augsburg *Wie wir arbeiten* 128 *The way we work*	19 BMW Verwaltungsgebäude 138 Dingolfing BMW Administration Building, Dingolfing
CAD als Arbeitsmittel 112 *CAD as a working tool*		20 Bundesanstalt für 148 Fleischforschung Kulmbach Federal Institute for Meat Research, Kulmbach

Anhang 150
Appendix

Zahlen und Daten der 152
Projekte 1 – 20
Facts and figures to projects
1 – 20

Arbeiten und Projekte 170
1970 – 2000
Works and projects
1970 – 2000

Biografien der Partner 184
Biographies of partners

Projektpartner und 186
Mitarbeiter
Project partners and
assistants

Rückblende: Nicht einmal zwei Jahrzehnte ist es her, da auch in Deutschland einige Wortführer des „Zeitgeistes" meinten, die Architektur der Moderne beerdigen zu können. Als Hauptstätte dieser versuchten Grablegung fungierte fünf Jahre lang das 1984 eröffnete Deutsche Architektur-Museum (DAM) in Frankfurt am Main. Schon in seiner ersten Ausstellung mit dem Titel „Die Revision der Moderne" rechnete Heinrich Klotz, der Gründungsdirektor des Museums, in einer simplen Schwarzweiß-Manier mit der gesamten modernen Architektur ab. Für seinen Generalangriff bediente er sich eines Kniffs: Er setzte die Moderne mit dem „Modernismus" gleich – und konnte somit behaupten, die Verheerungen des „Bauwirtschaftsfunktionalismus" seien auf die Programmatik der funktionalen Moderne zurückzuführen. Im gleichen Maße machte Klotz das DAM zu einem Haus der Propaganda für die Postmoderne. In mehreren Ausstellungen und Publikationen feierte er den neuen Eklektizismus als Befreiung, weil er das Prinzip „Funktion" durch das Prinzip „Fiktion" ersetzt habe.[1]

Trotz aller fundierten Kritik am schönen Schein der Postmoderne sind die Positionen von Klotz und seinen Mitstreitern auch in der Wissenschaft nicht ohne Wirkung geblieben. So hat Heinz-Günter Vester in seiner „Soziologie der Postmoderne" der postmodernen Architektur und Urbanität ein eigenes Kapitel gewidmet.[2] Neben zahlreichen US-amerikanischen Autoren fungiert Heinrich Klotz als Kronzeuge. Wie dieser unterscheidet auch Vester nicht zwischen Moderne und Modernismus – und kann dadurch die mit sozialem Anspruch weiter wirkende Moderne nahezu ausblenden. Besonders leichtfertig geht Vester mit der Kritik an der postmodernen Architektur um: An Stelle von Stimmen aus der Fachwelt lässt er mit Jürgen Habermas einen Philosophen und mit Klaus-Jürgen Bruder einen Psychologen zu Wort kommen. Vester will Habermas zudem mit dem merkwürdigen Vorwurf entkräften, er sei Beispiele für gelungene Werke der modernen Architektur schuldig geblieben – als gehörten nicht zahllose solcher Beispiele zum europäischen Bildungskanon, vor allem Bauwerke in der Schweiz, in Finnland und den Niederlanden. Gerade in diesen Ländern ist die Moderne derart lebendig geblieben, dass die Postmoderne überhaupt nicht Fuß fassen konnte.

Weltweiter Starkult

Mittlerweile hat in ganz Europa die Konjunktur für postmodernes Bauen nachgelassen. Im Rückblick wird der Aufstand der Eklektiker sogar belächelt. Nachhaltig beschädigt ist aber die Kultur des Gesprächs über Architektur und Städtebau. Weil die Missionare der Postmoderne in erster Linie ästhetische Kriterien geltend gemacht und dabei das Besondere, Spektakuläre, Aufreizende, „Fiktionale" propagiert haben, ist bei einem breiten Publikum das Verständnis für die Ganzheitlichkeit der Architektur aus technischer Leistung, kulturellem Auftrag, sozialer Verantwortung, politischer Bedeutung und wirtschaftlichem Handeln geschwunden. Kein Wunder also, dass die Publizistik weithin einem Starkult frönt. Dies betrifft aber nicht nur die populären Massenmedien bis hin zu den bildersatten Lifestyle-Magazinen.

Auch manche Feuilletons durchweht ein neuer Ton. Auf der Jagd nach „interessanter" Architektur wird weniger argumentiert denn fabuliert. Unter der Hand wird das Bauen zu einem Teil des Show-Business: Flüchtig erzählte Geschichten verdrängen so die Geschichte. Je bizarrer ein Projekt ist und je eigenartiger ein Architekt, desto mehr Aufmerksamkeit wird ihm zuteil. Auf diese Weise erscheinen dann Fassadenkünstler als Leitfiguren und Kuriositäten als Vorbilder.

Ein markantes Beispiel für publizistisch gestützte Prominenz bietet seit etlichen Jahren Frank Gehry, der noch

Einführung
Introduction

Architektur für die Stadt

Architecture for an urban context

von Wolfgang Jean Stock
by Wolfgang Jean Stock

Less than 20 years ago, even in Germany, some of the leading representatives of the "zeitgeist" were arguing that Modern Movement architecture could be laid to rest. For five years, the main venue of this attempted interment was the German Museum of Architecture (DAM), which opened in Frankfurt am Main in 1984. In the very first exhibition staged there, which bore the title "The Revision of the Modern Movement", Heinrich Klotz, the founding director of the museum, settled accounts with modern architecture in a rather simplistic, undifferentiated manner. To underpin his sweeping attack, he resorted to the strategem of equating the Modern Movement with "modernism", which allowed him to assert that the havoc wreaked by "economic functionalism in building" was attributable to the programme underlying functional modern architecture. At the same time, Klotz turned the DAM into a propaganda centre for postmodernism. In a number of exhibitions and publications, he celebrated the new-found eclecticism of this movement as a liberation, since it had replaced the principle of "function" with that of "fiction".[1]

In spite of all well-founded criticism of the superficial attractions of postmodernism, the positions adopted by Klotz and his comrades-in-arms had their effect even in the realm of science. Heinz-Günter Vester, for example, devoted a whole chapter of his book "Soziologie der Postmoderne" to postmodern architecture and urbanism.[2] Together with numerous US authors, Heinrich Klotz is a key spokesman in this area. Like him, Vester makes no distinction between the Modern Movement and modernism as a whole, which enables him virtually to ignore the continuing influence of the former in its pursuit of social goals. Vester also treats criticism of postmodern architecture in a particularly cavalier manner. Instead of seeking views from the professional world, he has Jürgen Habermas, a philosopher, and Klaus-Jürgen Bruder, a psychologist, present their views. Vester then seeks to invalidate Habermas' arguments with the curious accusation that he fails to cite successful works of modern architecture – as if there were not innumerable examples, many of which now belong to the canon of European culture, particularly in Switzerland, Finland and the Netherlands. In these countries especially, the Modern Movement has remained so vital that postmodernism was not able to establish itself at all.

Worldwide star cult

In the meantime, enthusiasm for postmodern construction has abated throughout Europe. In retrospect, the uprising of the eclectics now evokes a smile. The cultivated dialogue between architecture and urban planning, however, has suffered lasting damage as a result of this controversy. Because the apostles of postmodernism stressed mainly aesthetic criteria and propagated the special, spectacular, stimulating, "fictional" aspects of buildings, public awareness of the holistic nature of architecture – as a combination of technical achievement, artistic and cultural goals and social responsibility with a political and economic significance – has declined. It is hardly surprising, therefore, that the press and media pander in no small measure to the star cult. This is true not only of the popular mass media, but of the pictorially lavish lifestyle magazines as well.

mehr als andere zeitgenössische Architekten seine Arbeit weltweit wie ein Markenzeichen vermarktet. Der mediale Erfolg ist ihm stets gewiss: Sein Düsseldorfer Zollhof prangt auf dem Umschlag einer neueren Publikation zum Bauen für das 21. Jahrhundert – und eben kein Gebäude von Peter Zumthor, dessen „bodenständiger Minimalismus" nur im Innenteil des Heftes gepriesen wird.[3]

Zurückhaltung als Qualität

Dieser Starkult in der veröffentlichten Meinung hat Folgen für das öffentliche Bewusstsein, weil die Wahrnehmung von Architektur auf vorwiegend extravagante und bildhafte Bauten verengt wird – gleichsam auf die Spanne zwischen Helmut Jahn und Friedensreich Hundertwasser. Nicht wenige Bauherren haben sich dadurch schon verführen lassen: Bildhaftigkeit als Garant für Aufsehen, auch wenn die Funktionalität leidet. Auf der anderen Seite entsteht die übergroße Masse des Gebauten nach wie vor ohne jeden kulturellen Anspruch. Dazwischen behauptet sich jener Bereich, in dem die Traditionen der sachlichen Moderne auf vielfältige Weise fortgeführt werden. In ihm ist die Architektur von Koch + Partner angesiedelt: mit städtebaulich ausgerichteten und funktional ausgereiften Gebäuden, die auf jedes Spektakel in Gestalt, Farbigkeit und Materialität verzichten.

Solche Bauwerke mit der Qualität der Zurückhaltung erscheinen immerhin in Fachzeitschriften. Dort vor allem kommt noch eine Kritik zu Wort, die „den Gebrauchswert von Architektur für den Menschen berücksichtigt oder gar ins Zentrum setzt", wie Kristiana Hartmann eingefordert hat.[4] Und weil die Fachpresse mit der Praxis von Planen und Bauen vertrauter ist, pflegt sie in aller Regel auch keine wohlfeilen Vorurteile gegenüber privaten Investoren oder öffentlichen Verwaltungen. Schon gar nicht wird sie – bei aller Kritik an schlechten Ergebnissen – Wettbewerbe generell für untauglich erklären. Ihr ist nämlich bewusst, dass es kein besseres Instrument der Baukultur gibt als den möglichst offenen Wettstreit.

Erneuerung der Moderne

Die pauschale Kritik an der modernen Architektur nährt sich auch von der Legende, sie sei auf einer Art Einbahnstraße vorangeschritten. Der „Internationale Stil" habe schließlich alle Kontinente erfasst und weltweit das Antlitz vieler Städte entstellt. Verantwortlich dafür ist aber nicht die Moderne zu machen, sondern der Modernismus als ihre sinnentleerte Hülle, als rein wirtschaftlich determiniertes Bauen in quantitativ beliebiger Wiederholung. Bei der Moderne hingegen stand immer die Frage nach der kulturellen und sozialen Qualität des Bauens im Mittelpunkt. Deshalb hat sie sich auch auf mehreren Haupt- und zahlreichen Nebenwegen entwickelt. In nahezu allen europäischen Ländern ist mittlerweile die Geschichte der modernen Architektur eingehend erforscht. Dabei ist zu Tage getreten, wie sehr auch die Traditionen der jeweiligen Baukultur vom Dorf bis zur Stadt die modernen Strömungen beeinflusst haben. Am Beispiel von Bauformen, Materialien, Prinzipien der Raumorganisation, Kriterien der Lichtführung und im Verhältnis zur Landschaft lassen sich sogar regionale Unterschiede feststellen.

Von internationaler Gleichmacherei kann keine Rede sein. Umso weniger, als die beständige Erneuerung der Moderne auch von einer teilweise heftigen Selbstkritik begleitet war. Von Adolf Loos über Josef Frank und Alvar Aalto bis hin zu Herman Hertzberger warnten Protagonisten der Moderne immer wieder vor dem Abgleiten in einen Formalismus: Die Architektur sollte im Ausdruck reicher werden, um den Alltag von Arbeiten, Wohnen, Ausbildung und Freizeit zu steigern.

Dies bedeutet freilich auch den Abschied von den radikalen Forderungen der Avantgarden, die häufig an der Lebenswelt gescheitert waren, weil sie die Nutzer

A new mood prevails in a lot of feature departments. In pursuit of "interesting" architecture, there is less argumentation and more spinning of fables. Almost unnoticed, building is becoming part of show business: sketchy tales are replacing history. The more bizarre a project is and the more idiosyncratic an architect, the more attention will be devoted to them. Façade artists have become guiding lights, and curiosities now serve as models. For some years now, Frank Gehry has been a striking example of celebrity based on publicity. His work is marketed worldwide like a trademark, even more than that of other contemporary architects, and he can always be sure of media acclaim. It is his Zollhof scheme in Düsseldorf that gleams resplendently from the cover of a recent publication on building for the 21st century – not a work by Peter Zumthor, whose "vernacular minimalism" is praised only on the inside pages of the journal.³

Restraint as a token of quality

This star cult in the world of published opinion has an influence on public awareness; for the perception of architecture is thus reduced to extravagant buildings of bold visual quality, ranging perhaps from Helmut Jahn to Friedensreich Hundertwasser. A lot of building clients have been seduced by this: the temptation of resorting to bold visual effects as a sure means of attracting attention, even at the expense of functional needs. On the other hand, the vast mass of buildings erected today is still devoid of any artistic or cultural distinction. Between these two extremes lies a realm in which the tradition of an objective, functional Modern Movement continues to assert itself in a variety of forms; and it is here that the architecture of Koch + Partner is located: functionally well-considered buildings with an urban orientation; buildings that avoid spectacular gestures in their form, coloration and use of materials.

Buildings of this kind, distinguished by a quality of restraint, still command a place in specialist journals, where one can also find the kind of criticism that "takes account of the functional value of architecture for people, or that even makes this the centre" of its preoccupations, as Kristiana Hartmann once wrote.⁴ Since the professional press is more familiar with the practice of planning and construction, it does not generally harbour cheap prejudices against private investors or public authorities; and although it may criticize poor competition results, it certainly does not reject the competition system as a whole as inappropriate. It is aware that there is no better instrument in our building culture for achieving good design than the most open form of contest possible.

Renewal of modern architecture

The sweeping criticisms levelled against modern architecture thrive on the myth that it has gone down a one-way street. The International Style, it is argued, has finally reached every continent on earth and has disfigured the faces of cities all over the world. Responsible for this, however, is not the Modern Movement, but modernism as an empty container devoid of content, producing the kind of building that is subject to purely economic constraints and capable of endless repetition. In contrast, the Modern Movement was always centrally concerned with the cultural and social quality of construction. For that reason, it evolved along a number of different paths, both highways and byways.

The history of modern architecture has now been thoroughly researched in nearly all European countries. What has emerged in the process is how much the traditions of the respective cultures, from villages to cities, have influenced modern currents. Differences can be discerned in the forms of buildings, in the materials

überforderten. Besonders die nach dem Zweiten Weltkrieg in erster Linie von der Schweiz und von Skandinavien ausgehende „sanfte Moderne" hingegen hat es vielen Menschen ermöglicht, Bauten ihrer eigenen Zeit anzunehmen und in ihnen heimisch zu werden.

Wahrnehmung von Stadt

Zieht man Bilanz, so geht die Moderne aus dem 20. Jahrhundert nicht geschwächt, sondern gestärkt hervor. Wider ihre Absicht hat sogar die postmoderne Kritik dazu beigetragen. Deren Angriffe waren für die europäische Moderne eine Herausforderung, sich nochmals grundlegend zu erneuern. Dabei hat sie im Geiste der Dialektik durchaus Anstöße der Postmoderne aufgenommen. Auch im Städtebau ist die Zeit des von Aldo Rossi so bezeichneten „naiven Funktionalismus"[5] endgültig vorüber. Insofern ist die Moderne selbst schon historisch geworden. Was die Postmoderne vermitteln konnte, ist ein tieferes Verständnis für die Geschichtlichkeit der Stadt, für die Bedeutung der überlieferten Grundrisse und Raumbilder mit Straßen, Plätzen und Höfen, für die Rolle des Bestands im urbanen Zusammenhang. Brutale Flächensanierungen wie noch in den siebziger Jahren wären heute nicht mehr durchsetzbar. Sogar bei der Erneuerung von einzelnen Baublöcken muss man mit dem Widerstand der Öffentlichkeit rechnen.

Doch was sind die Gründe dafür, dass wir eine Stadt positiv wahrnehmen? Der Schweizer Architekturlehrer Martin Steinmann hat dies in seinem Essay über „Die Form des Gewöhnlichen, Täglichen"[6] sehr anschaulich beschrieben. Eine Stadt nimmt uns dann für sich ein, wenn sie durch ihre Bauten das Gemeinschaftliche ausdrückt, das Allgemeine des öffentlichen Raumes. Gewöhnlichen Zwecken dienende Häuser wie Wohngebäude oder Geschäfts- und Gewerbebauten, die durch Farben oder Formen „laut schreien", zerstören dieses Gewebe. Nicht die Häuser sollen das Ereignis sein, sondern das alltägliche Leben, das vor und in ihnen stattfinden kann. Neben den „Monumenten", welche die Stadt für unsere Erfahrung räumlich ordnen, braucht es die ruhigen Häuser als „Teig" der Stadt. Regelmäßige Straßenfronten und wahrnehmbare Blockeinheiten bilden den Hintergrund für die „Zeichen des Lebens".

Architektur für den Kontext

In diesem Sinne lassen sich jene Bauten von Koch + Partner verstehen, die in einem innerstädtischen Zusammenhang entstanden sind. Vorrang hat nicht das einzelne Projekt, sondern die Arbeit am Kontext. Diese Bescheidenheit bedeutet aber nicht, dass die Gebäude sich ducken – sie treten vielmehr vornehm zurück. An drei Fällen lässt sich exemplarisch zeigen, wie die Architekten Koch + Partner auf Herausforderungen geantwortet haben, welche die „europäische Stadt" in Zukunft noch vermehrt bieten wird.[7]

Beim Neubau des Arbeitsamtes in Augsburg (1989) bestand die Aufgabe darin, die Stadt außerhalb des Zentrums weiterzubauen. Das kompakte, hell verputzte Gebäude stellt das Pilotprojekt für eine Überbauung der angrenzenden Flächen dar. Die reizvolle topographische Lage unterstreicht es durch seine Position und Gestalt: Um einen alten Baumbestand zu schonen, ist der Eingangsbereich von der Straße zurückgesetzt, während die doppelt geschwungene Ostfassade einen Wasserlauf unmittelbar begleitet. Zum Außenraum hin ein markanter Körper, überrascht das Gebäude in seinem Kern durch die zentrale Halle, die als lichtdurchflutetes Glashaus den großen Innenhof teilt.

Wiederherstellung einer städtischen Blockbebauung war das Thema des Postsparkassenamtes in München (1993). Weil das Gelände zuvor nur provisorisch genutzt wurde, stand für den Neubau eine ganzes Quartier in der

used, in the principles of spatial organization, in the criteria governing lighting, and in the relationship between buildings and the landscape. This applies even on a regional scale.

There can be no question of international uniformity, especially since the constant process of renewal that went on within the Modern Movement was accompanied by an often quite violent process of self-criticism. The protagonists of modern architecture, from Adolf Loos and Josef Frank to Alvar Aalto and Herman Hertzberger, always warned against the dangers of drifting into formalism. Architecture should become richer in expression to enhance the everyday activities of working, living, education and leisure.

This, of course, also means bidding farewell to the radical demands of the avant gardes, which not infrequently foundered on the realities of life and asked too much of the users of their buildings. In contrast, the "gentle modernism", which had its roots in Switzerland and Scandinavia after the Second World War, has enabled many people to accept buildings of their own times and to feel at home in them.

Perception of the city
Taking stock, one may safely say that the Modern Movement emerges from the 20th century not in weakened form, but strengthened; and contrary to its intentions, postmodern criticism has been responsible for this in part. Its attacks posed a challenge to modern European architecture to subject itself to a fundamental process of renewal; and in the spirit of dialectics, it also adopted impulses from postmodernism. Even in the field of urban planning, the age of "naive functionalism"[5], as Aldo Rossi described it, is over. In that respect, the Modern Movement itself has become a historical phenomenon. What postmodernism did convey was a deeper understanding of the historical nature of the city; of the significance of traditional layouts and the spatial forms of streets, squares and courtyards; and of the role of the existing fabric in the urban context. It would no longer be possible to implement the brutal large-area clearance and redevelopment schemes that were still common in the 1970s. Today, one has to reckon with the opposition of the public to the renewal of even individual blocks.

What makes us perceive a city as something positive? The Swiss architectural teacher Martin Steinmann described this quite vividly in his essay on "Die Form des Gewöhnlichen, Täglichen" (The Form of Ordinary, Everyday Things)[6]. A town or city attracts us when it expresses a sense of community through its buildings: the universal quality of public space. Developments that serve ordinary everyday purposes, such as dwellings, offices or commercial buildings, and that "cry out loud" in their colours or forms destroy this tissue. It is not the buildings themselves that should be the central event, but the everyday life that can take place within them and in the space outside them. Alongside the monuments that structure the city spatially for our experience, one needs calm buildings as a matrix. The background for the "signs of life" that go to make up the city is formed by regular street fronts and perceptible block divisions.

Architecture in context
The buildings designed by Koch + Partner for inner-city contexts may be understood in this sense. Of paramount importance is the concept of work in a certain context, not the individual projects themselves. This act of restraint does not mean that the buildings deny their own identity, however. They stand back at a noble distance. Three examples demonstrate how the architects Koch + Partner react to the challenges that the "European city" of the future will increasingly pose.[7]

Nähe des Hauptbahnhofes zur Verfügung. Das „dualistische" Fassadenprinzip, das auch andere Projekte von Koch+Partner prägt (etwa der Neubau der Postbank in Leipzig, 1995), kommt hier besonders deutlich zum Ausdruck. Dezent gegliederte und deshalb großstädtisch wirkende Lochfassaden in hellem Putz haben den Straßenräumen eine neue Fassung gegeben. Nach innen hingegen sind die Fassaden weitgehend in Glas aufgelöst, wodurch die Arbeitsplätze an den ruhigen, fast intimen Höfen eine außergewöhnliche Qualität besitzen. Das große Gebäude ist jedoch kein monofunktionaler Bürobau: Urbanes Leben stimulieren die Geschäfte und gastronomischen Einrichtungen im Erdgeschoss.

Der Neubau der Chemischen Institute in Leipzig (1999) war mit dem Ziel verbunden, eine Stadtreparatur einzuleiten. Einerseits mit altem Baumbestand durchsetzt, ist der vorstädtische Bereich des künftigen Naturwissenschaftlichen Zentrums andererseits sehr heterogen bebaut. Sinnfällig orientiert sich der kammartig gegliederte Neubau zu einer vielbefahrenen Straßenkreuzung. Die beiden transparent geöffneten Flügel flankieren vor dem Haupteingang einen begrünten Hof, der zum Aufenthalt einlädt und von den Studenten sofort als kleiner Campus angenommen wurde. Verbunden werden die Flügel durch eine lange Querspange, die auch den viertelkreisförmigen Hörsaal enthält. Dahinter erhebt sich ein aus DDR-Zeiten stammendes Studentenheim in Plattenbauweise, das nicht nur saniert, sondern zugleich mit dem Institutsgebäude verbunden wurde. Durch ihre unaufgeregte Modernität stellt die neue Anlage ein Vorbild zum Weiterbauen dar.

Die Farbe des Erfolgs

„Es ist das Ziel (und auch die beachtenswerte Fähigkeit) erfolgreicher Büros einer bestimmten Größe, nicht das Außerordentliche zu bauen, sondern das im hohen Maße Ordentliche."[8] Mit diesem Satz ist das Selbstverständnis von Koch+Partner präzis umschrieben. Sie hängen nicht baukünstlerischen Träumen an, sondern verfolgen ganz offen eine Strategie des intelligenten Pragmatismus. Koch+Partner führen ein Büro, das als „Architekturfima" sozusagen mit beiden Beinen auf dem Boden steht und zugleich daran festhält, einen eigenen Beitrag zur Baukultur zu leisten. Dies ist den Architekten auch bei zahlreichen Projekten gelungen, die nicht im städtischen Raum entstanden sind – durch die Kultivierung moderner Konventionen ebenso wie durch eine sorgfältige Arbeit an Details. Die „Farbe des Erfolgs" (Olaf Winkler) zeigt sich nicht zuletzt darin, dass stets beide zufrieden sind, die Bauherren wie die Nutzer. Wenn Architektur soziales Wohlbefinden auslöst, dann ist ihre wichtigste Aufgabe erfüllt.

Anmerkungen
1
Siehe dazu Wolfgang Jean Stock, Vom Höhenflug zum Trauerspiel. Deutsches Architektur-Museum, Frankfurt am Main, in: Der Architekt, 1999, Heft 4, S. 18 ff.
2
Heinz-Günter Vester, Postmoderne Architektur und Urbanität, in: ders., Soziologie der Postmoderne, München, 1993, S. 153–173
3
Bauen für das 21. Jahrhundert, ZEIT Punkte, 1999, Heft 6
4
Kristiana Hartmann, Schmeckt Berlin nach Zukunft? in: Der Architekt, 1996, Heft 1, S. 15
5
Aldo Rossi, Die Architektur der Stadt. Skizze zu einer grundlegenden Theorie des Urbanen, Düsseldorf 1973, S. 10
6
Martin Steinmann, Die Form des Gewöhnlichen, Täglichen, in: Irma Noseda, Bauen an Zürich, Zürich 1992, S. 146–149
7
Zu den grundsätzlichen Unterschieden zwischen der europäischen und der amerikanischen Stadt siehe: New Urbanism, Stadtbauwelt 145, März 2000
8
Olaf Winkler, Die Farbe des Erfolgs oder die Strategie des Pragmatismus, in: Baumeister, 1999, Heft 9, S. 26

Notes
1
See Wolfgang Jean Stock, "Vom Höhenflug zum Trauerspiel. Deutsches Architektur-Museum, Frankfurt am Main", in: "Der Architekt", 1999, no. 4, pp. 18 ff.
2
Heinz-Günter Vester, "Postmoderne Architektur und Urbanität", in: Heinz-Günter Vester, "Soziologie der Postmoderne", Munich 1993, pp. 153–173
3
"Bauen für das 21. Jahrhundert", "ZEIT Punkte", 1999, no. 6
4
Kristiana Hartmann, "Schmeckt Berlin nach Zukunft?", in: "Der Architekt", 1996, no. 1, p. 15
5
Aldo Rossi, "Die Architektur der Stadt. Skizze zu einer grundlegenden Theorie des Urbanen", Düsseldorf 1973, p. 10
6
Martin Steinmann, "Die Form des Gewöhnlichen, Täglichen" in: Irma Noseda, "Bauen an Zürich", Zurich 1992, pp. 146–149
7
For a discussion of the basic differences between European and American cities, see: "New Urbanism", "Stadtbauwelt" 145, March 2000
8
Olaf Winkler, "Die Farbe des Erfolgs oder die Strategie des Pragmatismus", in: "Baumeister", 1999, no. 9, p. 26

The brief for the new Jobcentre in Augsburg (1989) required an urban extension outside the city centre. This compact building with its light-coloured rendered façades forms a pilot scheme for the development of the adjoining areas. In its location and form, the building brings out the attractive topography of the site. In order to preserve the fine stock of mature trees, the entrance area was set back from the road, while the double curve of the east face follows the course of a stream. The striking outward form of the building is contrasted with the interior, where visitors are taken by surprise by the central hall – a glazed structure filled with light that divides the large courtyard.

The theme of the Post Office Savings Bank in Munich (1993) was the reinstatement of an urban street block. Prior to this scheme, the site had been used for temporary purposes, so that a whole neighbourhood in the immediate vicinity of the main station was available for the new development. The "dual" façade principle, which Koch + Partner have used to good effect in other projects such as the new Post Office Bank in Leipzig (1995), is clearly evident in the Munich scheme. The restrained articulation of the closed façades with rectangular openings and light-coloured rendering lends the complex an urban dimension and gives the street spaces a new definition. On the inside, in contrast, the façades are largely dissolved into areas of glazing. As a result, the workplaces set out around the peaceful, almost intimate, courtyards are of exceptional quality. This large complex is not a monofunctional office development, however. Urban life is stimulated by the shops and gastronomic amenities on the ground floor.

The erection of the Institutes for Chemistry at Leipzig University (1999) was also meant to initiate a process of urban repair. The suburban setting for this future centre for the natural sciences was distinguished by a fine stock of old trees; on the other hand, it had an extremely heterogeneous built structure. Laid out in comb-like form, the new buildings are cogently oriented to a busy road junction. At the main entrance, two transparent, open wings flank an inviting landscaped courtyard, which students have readily adopted as a small campus. The new wings are linked by an elongated tract that terminates in a quadrant-shaped lecture hall. Behind this part of the development is a students' hostel dating from the time of the German Democratic Republic and built in prefabricated panel construction. This has not only been refurbished and converted in part, but also linked with the new institute buildings. The calm modernity of the new complex provides a model for further development.

The colour of success

"Successful offices of a certain size have the aim (and the remarkable ability) to build not incredible, but extremely credible and sound things."[8] These words accurately describe the way Koch + Partner view their role. The architects do not indulge in architectural dreams; they openly pursue a strategy of intelligent pragmatism. Koch + Partner is an office, an "architectural firm", so to speak, with both feet on the ground. At the same time, it seeks to make its own individual contribution to building culture. The architects have also succeeded in implementing these concepts in a large number of projects that are not situated in an urban context – through the cultivation of modern conventions and by paying careful attention to details. The "colour of success" (Olaf Winkler) is evident not least in the fact that the two groups for whom they design – clients and users – are happy with the outcome. When architecture helps to create a sense of social well-being, it has accomplished its most important task.

*Wettbewerb 1998
für Terminal 2:
Blick in die zentrale
Halle*

*Competition for
Terminal 2, 1998:
view into central hall*

Flughafen München

1   **Munich Airport**

1970   Plangutachten zum Masterplan
1975   Fortschreibung Masterplan
1976   Wettbewerb Betriebsbereich Nord · Ankauf
1987 – 1991 Allgemeine Luftfahrt · Terminal und Hangar · Planung und Realisierung
1998   Terminal 2 · Wettbewerb mit zwei Überarbeitungen · 1. Preis
1998 – 2003 Terminal 2 · Planung und Realisierung

1970   Planning report for master plan
1975   Development of master plan
1976   Competition for Technical Operations Area North: purchase of scheme
1987 – 1991 General aviation terminal and hangar: planning and construction
1998   Competition for Terminal 2, with two revision stages: first prize
1998 – 2003 Terminal 2: planning and construction

1970, das heißt 30 Jahre vor Erscheinen dieses Werkberichts, wurde mit den Planungen für den neuen Flughafen München im Erdinger Moos begonnen.

In 1970, thirty years before the publication of this review of work, the planning for the new Munich Airport in Erding Moor began.

Gesamtlageplan Flughafen München nach Inbetriebnahme 1992

General site plan for Munich Airport since the start of operations in 1992

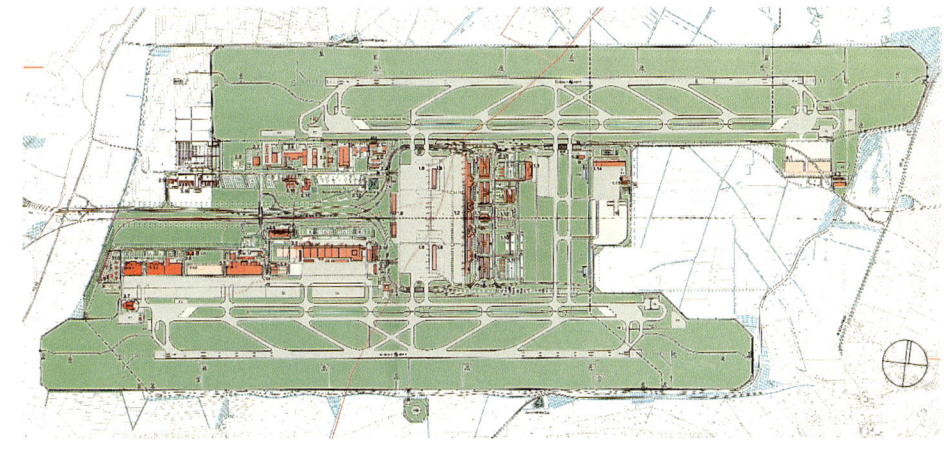

*Seite 16/17:
Die Abfertigungsebene in der Abflughalle nach der zweiten Wettbewerbsüberarbeitung: einfache Geometrie – Transparenz nach allen Richtungen*

*pp. 16/17:
Departures hall on passenger-handling level after the second revision of the competition scheme: simple geometry; transparency in all directions*

Plangutachten zum Masterplan

Sechs international zusammengesetzte Arbeitsgemeinschaften von flughafenerfahrenen Architektur- und Ingenieurbüros wurden 1970 beauftragt, Plangutachten für den künftigen Masterplan zu erstellen.

Norbert Koch war hierbei Partner der „Studiengruppe Luftfahrt", die aus den Ingenieurbüros Grube, Starnberg, Scott Wilson, Kirk Patrick und Partner, London, bestand. Norbert Koch bearbeitete im Wesentlichen die Bereiche „Städtebauliche Planung" sowie die Nahbereichsplanung. Die Studiengruppe legte zwei Lösungsvorschläge vor: neben einer klassischen „Terminal-Lösung" auch ein so genanntes Konzept „Mobil-Lounge".

Aus diesen „Urideen" für die Planung eines neuen Flughafens entstanden dann in den Jahren bis 1974 der Geländenutzungs- und Funktionsplan für die Gesamtanlage, der „Masterplan", sowie die Vorgaben zur Auslobung des ersten Terminal-Wettbewerbs. In diesem Zeitraum wurden die grundsätzlichen Leitlinien und Zielvorstellungen definiert, die das Erscheinungsbild des Flughafens bis heute maßgeblich geprägt haben.

Die wichtigsten Ergebnisse waren:
- Der Flughafen ist von West und Ost durch Straße (peripher) und Schiene (in der Mittelachse) erschlossen. Die Gesamtanlage und die Einzelbereiche bieten durch eine sinnfällige städtebauliche Ordnung sowie durch Offenheit und Großzügigkeit eine gute Orientierung.
- Übersichtlichkeit und Systemverständnis für die Passagiere.
- Erweiterungen sind unter Wahrung der städtebaulichen Ordnung und der Gestaltungsprinzipien ohne Beeinträchtigung durchführbar.
- Die Landschaftsgestaltung ist fester Bestandteil des Flughafengesamtkonzeptes.

Planning report for master plan

In 1970, six international ad hoc teams of architects and engineers, all with a wide range of experience in airport planning, were commissioned to draw up proposals and reports for the future master plan.

In this context, Norbert Koch was a partner in the Aviation Study Group, which also included the engineering offices Grube from Starnberg, and Scott Wilson and Kirk Patrick and Partners from London. Norbert Koch was basically responsible for the urban planning and the planning of the surrounding areas. The study group presented two sets of proposals: a classical terminal solution and a so-called "mobile lounge" concept.

These initial ideas for the planning of the new airport ultimately led to the Site Use and Functional Plan for the entire area – the master plan – completed in 1974, and to the formulation of the brief for the first competition for the terminal building. During this period, the basic guidelines and objectives were defined that were later to determine the appearance of the airport as one knows it today.

This resulted in the following main features.
- Road access to the airport is from the west and east via peripheral routes; rail access is along a central axis. The clear urban order, the openness and generous sense of space, evident in the overall site layout and in the individual sections of the scheme, ensure a good sense of orientation.
- A clear, easily comprehensible system was created for passengers.
- The facilities can be extended within the overall urban order and design principles without impairing the organization of the existing development.
- The landscape design forms an integral part of the overall airport concept.

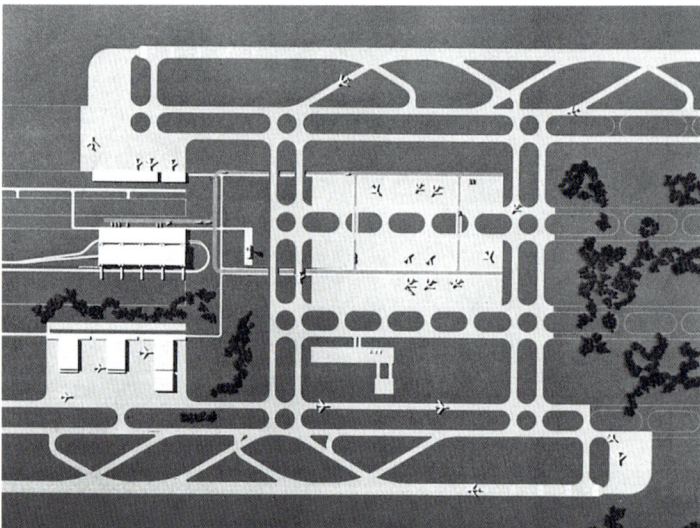

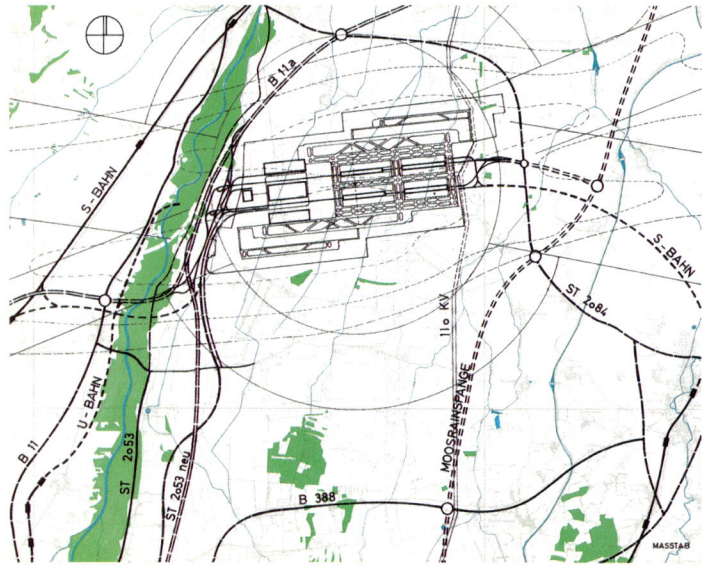

Aus dem Plangutachten 1970: Vorschläge für die innere und äußere Erschließung des neuen Flughafens

From the planning report, 1970: proposals for internal and external access routes for the new airport

Fortschreibung Masterplan – Städtebauliche Planung

Auf der Grundlage dieser Vorarbeiten wurde 1975 der „Geländenutzungs- und Funktionsplan" von der Planungsgruppe Koch-Dorsch-Grünplan fortgeschrieben (Städtebau und Projektkoordination: Norbert Koch; Verkehrsplanung: Dorsch-Consult; Landschaftsplanung: Grünplan GmbH, Professor Günther Grzimek). Im Rahmen dieses Planungsauftrags wurde der Schritt von der Planungsebene M 1:5000 in die Ebene M 1:2000 vollzogen. Auf der Grundlage der Raum- und Funktionsprogramme für die einzelnen Gebäudeanlagen im Betriebsgelände wurde zunächst ein „Städtebaulicher Entwurf" für diesen Bereich erstellt, der den westlichen Teil der Bebauungszone zwischen den nördlichen und südlichen Start- und Landebahnen umfasst.

In den fortgeschriebenen Masterplan wurden folgende Planungen bzw. Planungsergebnisse integriert: die Optimierung des Rollbahnsystems vom Mai 1975, das Raum- und Funktionsprogramm für den Passagierabfertigungsbereich, der städtebauliche Entwurf für das Betriebsgelände (hochbauliche Anlagen: Norbert Koch), Raum- und Funktionsprogramm für den Bereich „Allgemeine Luftfahrt", Rahmen- und Programmplanung für die Freiflächen (federführend: Grünplan GmbH), die Vorplanung der Deutschen Bundesbahn für den künftigen Fernbahnanschluss, die Funktionsplanung für die öffentlichen Flughafenstraßen (federführend: Dorsch-Consult).

Darüber hinaus wurde unter Beteiligung der Grünplan GmbH und Dorsch-Consult vom Architekturbüro Koch die Planfeststellungsunterlage „Plan der Baulichen Anlagen" erstellt, die Festlegungen zur städtebaulichen Ordnung und zur Grünordnung des gesamten Flughafengeländes enthält.

Damit waren alle wesentlichen Entscheidungen für die Gestaltung des künftigen Flughafens sowie die Voraussetzung zur Durchführung des Architekturwettbewerbs für den Terminal geschaffen.

Wettbewerb Betriebsbereich Nord

Auf dieser Grundlage wurde 1976 außerdem ein öffentlicher Wettbewerb für die Gestaltung des Betriebsgeländes Nord von der Flughafengesellschaft ausgeschrieben, an dem sich Norbert Koch zusammen mit Gabor Benedek beteiligte und einen Ankauf erhielt.

Bei allen diesen Planungsschritten war – von Anfang an – ganz wesentlich Michael Schneider beteiligt.

Ongoing development of master plan – urban planning

Based on this preliminary work, the Site Use and Functional Plan was drawn up in 1975 by the planning group Koch-Dorsch-Grünplan (urban planning and project co-ordination: Norbert Koch; traffic planning: Dorsch-Consult; landscape planning: Grünplan GmbH, Professor Günther Grzimek). Within the scope of this planning assignment, work progressed from a scale of 1:5000 to 1:2000. On the basis of the spatial and functional programme for the individual building tracts within the technical operations area, an initial "urban design" was drawn up for the western part of the development zone between the northern and southern runways.

The following planning concepts were adopted as part of the ongoing development of the master plan: the optimization of the runway and taxiway system dating from May 1975; the spatial and functional programme for the passenger-handling areas; the urban planning proposals for the technical operations area (building structures: Norbert Koch); the spatial and functional programme for the "general aviation" area; the outline planning and programming for the external landscape areas (overall responsibility: Grünplan GmbH); the preliminary planning of the German railways organization (DB) for the future main-line rail connection; and the functional planning for the public access roads within the airport (overall responsibility: Dorsch-Consult).

In addition, the Koch practice – in collaboration with Grünplan GmbH and Dorsch-Consult – prepared the planning documents for the statutory implementation of these measures (Building Development Plan), which regulates the urban and landscape planning for the entire airport site.

All main planning decisions affecting the design of the future airport and the conditions for the architectural competition for the terminal building were therewith taken.

Competition for Technical Operations Area North

Pursuant to these conditions, an open competition was held by the airport corporation in 1976 for the design of the Technical Operations Area North. Norbert Koch participated in this competition in collaboration with Gabor Benedek. Their scheme won a purchase prize.

From the very outset, Michael Schneider played a most important role in all these planning stages.

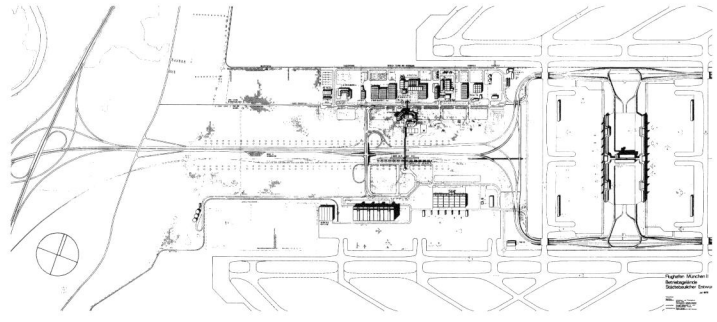

Geländenutzungs- und Funktionsplan 1975: endgültige Festlegung der städtebaulichen Ordnungsprinzipien

Site Use and Functional Plan, 1975: determination of principles of urban organization

Der Eingangsbereich zum Abfertigungsgebäude für die „Allgemeine Luftfahrt"

Entrance to "general aviation" passenger-handling building

Allgemeine Luftfahrt

1986 wurden wir – seit 1980 Koch+Partner – von der Flughafengesellschaft München mit der Planung der Anlagen für die „Allgemeine Luftfahrt" beauftragt. Dabei ergab sich die schwierige Aufgabe, wegen der zeitlich befristeten Unterbringung dieser Gebäude am derzeitigen Standort, trotz der wirtschaftlichen Zwänge, mit einfachen Mitteln etwas Anspruchsvolles zu schaffen.

Als „Allgemeine Luftfahrt" gilt der gewerbliche Flugverkehr mit Flugzeugen von Spannweiten zwischen 10 und 32 m. Die Gebäude der „Allgemeinen Luftfahrt", die aus einem Terminal und einer Flugzeugunterstellhalle bestehen, bilden einen kleinen separaten Flugplatz im großen Flughafen München. Sie liegen nord-östlich des Passagierabfertigungsbereichs mit einem eigenen Vorfeld und werden langfristig einer Terminalerweiterung weichen. Das Gebäude ist Anlaufstelle für Piloten und Passagiere im Privat- und Geschäftsreiseverkehr. Zoll, Grenzschutz, Sicherheitskontrollen, Wetterdienst, Flugberatung sowie Büroräume von Luftbildfirmen, Ambulanzdiensten und Regionalfluggesellschaften sind vorhanden. Die Unterstellhalle enthält außer den Hangars für Flugzeuge Wasch- und Wartungseinrichtungen sowie Werkstätten.

Die Bürobereiche des Terminals sind als Stahlbetonwandsystem für die Außenwände konzipiert, Stützen und Unterzüge in den Fluren. Die zentrale Erschließungs- und Wartungshalle ist eine eingestellte Stahlkonstruktion mit sichtbarem Tragwerk, die Stützen sind als Stahl/Beton-Verbundstützen ausgeführt. Die Fassaden von Terminal und Unterstellhalle sind mit großformatigen Keramikplatten hinterlüftet verkleidet, um den Anforderungen an reduzierte Radarreflektion zu genügen.

General aviation facilities

In 1986, our practice – known as Koch+Partner since 1980 – was entrusted by the airport corporation in Munich with the planning of the "general aviation" facilities. In view of the temporary status of this complex in its present location and the economic constraints that imposed, we were faced with the difficult task of creating high-quality architecture with simple means.

The term "general aviation" refers to commercial air traffic operating with planes that have wingspans of between 10 and 32 metres. The general aviation buildings, consisting of a terminal and aircraft hangar, form a small separate airport within the main Munich Airport. The complex is situated to the north-east of the passenger-handling zone and has its own apron area. In the long term, it will give place to an extension of one of the main terminals. The present buildings provide a check-in point for pilots and passengers travelling privately or on business and contain facilities for customs, border guards, security controls, a weather service and flight briefing, as well as offices for aerial photography firms, ambulance services and regional airlines. In addition to hangar space, the aircraft hall contains washing and maintenance facilities and workshops.

The office areas within the terminal were constructed in a system comprising reinforced concrete external walls, with columns and downstand beams in the halls. The central access and maintenance hall – inserted in the middle of the complex – consists of an exposed load-bearing steel structure. The columns are in a composite form of construction in concrete and steel. The façades of the terminal and the hangar are clad with large ceramic tiles with a ventilated cavity to the rear to meet requirements for reduced radar reflection.

Aus der zentralen Halle sieht man das Vorfeld und den Himmel über dem Flughafen.

From the central hall, one has a view of the apron area and the sky over the airport.

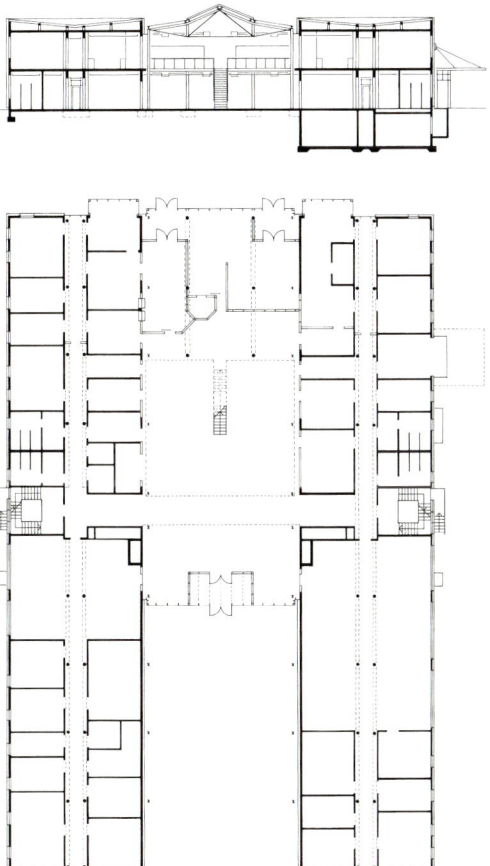

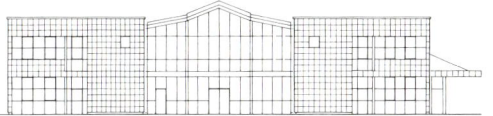

Grundriss Erdgeschoss, Schnitt und Ansicht zeigen das Konstruktionsprinzip.

Ground-floor plan, section and elevation reveal the structural principle.

Flughafen München | 21

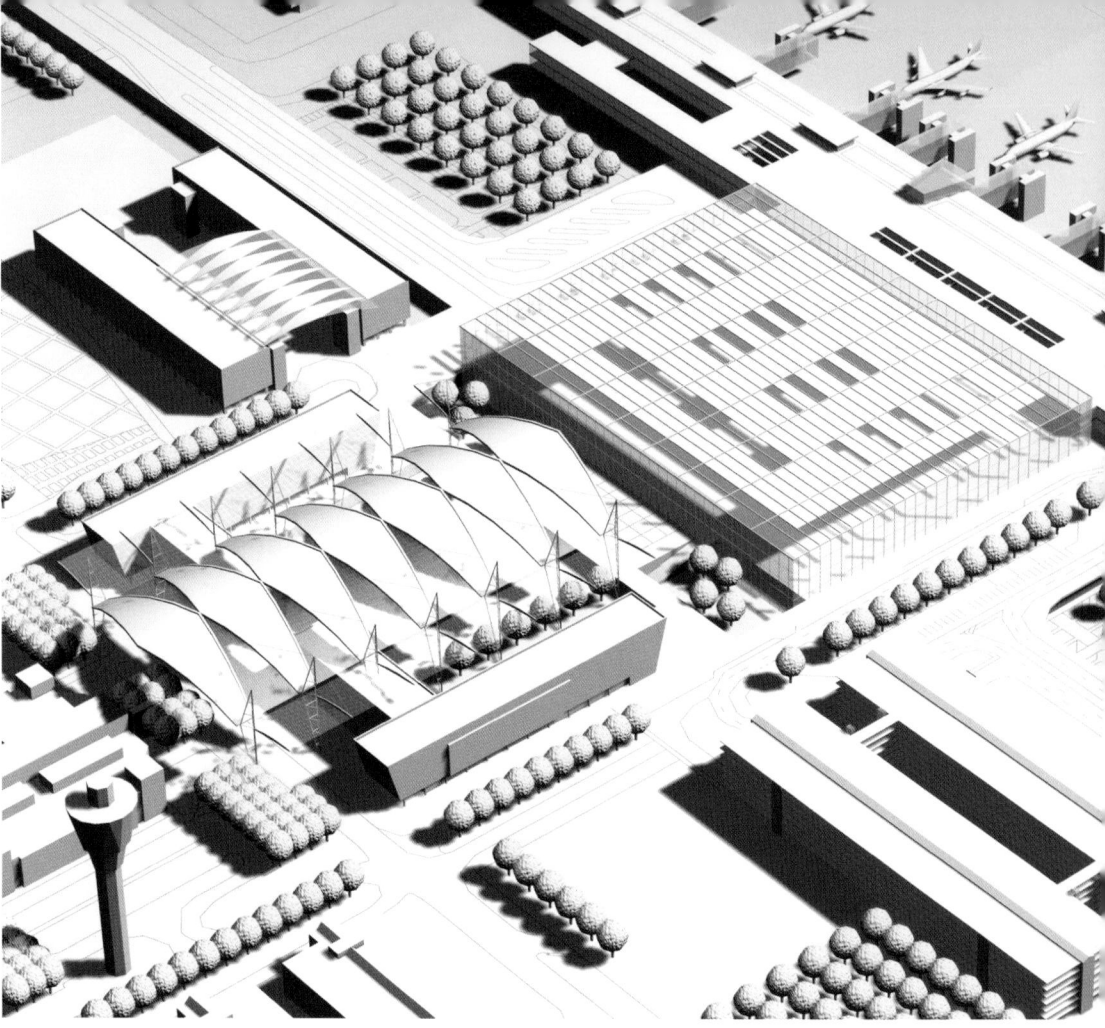

Wettbewerb Terminal 2

Das massive Verkehrswachstum hat den Münchner Flughafen früher als erwartet an die Grenzen seiner Kapazitäten geführt. Um für das mittelfristig zu erwartende Verkehrsaufkommen ausreichende Kapazitäten bereitzustellen, benötigt der Flughafen München spätestens im Jahr 2003 ein zweites Terminal mit der dazugehörigen land- und luftseitigen Infrastruktur.

Aus diesem Grund lobte die Flughafengesellschaft München im Dezember 1997 einen internationalen Architektenwettbewerb aus. Der Auslobung ging ein Teilnehmerwettbewerb voraus, der gemäß der EG-Sektorenrichtlinie europaweit ausgeschrieben war. Insgesamt wurden 15 Teilnehmer zugelassen.

Die funktionalen Anforderungen an dieses zweite Abfertigungsgebäude wurden im Vorfeld durch eine Reihe von Konzeptstudien festgelegt. Unter Berücksichtigung der bestehenden Gebäude und Anlagen des Terminals 1 sieht das Ausbaukonzept die Errichtung eines zentral organisierten Terminals 2 mit einem linearen Pier und die zukünftige Errichtung von Satelliten vor, die funktional dem Terminal 2 zugeordnet werden.

Die Wettbewerbsaufgabe umfasste das Terminal 2, die zugehörigen Parkgebäude mit den entsprechenden Straßenanbindungen und Vorfahrtsbereichen. Darüber hinaus waren Maßnahmen für eine zukünftige Satellitenanbindung aufzuzeigen.

Competition for Terminal 2

The enormous increase in flight traffic has brought Munich Airport to the limits of its capacity earlier than was anticipated. In order to cope with the volume of traffic expected in the medium term, the airport will require a second terminal – with all the ancillary land and air infrastructure this implies – at the latest by 2003.

The Munich Airport corporation therefore held an international architectural competition in December 1997. This was preceded by a preliminary contest, advertised throughout Europe in compliance with "EC sector guidelines", from which a total of 15 participants were admitted to the final competition.

The functional requirements for this second passenger-handling building were determined in advance by a series of conceptual studies. Taking account of the existing buildings that comprise Terminal 1 and the facilities it provides, the extension concept foresees a centrally organized second terminal with a linear pier and the erection, at a future date, of a number of

Die Modelle der drei Wettbewerbsbearbeitungsstufen: links das zur Ausführung vorgesehene, rechts die erste und zweite Stufe

Models of the three stages of the competition scheme: left, the proposals finally adopted for implementation; right, the first and second design stages

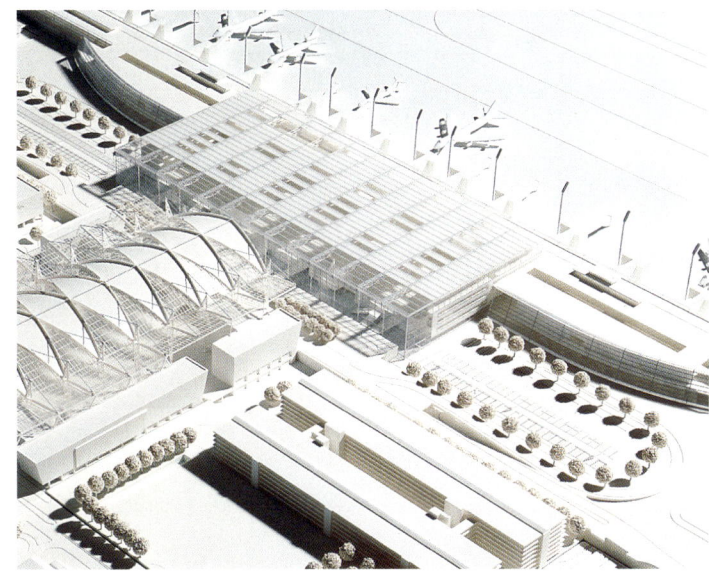

satellites that can be functionally connected to the new developments.

The competition brief included Terminal 2 and the ancillary parking structure, together with the necessary road links and approach areas. In addition, allowance was to be made for the creation of future satellite links.

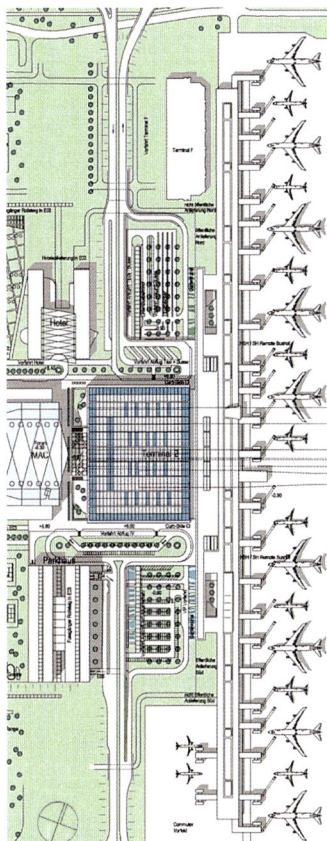

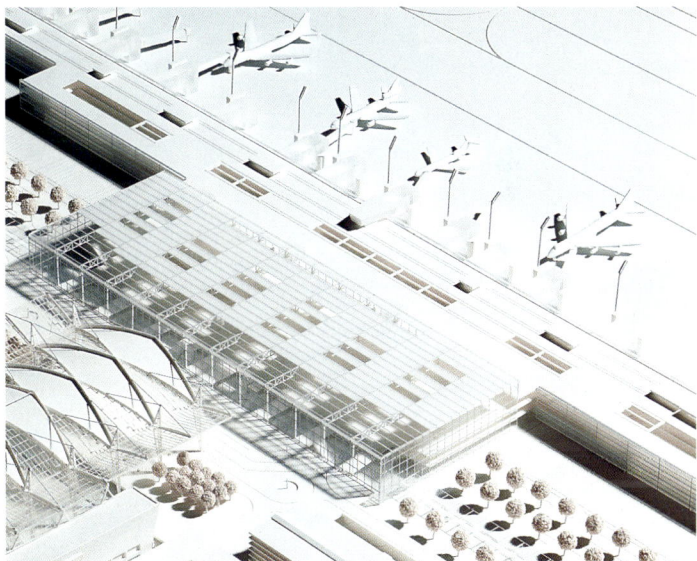

Lageplan und Modellfotos zeigen die zentrale Lage der neuen Terminalhalle, flankiert von MAC, Hotel und neuem Parkhaus.

Site plan and photos of model, showing the central location of the new terminal hall, flanked by the MAC, a hotel and a new parking block

Flughafen München | 23

Vorgaben für die Wettbewerbsaufgabe waren die zentral organisierte Passagierabfertigung, die Konzeption für Abflug und Ankunft auf zwei Ebenen, die Unterscheidung von Schengen- (ohne Passkontrolle) und Non-Schengen-Verkehr (mit Passkontrolle) auf zwei separaten Ebenen, die lineare Nord-/Südausrichtung des Piers nach den Vorgaben der Planfeststellung, die funktionale und architektonische Anbindung des Münchner Airport Centers (MAC) sowie eine direkte Fußwegverbindung zur S-Bahn.

Das Preisgericht empfahl dem Auslober einstimmig, die Architekten der 1. Preisgruppe, in der auch wir vertreten waren, mit einer Überarbeitung zu beauftragen. Dabei war der Einhaltung des Kostenrahmens unter Einbeziehung einer möglichen MAC-Erweiterung sowie unter Beibehaltung der vollen Funktionsfähigkeit von Hauptgebäude und Pier hohes Augenmerk zu schenken.

Daraufhin fanden zwei Überarbeitungen statt, die von einem Beratungsgremium bewertet wurden. Der Aufsichtsrat und die Gesellschafterversammlung der Flughafen München GmbH beschlossen im Juli 1998, uns auf der Basis des überarbeiteten Wettbewerbsentwurfs mit den Planungen für den Neubau des zweiten Terminals zu beauftragen.

The competition brief required the provision of centrally organized passenger-handling zones, a two-level departures and arrivals concept, a differentiation between Schengen traffic (without passport control) and non-Schengen traffic (with passport control) on two separate levels, a linear north-south alignment of the pier in accordance with the statutory planning requirements, tbe creation of a functional and architectural link to the Munich Airport Centre (MAC), and a direct pedestrian link to the rapid suburban railway (S-Bahn) station.

The jury unanimously recommended the clients to request the prize-winning architects – including our office – to revise their schemes. Special importance was attached to remaining within cost limits, while at the same time allowing for a possible extension of the MAC and maintaining the full functional efficiency of the main building and the pier.

The proposals underwent two revisions, which were evaluated by an advisory body. In July 1998, the supervisory board and a meeting of

Stahl, Glas, Transparenz, Großzügigkeit, Flexibilität und Einfachheit waren unsere Ziele beim Wettbewerb.

Steel, glass, transparency, ample space, flexibility and simplicity were our goals in the competition.

shareholders of the Munich Airport corporation decided to commission us with the planning of the new Terminal 2 building on the basis of the revised competition scheme.

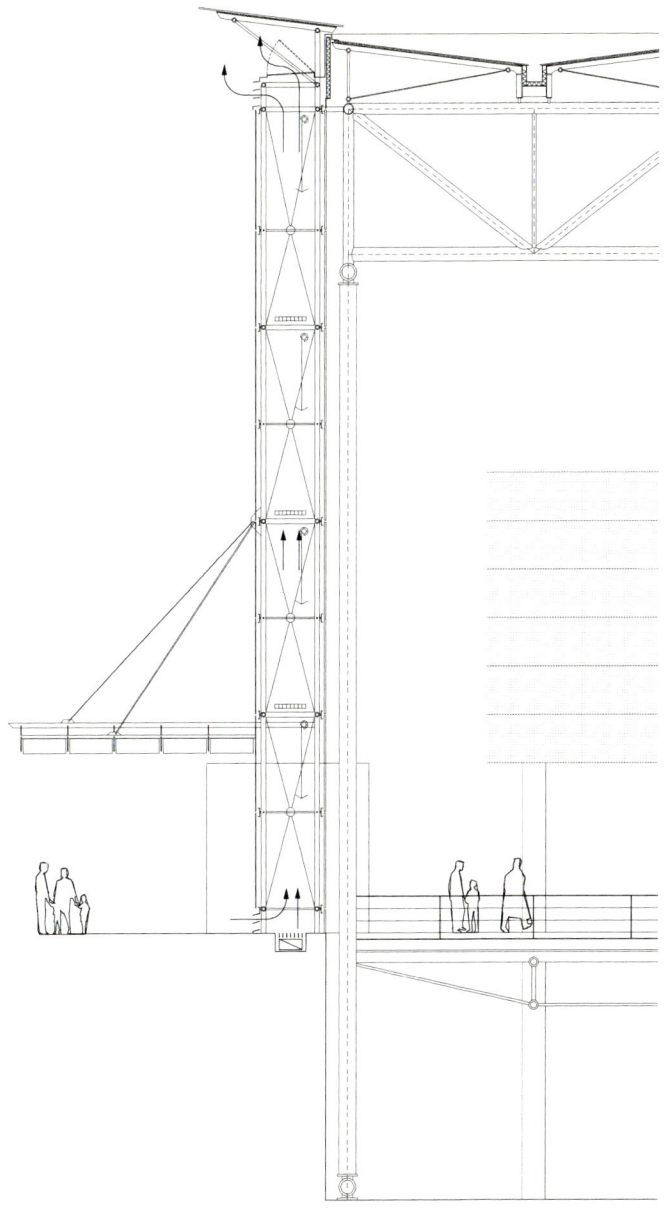

Glasdach und zweischalige Fassade – die wesentlichen Merkmale der Halle

The glass roof and the two-layer façade are the main features of the hall.

Flughafen München | 25

Die Durchfahrtsmöglichkeit auf der Abflugebene musste in der endgültigen Lösung entfallen.

The concept of a through-road on the departures level had to be abandoned in the final solution.

Landseitige Erschließung (erste Überarbeitung)

Access routes on the side facing away from the airfield (first revision)

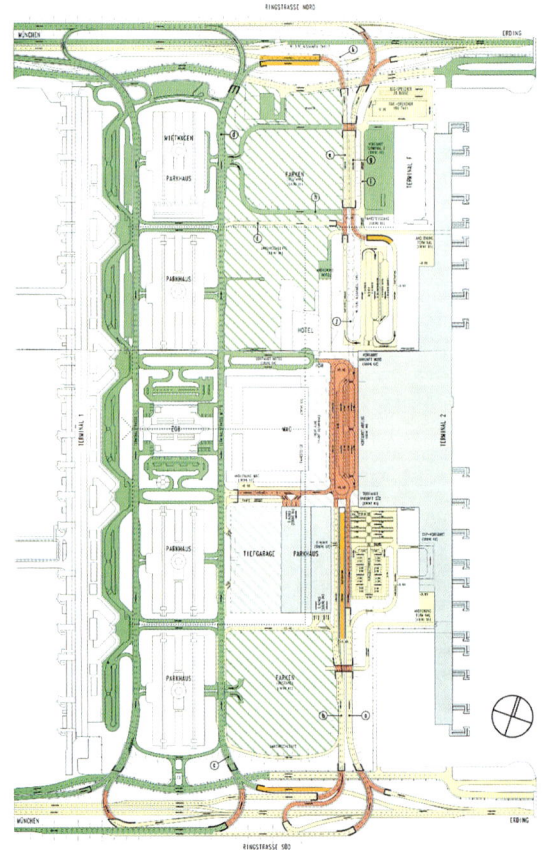

Der Terminal 2 ist als zentrales Zwei-Ebenen-Abfertigungsgebäude mit entsprechender Straßenanbindung und Vorfahrtsbereichen im Norden und Süden des zentralen Hauptgebäudes konzipiert. Landseitig sind das Erdgeschoss (Ebene 03) als Ankunftsebene und die Ebene 04 als Abflugebene organisiert. Luftseitig werden auf der Ebene 04 Schengen-Passagiere und auf Ebene 05 Non-Schengen-Passagiere abgefertigt. Die Ebene 03 (Vorfeldebene) wird luftseitig hauptsächlich für betriebliche Zwecke genutzt. Funktional und architektonisch schließt der neue Terminal im Westen unmittelbar mit dem zentralen Hauptgebäude an das MAC an und ist über dessen Forum fußläufig direkt mit der S-Bahn sowie über das Zentralgebäude mit dem Terminal 1 verbunden. Der Pier ordnet sich funktional dem neu geplanten Vorfeld Ost zu. Im Süden und Norden sind, dem Pier westlich vorgelagert, Verwaltungsbereiche organisiert.

Neben den Einrichtungen für die Passagierabfertigung und den dafür erforderlichen betrieblichen und technischen Einrichtungen liegt eine große Bedeutung in der Integration der kommerziellen Flächen.

Das erste Untergeschoss dient im Wesentlichen der technischen Ver- und Entsorgung sowie der Anlieferung. Darüber hinaus ist dem Terminalgebäude unter dem Vorfeld ein Bahnhof für ein Personentransportsystem vorgelagert, der die zukünftige Anbindung an die Satelliten gewährleistet. Über Rolltreppenanlagen sind die Schengen- und die Non-Schengen-Ebene des Piers erreichbar. Unterhalb der Ebene 02 werden im Westen ein Gepäcktunnel und ein zentraler Medienkanal an den Bestand angeschlossen und östlich unter dem Vorfeld zum Satellitenbereich weitergeführt. Ebenso werden Vorabmaßnahmen für einen späteren Fernbahnanschluss in die Planung integriert, der bestehende S-Bahn-Tunnel muss berührungsfrei überbaut und verlängert werden.

*Ankunfts- und Abflug-
ebene im räumlichen
Zusammenhang
(Wettbewerb)*

*Spatial relationship
between arrivals and
departures levels
(competition)*

Terminal 2 was conceived as a central, two-level passenger-handling building with the necessary road links and access areas to north and south of the central section of the main tract. The arrivals area is situated on the ground floor (level 03) on the side facing away from the airfield; the departures area is on level 04. On the side facing the airfield, level 04 is designated for Schengen passengers; level 05 for non-Schengen passengers. On the airfield face, level 03 (apron level) will be used largely for operational purposes. The central tract of the new terminal is closely linked, both functionally and architecturally, with the MAC to the west. Pedestrians also have direct access to the S-Bahn station via the MAC forum and to Terminal 1 via the central building. The pier is functionally oriented to the newly planned apron area to the east. On the western side of the pier, to the north and south of the terminal, are administration buildings.

In addition to the design of the passenger-handling areas and the requisite operational and technical facilities, great importance was attached to the integration of the commercial areas.

The first basement level accommodates mainly technical supply and waste-disposal services and the deliveries area. In addition, in front of the terminal building beneath the apron area is a station for a passenger transport system which will provide a link to the future satellites. The passport and non-passport passenger levels of the pier are reached via escalators. Beneath level 02 at the western end, a luggage tunnel and a central media duct will be connected to the existing facilities and extended eastwards beneath the apron to the satellite area. Similarly, preparatory steps will be taken to implement the planning for a later main-line railway link. This would necessitate building over the existing S-Bahn tunnel and extending it without interfering with the present structure or the transport service.

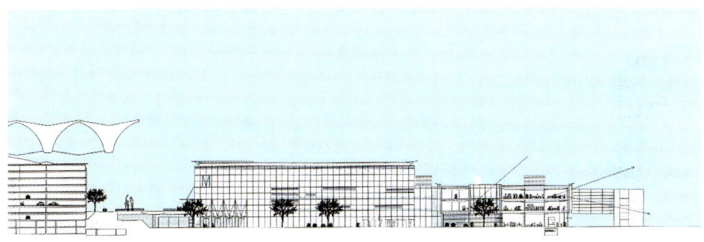

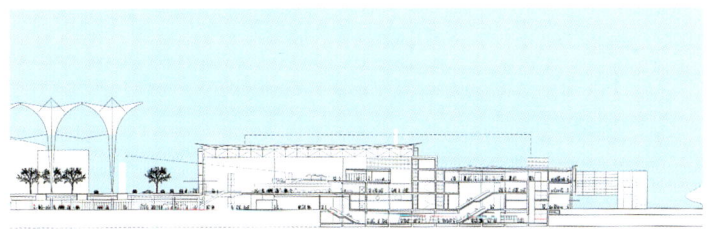

*Ansicht und Schnitt
von Süden*

*South elevation and
section*

Seite 28/29:
Fotomontage: Das Hallendach mit „Lichtsegel" und die zweischalige Fassade mit Blick auf MAC und Hotel Kempinski

pp. 28/29:
Photomontage of hall roof with "light sail" and the two-layer façade, with views to the MAC and the Kempinski Hotel

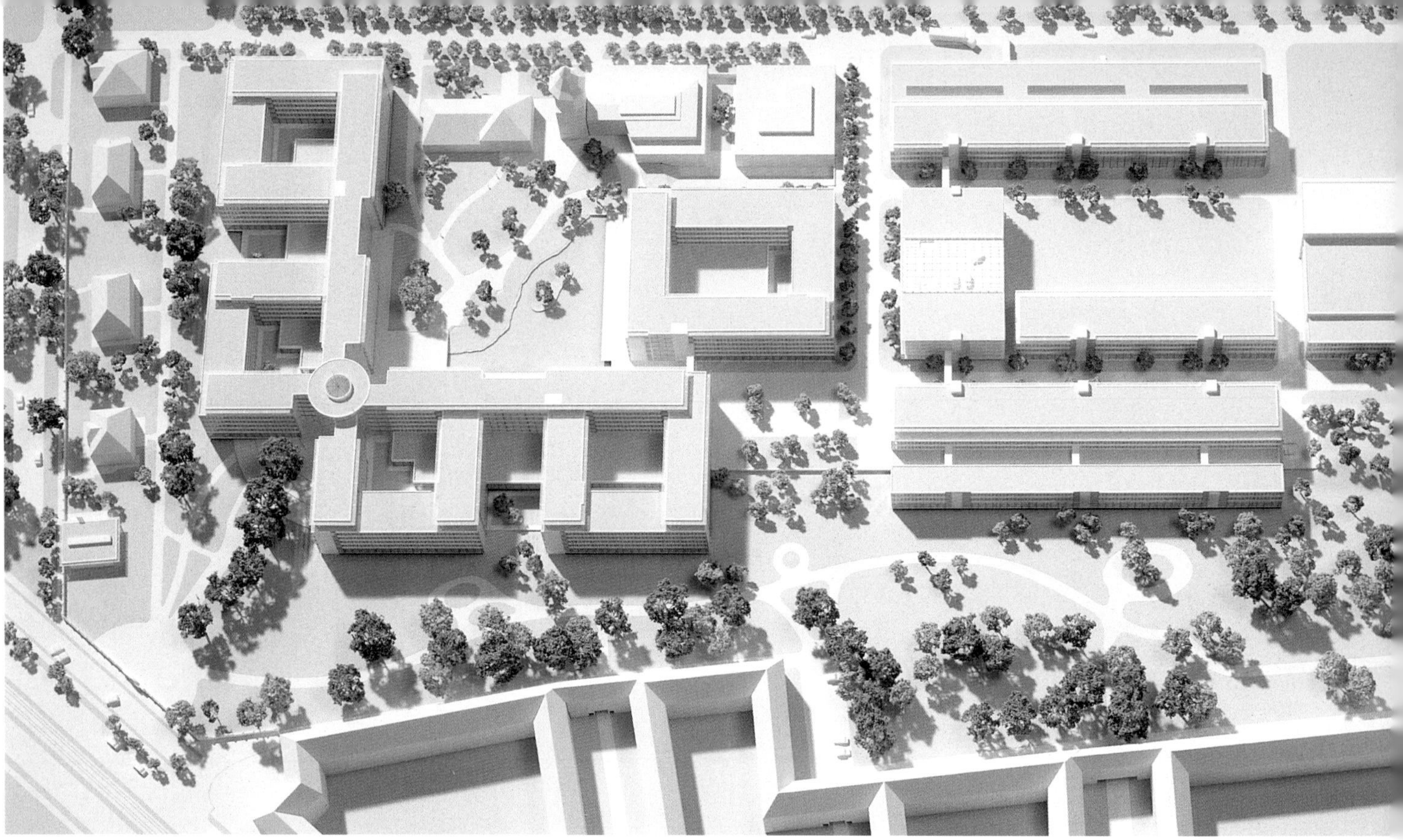

*Modellfoto
Stand Entwurf 1997.
Fünf Baublöcke formen zusammen mit den Bestandsgebäuden und dem Wasserturm einen zentralen Innenhof mit Grünanlagen und einem See.*

*Photo of model: design stage, 1997.
In conjunction with the existing structures and the water tower, the five new blocks form a central, enclosed, landscaped courtyard with a lake.*

Bürozentrum Ostansicht

East elevation of administration centre

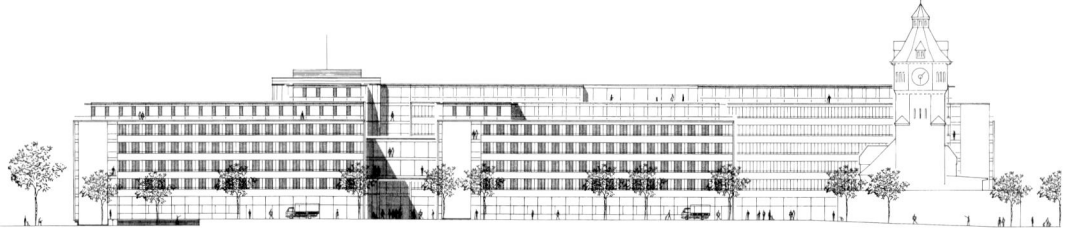

Die neue Zentrale für die Stadtwerke München wird von bestehenden Bäumen eingerahmt. Im Süden der Gesamtanlage wurde eine öffentliche Grünanlage geschaffen. Der Hauptzugang zum zentralen, gläsernen Eingangsbauteil erfolgt über die vorhandene Toranlage an der Dachauer Straße. Hiermit ergeben sich drei übergeordnete städtebauliche Bezüge:

- Nach Norden: Entlang der bestehenden Dienstvillen und dem alten Baumbestand erschließt sich die zukünftige Anbindung zum Georg-Brauchle-Ring.
- Nach Nordosten in der Diagonalen: zum alten Wasserturm, der vom Eingangsbauteil aus sichtbar ist und der dem zentralen Innenhof als Orientierungsmerkmal dient.
- Nach Osten: öffentlicher Grünzug, denkmalgeschützte Fassade der „Borstei" und Zugang zum Olympiagelände.

The new centre for the Municipal Department of Works in Munich is set off by the existing stock of trees on the site and by a newly created public landscaped area to the south of the complex. The principal line of access to the central glazed entrance structure is via an existing gateway in Dachauer Strasse. The layout has three main urban points of reference.

- To the north: the future link to the Georg-Brauchle-Ring road leads past the existing staff villas and the old stock of trees.
- On the diagonal to the northeast: to the old water tower, which is visible from the entrance structure and serves as a point of orientation within the central courtyard.
- To the east: to the public landscaped strip, the listed façade of the "Borstei" housing development, and the 1972 Olympics site.

Stadtwerkszentrale München

2 Municipal Department of Works, Munich

1980 Wettbewerb · 1. Preis
1989 – 1995 Labor · Planung und Realisierung
1992 – 1995 24-Stunden-Trakt · Planung und Realisierung
1995 – 1997 Gasdruckregler · Planung und Realisierung
1994 – 2001 Büro- und Betriebszentrum
 Planung und Realisierung

1980 Competition: first prize
1989 – 1995 Laboratory: planning and construction
1992 – 1995 24-hour tract: planning and construction
1995 – 1997 Gas-pressure control centre:
 planning and construction
1994 – 2001 Administration and works centre:
 planning and construction

Fünf Baublöcke im Zusammenschluss bilden eine Büro- und Betriebszentrale im Grünen.

An ensemble of five blocks, forming a works and administration centre in a landscaped setting

Blick vom Olympiaturm in Richtung Westen auf die Baustelle der Stadtwerkszentrale

View from Olympic Tower looking west towards the Municipal Department of Works building site

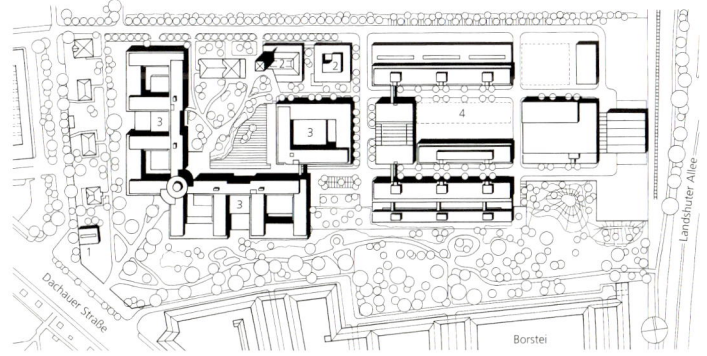

Lageplan
1 Gasdruckregler
2 Labor und 24h-Trakt Gas/Wasser
3 Bürozentrum
4 Betriebszentrum

Site plan
1 Gas-pressure control centre
2 Laboratory and 24-hour tract
 gas/water
3 Administration centre
4 Works centre

Die vorgezogen realisierten Bauteile Labor und 24-Stunden-Trakt formen einen Hof mit filigraner Stahl-Verbindungsbrücke.

The laboratory and the 24-hour tract, erected before the other structures, are linked by a slenderly dimensioned steel bridge and form a courtyard space.

Vorgeschichte

Schon seit Ende der 50er Jahre waren die Stadtwerke bestrebt, ihre Büro- und Betriebseinheiten in einem zentralen Standort zusammenzufassen. Nach mehreren Standortvarianten wurde 1979 das Gelände an der Dachauer Straße für den zukünftigen Standort bestimmt.

Auf der Basis eines dazu erarbeiteten Raum- und Funktionsprogrammes wurde 1980 ein Wettbewerb durchgeführt und der 1. Preis dem Architekten Norbert Koch zuerkannt. Dieser Wettbewerbsentwurf bildete die nahezu unveränderte Grundlage für den Vorentwurf, der im Mai 1981 vorgelegt wurde. Nach einer zwischenzeitlichen Überarbeitung des Vorentwurfs, zur Vereinfachung und Einsparung, wurde der Entwurf bis Mai 1983 bearbeitet und abgeschlossen.

Nach einer Planungsunterbrechung wurde, auf Basis des Entwurfskonzeptes, der Bebauungsplan für die Stadtwerke 1987 rechtskräftig. Nach Wiederaufnahme der Planungsarbeiten im Juli 1994 legten die Architekten Koch+Partner im Juli 1995 den aktuellen Nutzeranforderungen entsprechende Bebauungskonzepte vor, die eine Zentralisierung aller nicht standortgebundenen betrieblichen Einrichtungen ermöglichen. Im Vorfeld der gesamten Baumaßnahme entstanden die zunächst notwendigen Bauten, ein Gasdruckregler, ein Labor und ein so genannter 24-Stunden-Trakt, die Leitzentrale der Gas- und Wasserversorgung Münchens.

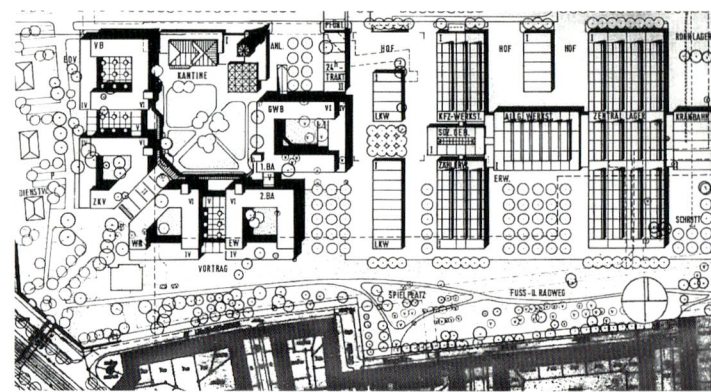

oben:
Wettbewerb 1980

Top: competition scheme, 1980

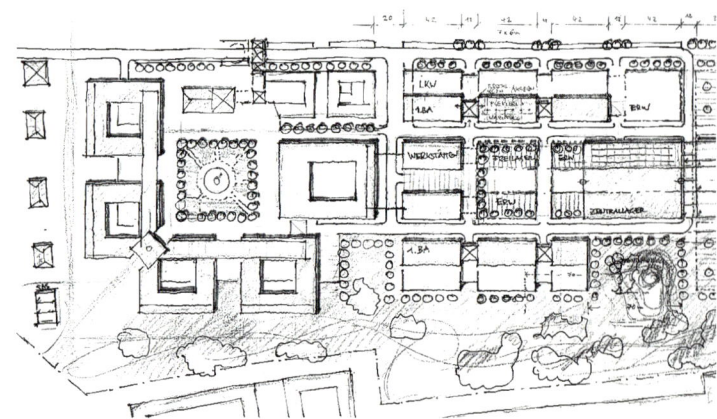

unten:
Planungszwischenstand 1995

Bottom: intermediate stage of planning, 1995

Geordnete Installationen und technische Strukturen prägen das Bild des Gasdruckreglers.

The appearance of the gas-pressure control building is dominated by the technical structures and the systematic layout of the plant.

Gasdruckregler

Der Neubau der Gasdruckregelanlage wurde durch den Neubau der Stadtwerkszentrale aus städtebaulichen Gründen und wegen der Betriebssicherheit erforderlich. Das pavillonartige Gebäude liegt in der Flucht der ehemaligen Dienstvillen im Eingangsbereich und setzt sich aus dem eigentlichen Reglerraum und den im Untergeschoss angeordneten Technikräumen zusammen. Transparent gestaltete Abschnitte der Fassade gewähren Einblick in das Gebäudeinnere und dessen hochtechnische Ausstattung. Die geschlossenen Flächen sind mit Keramikplatten System „Argeton" verkleidet und bilden einen gestalterischen Bezug zu den Fassaden des Neubaus der Stadtwerkszentrale.

History

Since the late 1950s, the Municipal Department of Works had sought to unite its administration and works buildings in a central position.
In 1979, after exploring a number of alternative sites, the authorities decided in favour of a location in Dachauer Strasse.

A functional and spatial programme was drawn up that formed the basis of the architectural competition held in 1980, in which Norbert Koch won first prize. The preliminary design presented in May 1981 was, in turn, based on the competition scheme, which remained virtually unaltered. The subsequent simplifications and savings that were required led to a reworking of the preliminary design. Planning then continued until the completion of the design work in May 1983.

In 1987, after an interruption in the planning process, the development plan – based on the design concept – came into force for the Department of Works' site. The architects, Koch + Partner, resumed planning work in July 1994 and presented a building concept in July 1995 that took account of the latest user needs. All works operations that are not tied to specific locations are now united on this central site. Certain key buildings were erected prior to the main construction programme. These included a gas-pressure control plant, a laboratory and a so-called "24-hour tract", the computer centre that monitors Munich's gas and water supplies.

Gas-pressure control centre

With the construction of the Municipal Department of Works, a new gas-pressure control building became necessary in response to urban planning needs and for reasons of operational safety. This pavilion-like structure is situated in the entrance area on the axis of the former staff villas and consists of a main control room, with service rooms in the basement. Transparent façade areas afford a view into the interior of the building with its technical equipment. The closed areas of the outer skin are clad in Argeton tiles, which thus establish a relationship to the façade design of the new municipal works centre.

Die großen Glasflächen der Bürogebäude spiegeln sich über die vorgesetzten Terrassen im See.

The large areas of glazing to the office tracts are reflected in the lake beyond the projecting terraces.

Blick vom Haupteingang Dachauer Straße auf den verglasten Eingangsbauteil

View from the main entrance in Dachauer Strasse to the glazed entrance structure

Bürozentrum

Der gläserne Eingangsbauteil erschließt über gekoppelte Verbindungsbauwerke zentral und geschossweise die fünf Baublöcke. Im Erdgeschoss erfolgt die Verteilung über großzügige Foyerzonen mit Ausstellungsflächen zu den einzelnen Baublöcken.

Das Bürozentrum beherbergt im Erdgeschoss kundenorientierte und großflächige Sondernutzungen. Mittig in der Gesamtanlage befindet sich die für die Mitarbeiter gut erreichbare Kantine. Die Lage am zentralen Innenhof mit vorgelagerter Terrasse am See und mit Blick auf die Skulptur aus Verkehrsampeln der Künstler Brunner + Ritz bietet eine beziehungsreiche Gesamtsituation.

Vertikale und horizontale Scheiben mit Ziegelverkleidung System „Argeton" in hellem Farbton setzen sich auf der im übrigen verglasten Fassade deutlich ab und verleihen dem Projekt eine gerichtete Struktur. Die Metallkonstruktion der verglasten Flächen tritt mit der Farbe Grau-Aluminium zurück.

Die großflächig verglasten Verbindungsbauteile mit Stahltreppen zur vertikalen Erschließung und mit angelagerten Besprechungsräumen machen in Gestalt und Funktion die Strukturierung des Bürobereiches deutlich.

Jeder der Baublöcke umfasst ringförmig einen Innenhof, der intensiv begrünt ist. Je nach Besonnung und Lage variiert das Bepflanzungsthema.

Alle Obergeschosse sind seit der Vorgabe aus dem Wettbewerb unverändert für eine konventionelle Büronutzung mit Ein- und Mehrpersonenräumen zweibündig geplant.

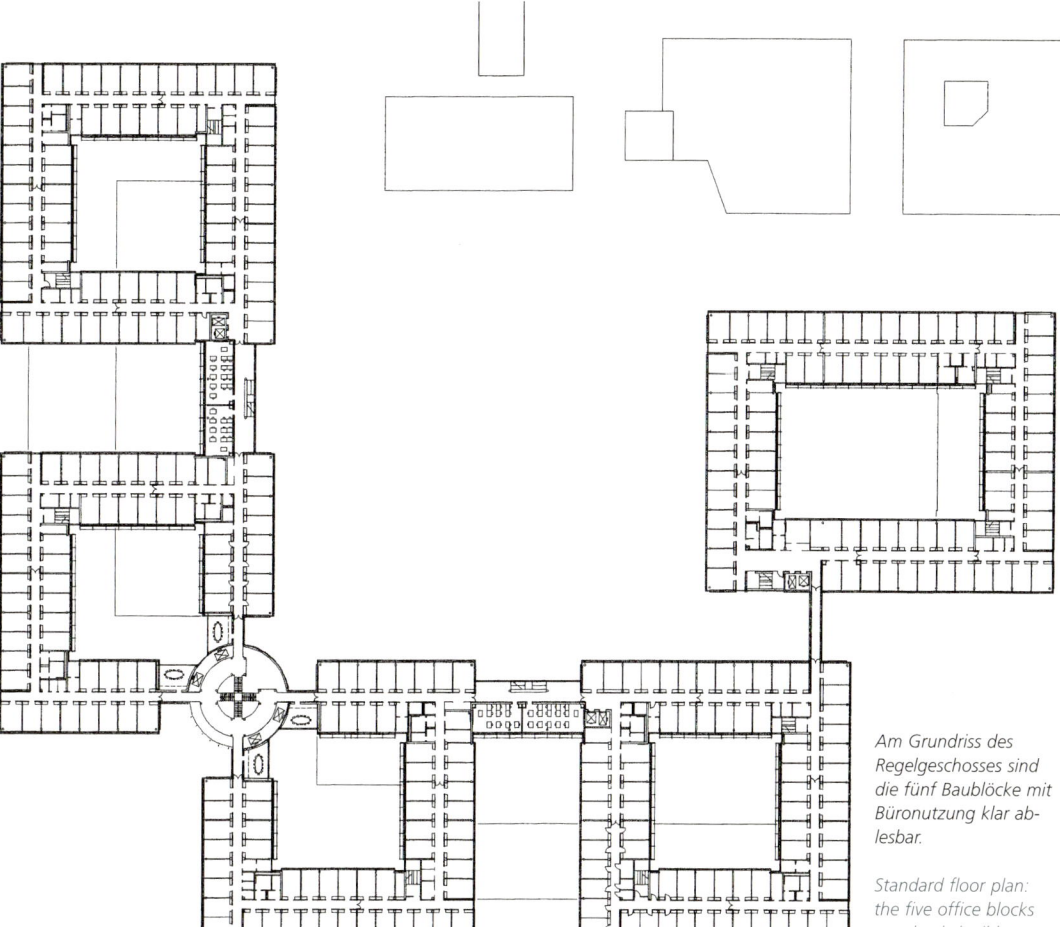

Im Rohbauzustand wird die filigrane Baustruktur und Transparenz des Eingangsbauteils besonders deutlich.

Carcass structure: the slender form of construction and the transparency of the entrance tract are immediately evident.

Am Grundriss des Regelgeschosses sind die fünf Baublöcke mit Büronutzung klar ablesbar.

Standard floor plan: the five office blocks are clearly legible.

Administration centre

The glazed entrance tract provides central access to the five blocks of the complex, which are connected on every floor by linking structures. On the ground floor, spacious foyer zones facilitate circulation to the individual blocks. The foyers also contain exhibition areas.

Customer-related functions and special uses that require greater space are situated on the ground floor of the administration centre. The canteen at the heart of the complex is easily accessible to staff. Located in the central courtyard, with a terrace overlooking the lake and a view to a traffic-light sculpture by the artists Brunner + Ritz, the canteen has an evocative general ambience.

The vertical and horizontal areas of pale Argeton brick-tile cladding are distinctly contrasted with the glazed areas of the façade and lend the scheme a directional structure. The aluminium supporting construction to the glazing is in a restrained grey tone.

In their form and function, the linking tracts – with large areas of glazing and steel stairs for vertical circulation – together with the adjoining conference and discussion spaces, articulate the structural layout of the office areas.

Each of the building blocks encloses an intensively landscaped courtyard. The theme of the plantings varies, depending on the aspect and the amount of sunshine to which each situation is exposed.

Since the time of the competition brief, all upper floors have had a two-bay layout for conventional office use with single- and multi-person units.

Der Bandfassade vorgesetzte, punktgehaltene Glasscheiben dienen als Wind- und Wetterschutz für das geöffnete Fenster während der Nachtauskühlung.

The panes of point-fixed glass in the outer skin of the horizontally banded façade screen the opened casements against the weather during the period of night-time cooling.

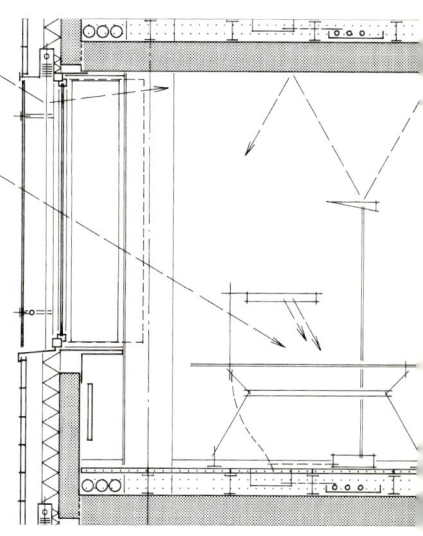

Stadtwerkszentrale München | 35

Der Büroflügel orientiert sich nach Süden zur Grünanlage.

The office wing, oriented to the south, overlooks the landscaped area.

Betriebszentrum

Das Betriebszentrum ist modular aufgebaut. Jedes der viergeschossigen Werkstattmodule stellt eine selbstständige Funktionseinheit dar und wird je einzeln mit Haus- und Betriebstechnik versorgt. So ist vermieden, „maßgeschneiderte" Werkstattkörper zu entwickeln, die Nutzungsänderungen gar nicht oder nur mit großen Schwierigkeiten ermöglichen. Im Betriebszentrum befinden sich Werkstätten und Prüfeinrichtungen für Gas, Wasser, Elektro und Fernwärme sowie werkstattbezogene Büroeinheiten.

Das einzelne Werkstattmodul ist durch zwei aussteifende Treppen- und Versorgungskerne erschlossen. Die Tragstruktur des Gebäudes basiert auf einem 8,40 m x 8,40 m Achsraster, das alle unterschiedlichen betrieblichen Anforderungen zulässt.

Works centre

The works centre is designed on a modular basis. Each of the four-storey workshop modules represents an independent functional unit individually served by mechanical services and operating systems. In this way, it was possible to avoid building tailor-made workshop structures that could not be adapted to subsequent changes of use – or only with great difficulty. The centre contains workshops and testing facilities for gas, water, electricity and district-heating supply services, as well as office units specifically related to the workshops.

The individual workshop modules are served by two staircase and service cores that also act as bracing elements. The load-bearing structure of the building is based on a 8.40 x 8.40 m axial grid that accommodates the many different operational needs.

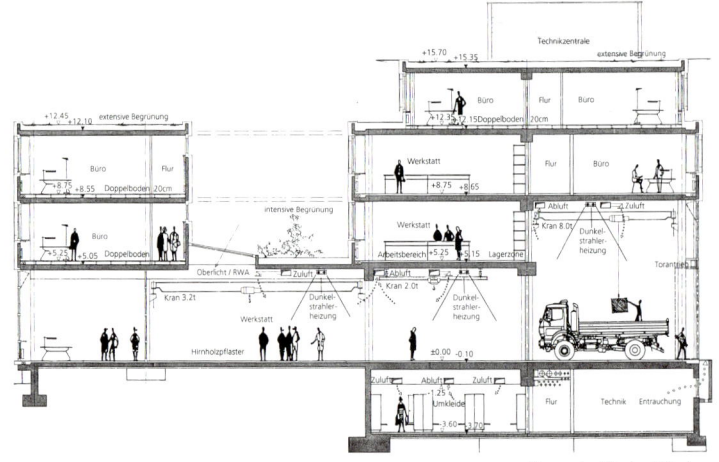

Querschnitt des Werkstattmoduls mit vorgelagerten Büros

Cross-section through workshop module with offices at front

Test und Optimierung der Glasvorsatzscheibe mit einem Institut für Fensterbau

Testing and optimizing outer glass skin in collaboration with an institute for window construction

Musterhaus

Model building

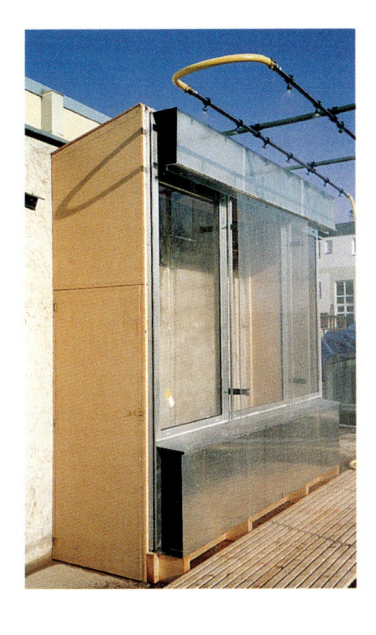

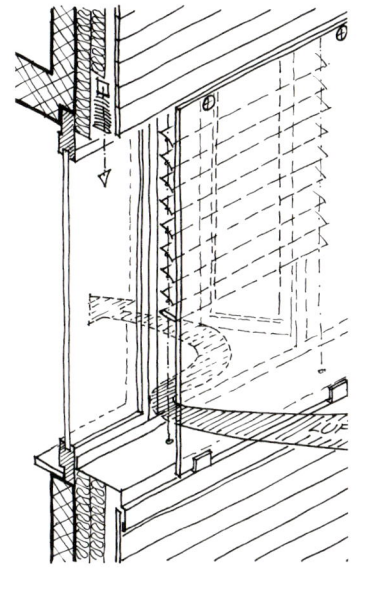

Ökologie

Zentrales Ziel war es, ein Projekt mit einem besonders niedrigen Gesamtenergiebedarf in einer ökologischen Bauweise zu erstellen. Insbesondere berücksichtigte die Planung den ganzen Lebenszyklus des Gebäudes mit den Aspekten Ökologie, Wirtschaftlichkeit, Nutzung und Energie.

Anhand eines theoretischen Gebäudemodells wurde in Verbindung mit einer Datenbank das Potenzial bezüglich der Umweltbelastungen und Primärenergieeinheiten der Materialien aufgezeigt und optimiert umgesetzt.

Optimale Tageslichtausnutzung und natürliche Lüftung war ein wesentlicher Aspekt bei der Planung und Konzeption. Die Büroflächen in den Obergeschossen sind natürlich belüftet. Auf eine Lüftungsanlage und die damit verbundene abgehängte Decke konnte zugunsten einer Optimierung der Geschosshöhe verzichtet werden. Die Stahlbetonrohdecke wirkt als Temperaturspeicher und kann zur Nachtauskühlung aktiviert werden.

Im gesamten Projekt ist durchgängig Doppelboden eingesetzt. Sämtliche Installationen sind am Boden geführt; die Geräte und die Beleuchtung sind von unten versorgt.

Musterhaus

Zum Überprüfen der Gebäudetechnikkonzepte und zum Veranschaulichen gegenüber den Nutzern wurde während der Planungsphase ein Musterhaus im Maßstab 1:1 errichtet. Mit Hilfe eines Raummoduls im Musterhaus ließen sich die Gebäude- und Gebäudetechnikkonzepte untersuchen und aufeinander abstimmen.

Ecological aspects

One of the central aims of the design was to create a complex with extremely low overall energy needs in an ecologically friendly form of construction. The planning took account of the entire anticipated life cycle of the buildings, including ecological, economic, functional and energy-related aspects.

Using a theoretical construction model and a databank, it was possible to demonstrate, optimize and implement the potential of the building with an eye to the environmental damage and primary energy consumption associated with the use of specific materials.

The optimum exploitation of daylight and natural ventilation was a major aspect of the concept and planning. The office areas on the upper floors are ventilated by natural means. As a result, it was possible to obviate ventilation plant and the suspended soffits this would have necessitated and to create spaces with an ideal storey height instead. The unclad reinforced concrete floor slabs function as thermal storage masses that can be activated for night-time cooling.

A double-floor construction was used throughout the project. All service runs are installed in the floors. Fittings and the lighting installation are served from below.

Model structure

To test the technical concepts of the buildings and as a means of demonstrating them to users, a full-scale model structure was erected during the planning phase. With the aid of a spatial module in this building, it was possible to investigate the underlying concepts of the construction and mechanical services and to co-ordinate them with each other.

Im Herbst 1994 wurde durch den Freistaat Thüringen in Zusammenarbeit mit der Stadt Erfurt ein europaweiter städtebaulicher Ideenwettbewerb, kombiniert mit einem Realisierungswettbewerb, für die Universität Erfurt ausgelobt. Ziel der Planung war die Entwicklung eines Gesamtkonzepts mit der Integration der bestehenden Pädagogischen Hochschule sowie die Planung der neuen Universitätsbibliothek.

Als erste Preisträger des Wettbewerbs wurden wir mit der Planung des Bibliotheksgebäudes (1. Bauabschnitt) und dem Umbau eines bestehenden Wohnheims der Pädagogischen Hochschule in das erste Dienstgebäude für Professoren und Seminarräumen beauftragt. Für die städtebauliche Entwicklung der gesamten Universität einschließlich der Pädagogischen Hochschule erstellten wir ein Entwicklungsgutachten.

In the autumn of 1994, the Free State of Thuringia and the city of Erfurt advertised a European urban planning ideas competition together with a competition for the construction of the University of Erfurt. The planning brief called for an overall concept, including the integration of the existing college of education into the scheme and the design of a new university library.

As winners of the first prize in the competition, we were entrusted with the planning of the library (first stage of construction) and with the conversion of an existing hostel for students of the college of education into a building with seminar rooms and office space for professors. We also prepared an urban development study for the university as a whole, including the college of education.

Universität Erfurt

3 University of Erfurt

1995   Wettbewerb · 1. Preis
1997 – 1999 Städtebauliches Entwicklungsgutachten
1996 – 1999 Dienstgebäude · Umbau
  Planung und Realisierung
1995 – 2000 Universitätsbibliothek · Neubau
  Planung und Realisierung

1995   Competition: first prize
1997 – 1999 Urban development study
1996 – 1999 Conversion of hostel into administration
  building: planning and construction
1995 – 2000 New university library: planning and
  construction

Die Universitätsbibliothek ist Kristallisationspunkt der Entwicklung der neuen Universität Erfurt.

The library forms the nucleus of the new University of Erfurt.

Modelleinsicht in die Freihand- und Publikumszonen der Universitätsbibliothek

View of interior of model, showing the open-access and public zones of the university library

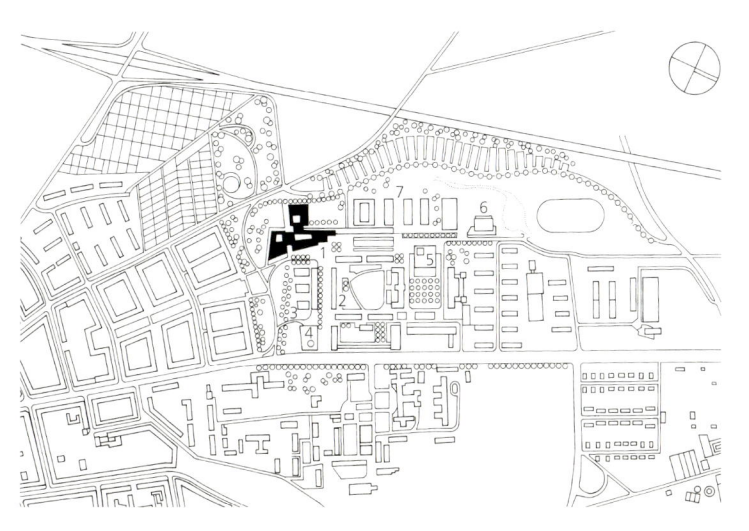

Das Campusgelände im Stadtgefüge

The campus in its urban context

1 Bibliothek
2 Dienstgebäude
3 Institutsgebäude
4 Hörsaalgebäude
5 neue Mensa
6 neue Sporthalle
7 langfristige Erweiterung

1 Library
2 Seminar rooms / offices for professors
3 University institute
4 Lecture-hall tract
5 New dining hall
6 New sports hall
7 Long-term extension

Städtebaulicher Wettbewerb und Realisierungswettbewerb Universitätsbibliothek

Die wohl wichtigste Frage bei der Neugründung der Universität Erfurt war die Entscheidung über den Standort der Universitätsbibliothek. Diese sollte Kristallisations- und Ausgangspunkt für das Entstehen der neuen Universität sein; sie sollte auch als öffentliche Einrichtung die Verbindung zur Stadt herstellen.

Der von uns gewählte Standort der Bibliothek bezeichnet einen Dreh- und Angelpunkt der beiden zukünftigen Entwicklungsachsen der Universität. Eine Achse nimmt in Nord-Süd-Richtung zwischen Bibliothek, Mensa und Sportzentrum die Verbindung zur Stadt auf, die andere schafft in West-Ost-Richtung zwischen Bibliothek und Hörsaalgebäude die Verbindung zur Nordhäuser Straße.

Die Fahrerschließung erfolgt ausschließlich von Westen, wo auch der ruhende Verkehr in einer schrittweise auszubauenden Parkharfe Platz findet. Damit kann eine innere Urbanität mit Plätzen sowie verkehrsfreien Aufenthaltszonen geschaffen werden. Die landschaftlichen Freiräume zwischen Parkharfe und Universität sind parkartig, zwischen vorgesehener Wohnbebauung und Universität als Universitätsgarten gestaltet.

Urban planning competition and university library competition

Probably the most important issue in founding the new University of Erfurt was the location of the library building. This was to form the nucleus for the entire development of the future university. As a public institution, it was also meant to establish a link with the city itself.

The location we proposed for the library is a focal point and pivot between the two future development axes of the university. The north-south axis between the library, the dining hall and the sports centre forges a link with the city. The east-west axis extends from the library to the lecture-hall building and links the development with Nordhäuser Strasse. Vehicular access is solely from the west, where parking space is also provided in an irregular curved area that will be extended in a series of stages. These measures help to create a sense of urbanity within the site, with public squares and traffic-free leisure zones. The landscaped spaces between the curved parking area and the university are designed as a park-like zone. The areas between the proposed housing development and the campus will be laid out as university gardens.

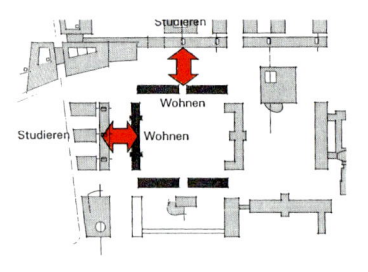

Räumliche Beziehung zwischen bestehenden Wohn- und neuen Institutsbauten

Spatial relationships between existing housing and new institute buildings

Der Bau der Universitätsbibliothek ist in drei Abschnitten konzipiert.

The university library is conceived in three construction stages.

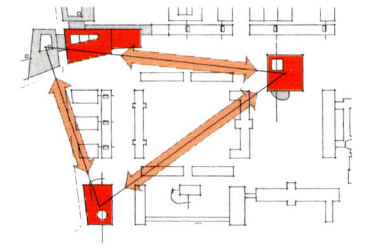

Bibliothek, Mensa und Hörsaalzentrum im übergeordneten „Dreieck" unterstützen durch ihre Besucherfrequenz die Verknüpfung der bestehenden mit den neuen Institutsbauten.

The library, dining hall and lecture-hall centre form a triangular set of co-ordinates. Through their visitor frequency, they help to unite the existing structures and the new institute buildings.

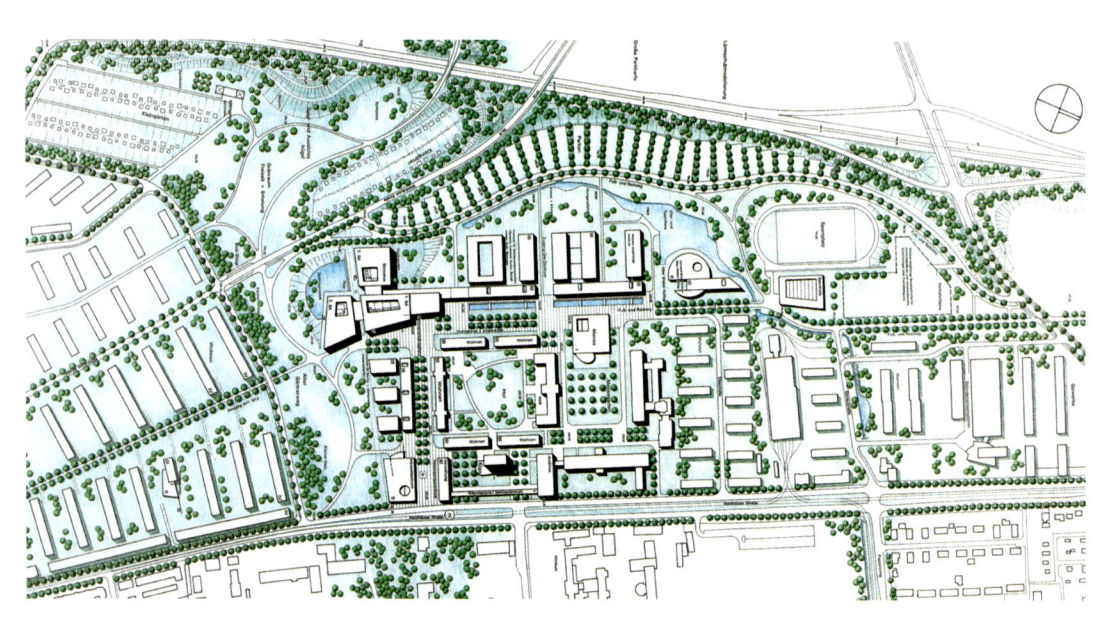

Die Gesamtanlage der Universität im städtebaulichen Kontext, Wettbewerb 1995

Overall layout of the university in its urban context; competition, 1995

Städtebauliches Entwicklungsgutachten

Wesentliche Parameter haben sich nach Abschluss des städtebaulichen Wettbewerbs geändert. Beim Wettbewerb 1995 wurde von 6.000 flächenbezogenen Studienplätzen und einem Neubauprogramm von 40.000 m² Hauptnutzfläche ausgegangen, anschließend nur noch von 3.000 Studienplätzen bis zum Jahre 2005 und einem Langfristziel von lediglich 4.000 flächenbezogenen Studienplätzen.

Auf dieser Grundlage haben wir eine Zeitschiene erarbeitet und die Entwicklung der Universität mit Integration der Bausubstanz der Pädagogischen Hochschule in fünf Stufen aufgezeigt.

Trotz reduzierter Vorgaben kann der Wettbewerbsentwurf mit seinen städtebaulichen Zielvorstellungen für die Gesamtmaßnahme Universität weitgehend aufrechterhalten und langfristig schrittweise umgesetzt werden. Vor diesem Hintergrund lässt sich die Entwicklung der Universität flexibel an die jeweiligen wirtschaftlichen Rahmenbedingungen anpassen.

Der erste Bauabschnitt der Universitätsbibliothek Erfurt mit ca. 900.000 Bänden und 360 Leseplätzen ist in einem drei- bis viergeschossigen Baukörper mit einem Untergeschoss untergebracht.

Urban development study

Some of the main parameters of the scheme have changed since the urban design competition held in 1995. The competition brief was based on a total of 6,000 study places – with the requisite area per student – and on a programme of new construction to provide a functional floor area of 40,000 m². Present plans envisage only 3,000 study places by 2005 and a long-term goal of 4,000 places (with the requisite area per student).

In accordance with these requirements, we drew up a time frame for the development of the university, including the integration of the existing college of education buildings, in five stages.

Despite the reduction in scale, it was possible to adhere in large part to the competition design, with its urban planning goals for the overall university scheme, and to implement this step by step in the long term. Within this framework, the university development can be flexibly adapted to meet specific economic constraints.

The first phase of construction of the university library in Erfurt – to accommodate roughly 900,000 volumes and 360 reading places – comprises a three- to four-storey building with a basement.

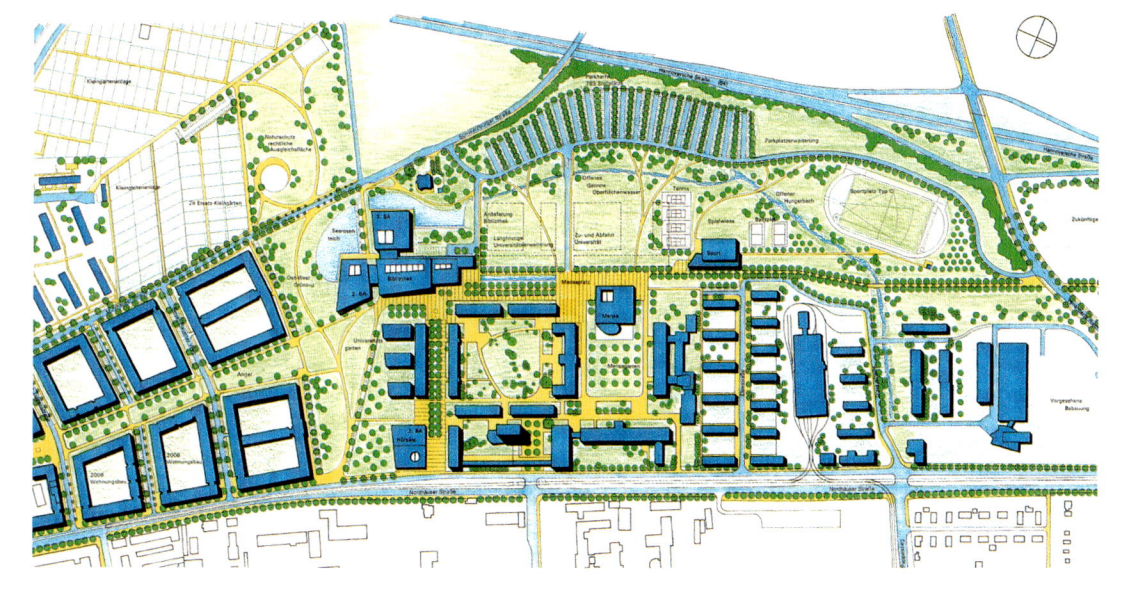

Langfristige städtebauliche Zielvorstellungen nach geänderten Vorgaben, Entwicklungsgutachten 1999

Long-term urban goals, reflecting changes in the brief; development study, 1999

Seite 42/43: Modellansicht der Universitätsbibliothek

pp. 42/43: Model of university library

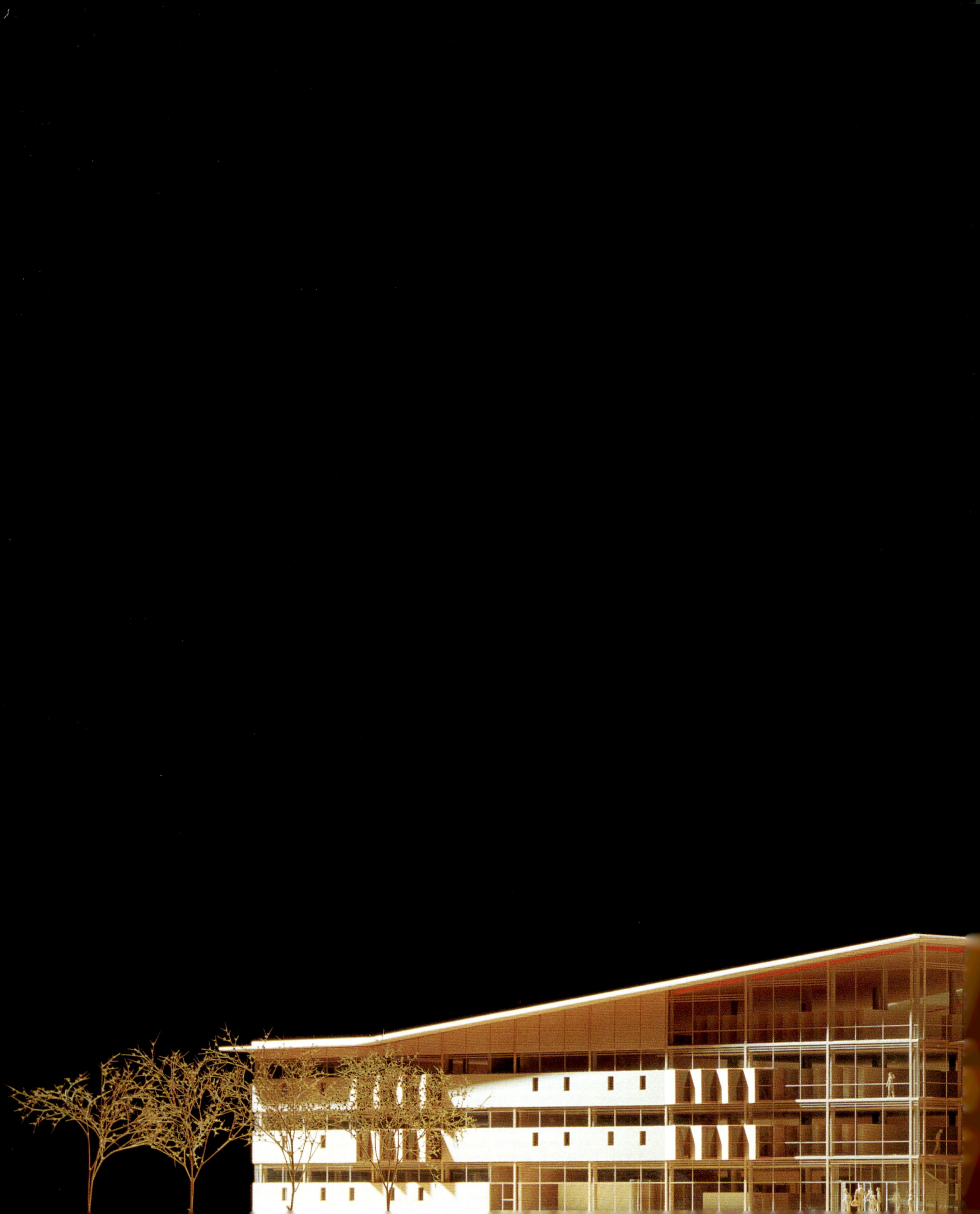

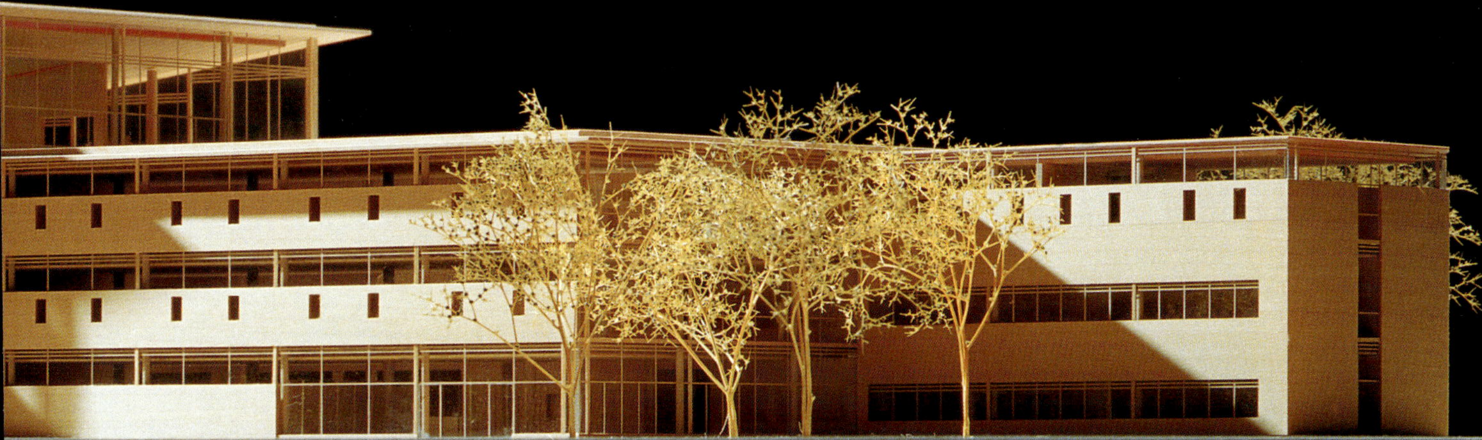

Das fertiggestellte Bibliotheksgebäude auf dem zukünftigen Campus bei Nacht

View of finished library at night in future campus

Carrels – in der Fassade integrierte Lesekabinen

Reading carrels integrated in the façade

Fassadenschnitt im Freihandbereich

Section through façade to open-access library area

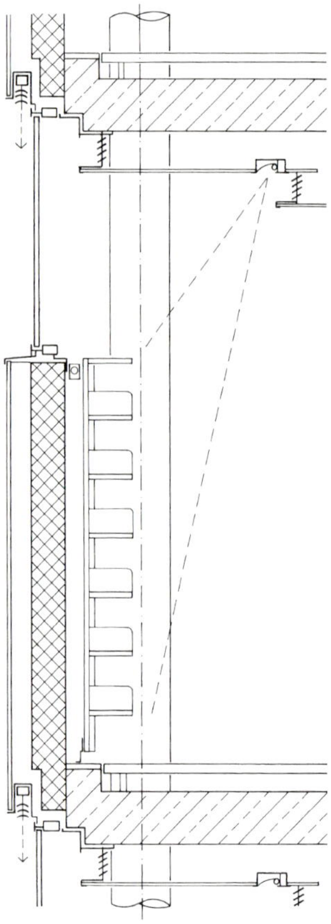

Universitätsbibliothek

Ein wichtiges Gestaltungsziel war die flexible Großraumkonzeption der Freihandbereiche und eine spannungsvolle Schnittführung im Gebäude. Dies wird vor allem in den drei zentralen Lichthöfen mit Oberlicht erreicht. Die Lichthöfe sind auf einer Seite von einer differenziert gestalteten Wandscheibe mit einer großzügigen Treppenanlage flankiert. Über Brücken und Öffnungen gibt es Sicht- und Wegebeziehungen zur angelagerten Verwaltungsspange. Entlang der Lufträume, wo die meisten Publikumsbewegungen stattfinden, sind die Freihandbereiche mit ihren Regalzonen trapezförmig aufgefächert. Durch die klare Zonierung und durch die innere Lichtführung über die drei Lufträume ist eine leichte Orientierung innerhalb des Gebäudes gewährleistet.

Es gibt ruhig gelegene Leseplätze – abgeschirmt durch die Regalzonen – entlang der Fassade mit kleinen Ausguckfenstern und Lesepools mit geschosshohen Glasfassaden und Blickbeziehung zur Stadt, zum Campus und zur Landschaft.

University library

The concept of large flexible spaces for the open-access library areas and the creation of a structure with a dynamic profile were two of the main design goals for this building. They were achieved in the first instance by forming three central atria with roof lights. The atria are flanked on one side by a wall slab of changing design and with sweeping staircase structures. Openings and bridges create visual links and connecting routes to the adjoining administration tract. The open-access library areas are situated in the tall spaces where the greatest volume of public traffic occurs. Here, the bookshelf areas are fanned out on plan. The clear zoning and the natural lighting in the three atria ensure a good sense of orientation within the building.

Along the façade, screened off by the shelf zones, are quiet reading spaces with small windows that allow a glimpse out of the building, as well as reading pools with storey-height glazing that affords views to the city, the campus and the landscape.

Die Rückseite der Bibliothek mit der Verwaltungsspange

The rear face of the library with the administration tract

Das Oberlicht verteilt gleichmäßig das Licht über drei Lufträume.

Roof lights ensure an even distribution of daylight in the three atrium spaces.

Schnitt durch die drei Lichthöfe

Section through the three atria

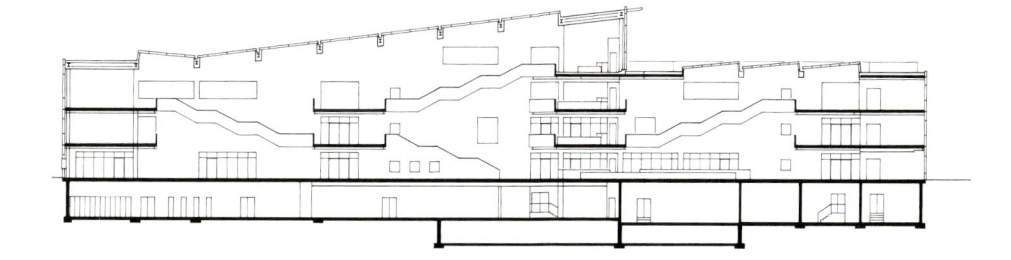

Grundriss der ersten Bibliotheksebene mit großflächigen Freihandbereichen

Plan of first library level with extensive open-access areas

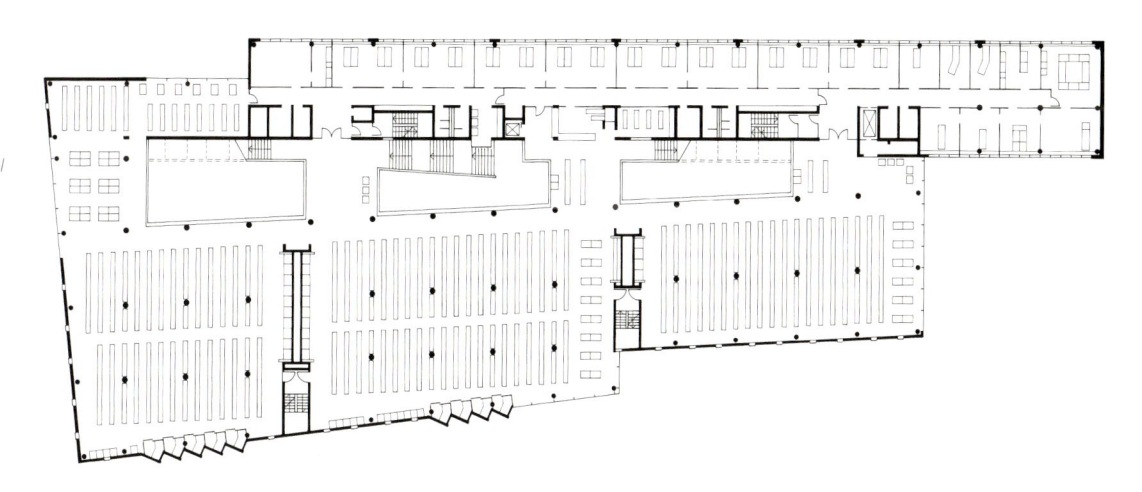

Universität Erfurt | 45

Computersimulation, 1998

Computer simulation, 1998

Lichthof mit der großzügigen Treppenanlage, 2000

Atrium with broad staircase structure, 2000

Computersimulation, 1998

Computer simulation, 1998

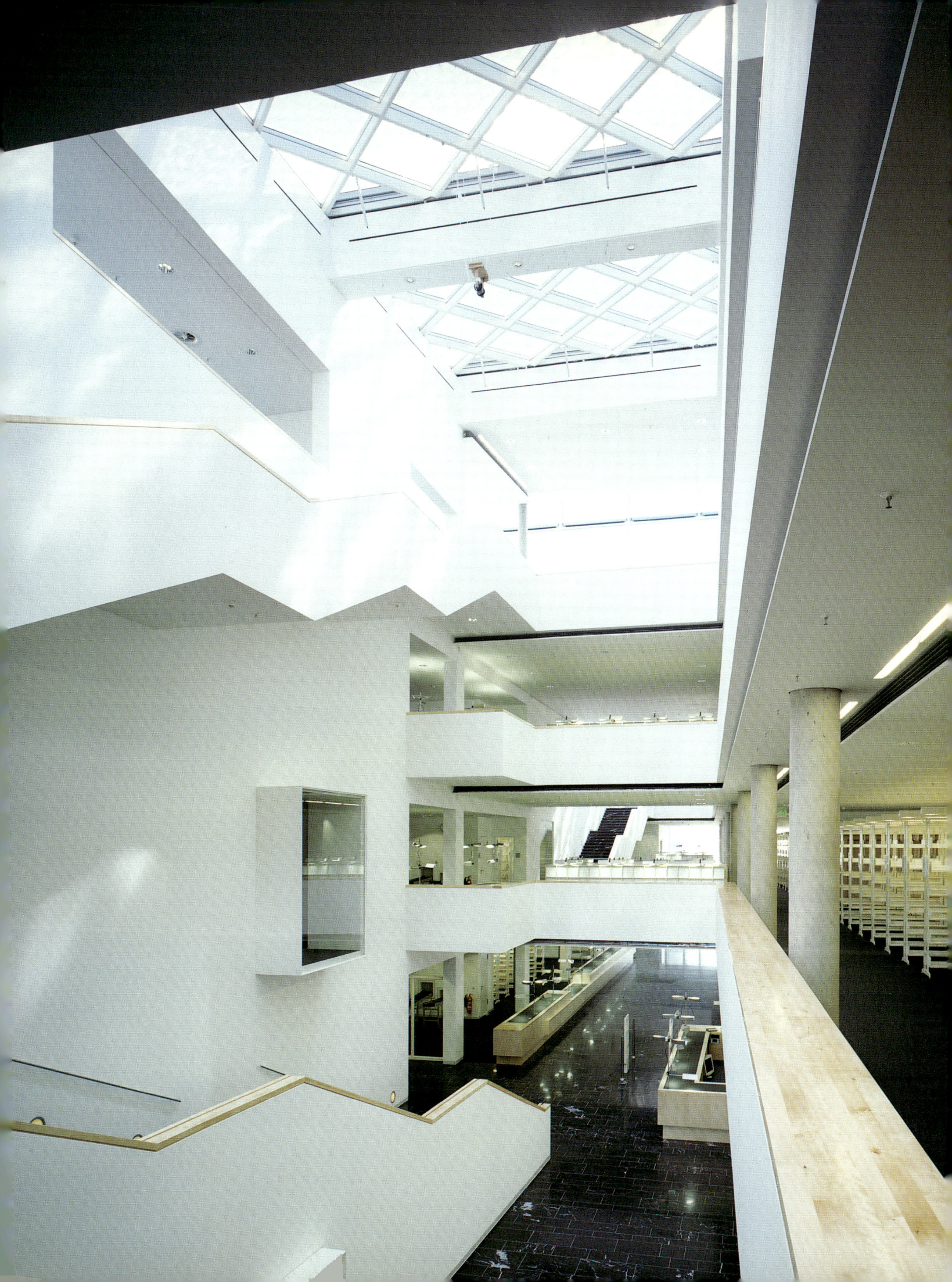

Mit der Verlagerung des Flughafens München-Riem ergab sich die einmalige Chance für eine großräumige Stadterweiterung an der östlichen Stadtgrenze von München. Aus der Folgeentscheidung, die Messe München von der Innenstadt nach Riem zu verlegen, entstand auch der Name für das Gesamtprojekt: Messestadt Riem.

Die Planung für die Messestadt Riem hatte das Ziel, ein vielfältiges, weitgehend eigenständiges und attraktives Stadtgebilde entstehen zu lassen. Ein Miteinander von Wohnen, Arbeiten, Kultur und Natur soll Wirklichkeit werden. Die Messestadt Riem ist entsprechend Standort für die Neue Messe München und bietet Wohnraum für 16.000 Menschen sowie bis zu 13.000 wohnungsnahe Arbeitsplätze.

Seit 1987 wirken wir bei allen Planungsphasen der Messestadt Riem mit. Als Mitglied der Beratergruppe „Stadtgestaltung und Ökologie" beschäftigen wir uns insbesondere mit Gestaltungsfragen.

With the relocation of Munich Airport from Riem to a site north of the city, a unique opportunity arose to create a large-scale urban extension on the eastern edge of the Bavarian capital. The ensuing decision to relocate the Munich Trade Fair from the city centre to the former airport site in Riem provided the name for the overall project: Messestadt (Trade-Fair City) Riem.

The planning of this new town centre had as its aim the creation of an attractive, varied and largely autonomous urban entity with a mixture of living and working amenities, cultural activities and natural areas. The Messestadt Riem is, therefore, not only the location of the New Munich Trade Fair; it also provides residential accommodation for 16,000 people and up to 13,000 workplaces in close proximity to each other.

Since 1987, we have collaborated on all phases of the planning for the Messestadt. As a member of the advisory group for "Urban Design and Ecology", we are concerned especially with questions of design.

Messestadt Riem, München

4   Messestadt Riem, Munich

1987 Kooperatives Verfahren · Künftige Nutzung
     des Flughafengeländes München-Riem
1991 Wettbewerb Gesamtgelände · Ankauf
1991 Wettbewerb Neue Messe München · 4. Preis
1993 Wettbewerb Neuriem Mitte Stufe 1 · 3. Preis
1993 Wettbewerb Neuriem Mitte Stufe 2
1994 – 1998 Städtebaulicher Entwurf und Bebauungsplan
     Gewerbegebiet Nord/West
1998 Wettbewerb Park+Ride-Anlage · 2. Preis
seit 1998 Beratertätigkeit

1987 Collaboration on drawing up proposals for future use of the former airport site in Riem, Munich
1991 Competition for development of entire site: purchase of scheme
1991 Competition for New Trade Fair, Munich: fourth prize
1993 Competition for district of Neuriem Mitte, stage 1: third prize
1993 Competition for district of Neuriem Mitte, stage 2
1994 – 1998 Urban planning and development plan for north-west commercial area
1998 Competition for park-and-ride facilities: second prize
since 1998 Consultancy for scheme

Messestadt Riem –
ein neuer Stadtteil entsteht

Mitwirkung an allen Planungsphasen über
einen Zeitraum von mehr als zwölf Jahren

Messestadt Riem –
the creation of a new urban district

Collaboration on all phases of planning over
a period of more than 12 years

Planungsumgriff der Messestadt Riem

Designated planning area for Messestadt Riem

Städtebaulicher Konzeptplan der Messestadt Riem; Stand 1998

Urban planning concept for Messestadt Riem; state of development in 1998

1 Erster Bauabschnitt Wohnen
2 Zukünftige Baugebiete Wohnen
3 Gewerbegebiet Nord/West
4 Gewerbegebiet Nord/Ost
5 Messe
6 Landschaftspark

1 First stage of construction: housing
2 Future development areas: housing
3 North-west commercial area
4 North-east commercial area
5 Trade-fair area
6 Landscaped park

Gutachten
Künftige Nutzung des Flughafengeländes

In einem kooperativen Verfahren erarbeiteten 1987 sieben Arbeitsgruppen aus Stadt- und Landschaftsplanern Vorschläge, wie die vom Stadtrat beschlossene Kombination von Wohnen, Gewerbe, Messe und Grünraum auf dem alten Flughafenareal verwirklicht werden kann.

Unsere Empfehlung war, die Gesamtanlage der Neuen Messe als ablesbare stadtteilprägende Großform in visuelle Korrespondenz zur Innenstadt zu setzen. Die städtebauliche Großform „Messe" findet in nordöstlicher Richtung eine Fortsetzung: eine ablesbare Baukante im Verlauf der ehemaligen Start- und Landebahn mit einer Bauzone für Forschung, Entwicklung und Dienstleistung. Lage und Form des zentralen Grünzuges entsprechen der Achse der ehemaligen Start- und Landebahn. Die südliche Begrenzung des Grünzuges ist geprägt durch dichte Vegetation in lockerer, den Dorfrändern nachgebildeter Form. Hier haben wir auch das Wohnen in überschaubaren Einheiten vorgeschlagen.

Study on the future use of the former airport site

In 1987, seven working groups collaborated in drawing up a series of urban and landscape planning proposals in response to the city council's requirements for a combination of housing, commercial uses, trade-fair facilities and landscaped space on the former airport site in Riem.

Our recommendation was to realize the entire New Trade Fair development as a comprehensible, large-scale urban entity that would form a visual counterpart to the city centre. The trade-fair complex itself is continued to the north-east in the form of a clear built demarcation line along the former runway, with a zone for the construction of research, development and service facilities. In its location and form, the central green strip also follows the axis of the former runway. The southern edge of this landscaped strip is marked by dense vegetation and an open form of development reminiscent of the outskirts of a village. We also suggested areas of housing here that would be articulated into clearly identifiable units.

Städtebaulicher Ideenwettbewerb Gesamtgelände

1990 wurde ein internationaler Ideenwettbewerb ausgeschrieben. Es galt nun, die für die Messestadt aufgestellten Anforderungen – Identität, Ökologie, Infrastruktur, Wohnen, Gewerbe – und den Standort der Neuen Messe in einem Gesamtplan zu bearbeiten.

Unser städtebauliches Konzept sah einen Stadtteil im Grünen vor, der mit drei Grünachsen durchdrungen wird und deshalb den Namen MesseParkStadt erhält. Gewerbe und Messe sind im Norden zur Autobahn orientiert, das Wohnen ist der Landschaft und einem geplanten großen See zugeordnet. Der zentrale Boulevard nimmt den Verlauf der ehemaligen Startbahnachse auf. Im Zentrum werden Messe, Hightech-Verwaltung und Wohnen mit Freiraum und Wasser verknüpft.

Urban planning ideas competition

In 1990, an international ideas competition was held. The brief required the goals laid down for the Messestadt – in respect of identity, ecological sensitivity, infrastructure, housing and commercial uses – and the site for the New Trade Fair itself to be incorporated in an overall plan.

Our planning concept envisaged an urban district in landscaped surroundings. The new development was to be dissected by three landscaped axes and, therefore, to bear the name MesseParkStadt (Trade Fair Park City). Commercial and trade-fair functions are situated to the north in close proximity to the autobahn. The housing areas, in contrast, are oriented to the open landscape and a large lake, which also formed part of our proposals. The central boulevard follows the line of the former airport runway. At the centre, the trade fair, the high-tech administration and the housing are linked to open landscaped spaces and areas of water.

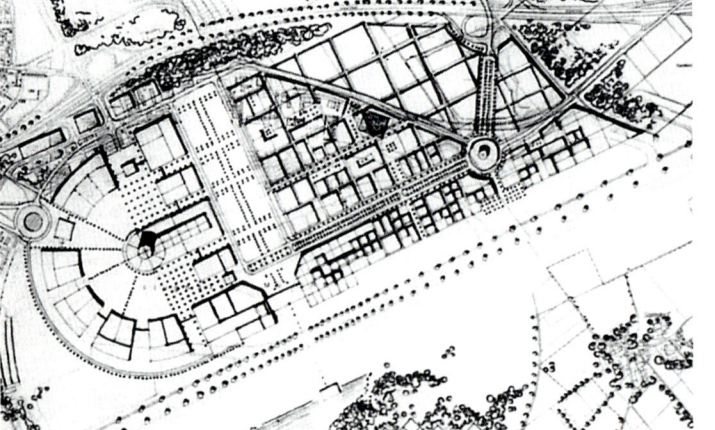

Entwurfsidee: Durchdringung des Stadtteils mit drei Grünachsen

Design idea: urban development intersected by three landscaped axes

Lage und Form des zentralen Grünzugs orientieren sich an der Achse der ehemaligen Start- und Landebahn.

The location and form of the central landscaped strip reflect the alignment of the former airport runway.

Grundkonzept der MesseParkStadt

Basic concept for the MesseParkStadt

Realisierungswettbewerb Neue Messe

1991/1992 schloss sich ein beschränkter Wettbewerb unter den Preisträgern für den Bau der Neuen Messe an. Das Erscheinungsbild unseres Messekonzeptes ist geprägt durch die schleifenförmige Anordnung der Ausstellungshallen, die sowohl eine gleichmäßige Beschickung aller Hallen von außen als auch eine optimale Erreichbarkeit durch die Besucher gewährleistet, und zwar bei Großmessen wie auch bei kleineren und parallelen Veranstaltungen. Wichtig war uns auch die Ausbildung unterschiedlich großer und gestalteter Frei- und Erholungsräume für die Besucher.

Bestimmendes Element ist eine große Magistrale, die „Mall", die T-förmig auf kurzem Weg die Haupteingänge mit den Hallen wie mit den zentralen Einrichtungen verbindet und die wichtigste Orientierungshilfe für den Besucher darstellt. Der typische Querschnitt der offenen und großen transparenten Dachkonstruktion ist gleichzeitig das unverwechselbare Signum der Neuen Messe.

Competition for the New Trade Fair

In 1991/92, a competition was held among the earlier prizewinners for the design of the New Trade Fair. Our concept is distinguished by the U-shaped layout of the exhibition halls. This guaranteed an even distribution of supplies and services to all halls from the outside, and optimum access for visitors during large-scale fairs as well as during smaller events that might be held parallel to the major exhibitions. Another important aspect of the design was the provision of outdoor and recreational spaces of various sizes and forms for visitors.

The dominant element is a large thoroughfare, the "Mall", which links the main entrances with the halls and the central amenities via a series of short, T-shaped routes. The Mall also serves as a main line of orientation for visitors. The standard cross-section of the large, open, transparent roof construction of the halls is a landmark of the New Trade Fair.

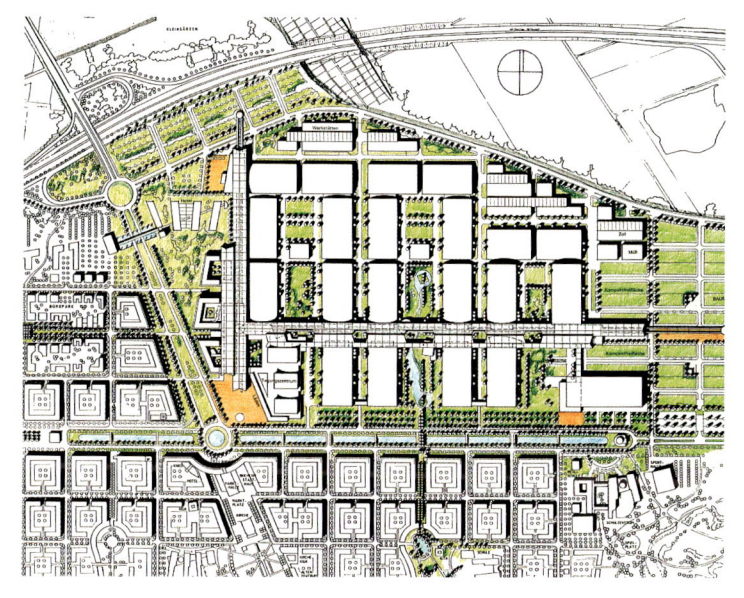

Städtebauliche Einbindung der Messe in den neuen Stadtteil

Integration of trade-fair site into new urban district

Schleifenförmig angeordnete Messehallen, T-förmige Erschließungs-Magistrale sowie differenzierte Freiflächen zwischen den Hallen prägen das Erscheinungsbild.

The development is distinguished by the U-shaped layout of the trade-fair halls, the T-shaped lines of access from the thoroughfare, and the variety of open spaces between the halls.

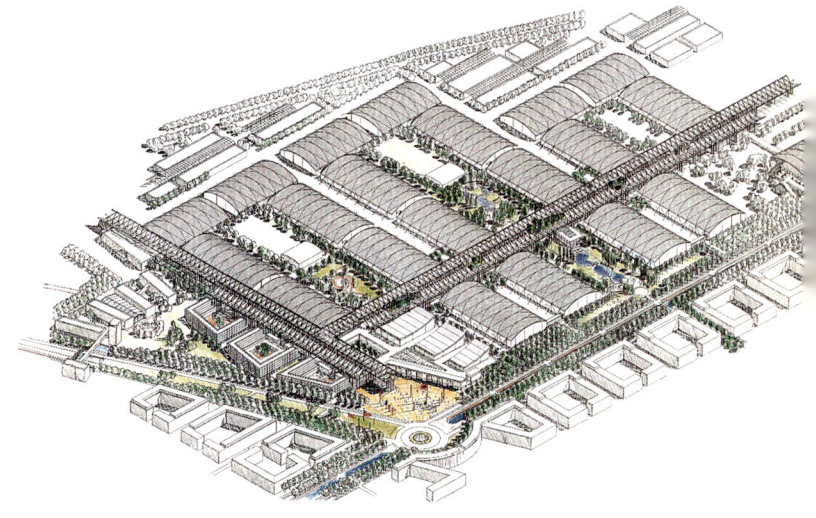

Wettbewerb Neuriem Stufe 1

Das städtebauliche Konzept des Zentrums der Messestadt Riem und des 1. Bauabschnittes Wohnen wurde in einem zweistufigen, ebenfalls auf die vorangegangenen Preisträger beschränkten Ideen- und Realisierungswettbewerb 1993 bearbeitet. In der ersten Stufe war die räumliche Ausformung und die Gestaltung des zentralen Platzes zu klären.

Hier wollten wir die mittlerweile vorgegebene „strenge", von straßenraumbestimmenden Blockkanten geprägte Ost-West-Allee um eine lockere, von der Abfolge von Freiräumen (Messeplatz, Marktplatz, Kirchenplatz) definierte Nord-Süd-Achse ergänzen. So wird an jeder Stelle im Zentrum der Messestadt eine unverwechselbare Situation geschaffen, die die großen Zusammenhänge spürbar macht und zwischen den unterschiedlichen Ansätzen der bisherigen Stadtteil- und Messeplanung vermittelt.

Diesem Gedanken folgend, wird die strenge Blockstruktur längs dieser Freiraumzone aufgelockert, so dass kleinere, differenzierte, der besonderen Zweckbestimmung entsprechende Teilräume (Schulen, Kirchen, Passagen und Galerien) entstehen.

Competition for Neuriem, stage 1

The urban planning concept for the centre of the Messestadt Riem and for the first phase of the housing construction was developed in two stages on the basis of an ideas and construction competition held in 1993 – again limited to the previous prizewinners. The spatial form and the overall design of the central square were the subject of the first stage of the competition.

In this context, we wished to complement the spatial "strictness" of the east-west avenue – required by the brief and defined by the edges of the building blocks – with a north-south axis, consisting of a looser sequence of open spaces (trade-fair square, marketplace, church square). In this way, a unique situation is achieved at every point in the centre of the Messestadt, allowing visitors to perceive the overriding relationships that exist within the area and mediating between the planning of the earlier development and that of the trade fair itself.

Pursuing this idea, the strict block structure along this open spatial zone is enlivened by a series of smaller, contrasting part-spaces with special uses (schools, churches, arcades and galleries).

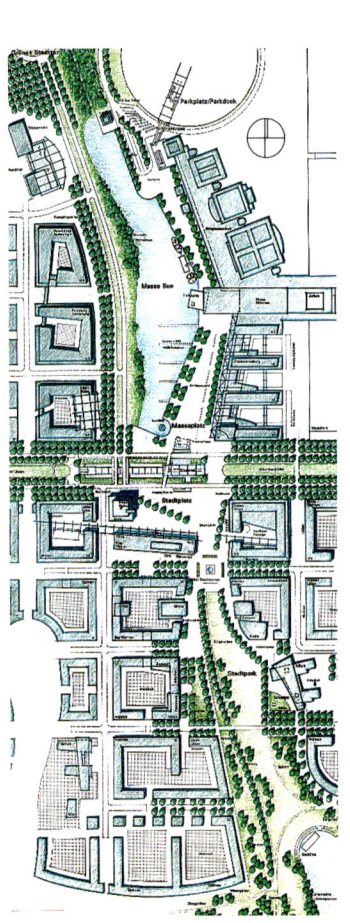

Skizze, Plan und Modell zeigen die lockere, durch die Abfolge von Freiräumen definierte Nord-Süd-Achse.

Sketch, plan and model, showing the informal north-south axis defined by a sequence of open spaces

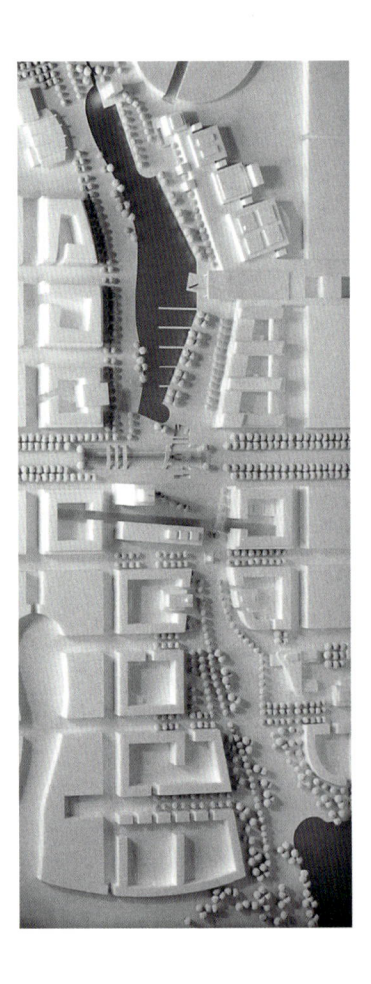

Wettbewerb Neuriem Stufe 2

In der zweiten Stufe des Wettbewerbs Neuriem Mitte sollte nun ein Konzept für die Wohngebiete in Ergänzung zur mittlerweile festgeschriebenen Messeplanung gefunden werden.

Dementsprechend haben wir das Rastermaß für die Wohnquartiere unter Aufnahme der Messeachsen modifiziert. Die nach Süden aufgefächerten Achsen ermöglichen eine bessere Verzahnung mit dem übergeordneten Grünzug im Süden; die leicht gebogenen Ost-West-Achsen (Meridiane) schaffen räumliche Zusammenhänge und lebendige Perspektiven. Die Überlagerung dieser beiden Achssysteme führt zu geringfügig, aber erkennbar unterschiedlichen Blockgrößen, erleichtert damit die Orientierung innerhalb des Quartiers und ermöglicht letztlich die Identifikation mit der eigenen Wohnumgebung.

Ein weiteres wesentliches Ziel war es, den Südrand des neuen Stadtteils so intensiv wie möglich mit der freien Landschaft zu verzahnen. Dies kommt der Durchlüftung des Wohngebietes zugute und soll möglichst vielen Wohnungen den freien Blick nach Süden ermöglichen.

Competition for Neuriem, stage 2

In the second stage of the competition for Neuriem Mitte, a concept was required for the housing areas that were to supplement the trade-fair planning – which, in the meantime, had been determined.

We adopted the axes of the trade-fair layout and modified the grid dimensions for the housing neighbourhoods. The axes, fanning out radially towards the south, allow a tighter linking of the development with the dominant landscaped strip to the south. In addition, the slightly curved east-west axes (meridians) create a series of spatial links and attractive perspectives. By overlaying these two axial systems, minor, but perceptible, differences in the sizes of the blocks were achieved. This facilitates a sense of orientation within the neighbourhood and a feeling of identification on the part of residents with their own immediate housing environment.

Another major goal of the planning was to knit together as tightly as possible the southern edge of the new district and the open landscape. This improves the flow of air through the residential area and was designed to provide as many dwellings as possible with an unimpeded view to the south.

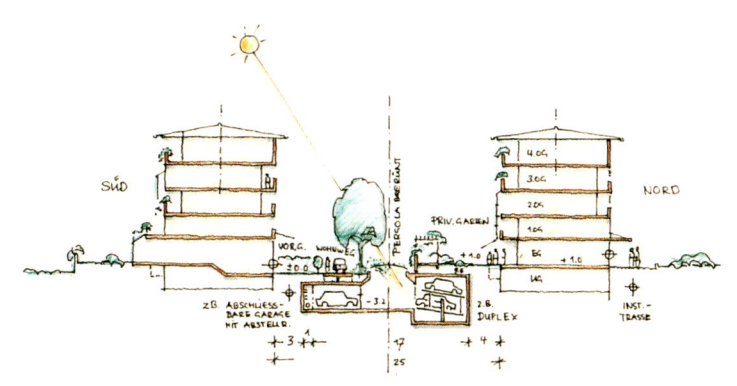

Stadtweg mit Unterflurgarage

Urban route with basement garage

Die leicht gebogenen Ost-West-Achsen (Meridiane) schaffen räumliche Zusammenhänge und lebendige Perspektiven.

The gently curving east-west axes (meridians) create spatial links and attractive perspectives.

Städtebaulicher Entwurf und Bebauungsplan Gewerbegebiet Nord/West

1994 wurden wir mit der Strukturplanung und anschließend mit der Bebauungsplanung für das Gewerbegebiet Nord/West beauftragt. Es ist als moderner Gewerbepark für innovative und wachstumsorientierte Branchen vorgesehen. Insbesondere Betriebe aus dem Medien- und Hightech-Umfeld sowie aus den Bereichen Umwelt- und Biotechnik sollen hier einen geeigneten Standort finden.

Begrenzt wird der Gewerbepark im Norden, Osten und Süden durch städtebaulich wirksame „harte" Ränder, im Westen ist er eingegrünt. Die orthogonale Grundstruktur ist durch eine Wiederaufnahme des ehemaligen Flughafen-Ovals überlagert, das sich als übergeordnete Grünspange von der denkmalgeschützten Tribünenanlage im Westen über die Wappenhalle zum Tower erstreckt. Dieses „Grünoval" sichert somit einen zusammenhängenden, unbebauten und für die Öffentlichkeit zugänglichen Freiraum.

Urban planning and development plan for the north-west commercial area

In 1994, we were entrusted with the structural planning and, following this, with drawing up the development plan for the north-west commercial area. This was conceived as a modern commercial park for innovative and growth-oriented activities. In particular, firms working in media and high-tech industries and in areas concerned with the environment and biotechnology were to find a suitable location here.

The commercial park is bordered to the north, east and south by "hard" urban edges. Along the western edge is a landscaped space. The former airport oval, readopted and superimposed on the orthogonal layout in the form of a dominant green strip, extends from the listed viewing terraces at the western end, past the heraldic hall, to the former airport tower. This "green oval" forms a continuous undeveloped open space that is accessible to the public.

Der öffentliche Straßenraum ist geprägt durch definierte Baufluchten und Vorgärten.

The public street space is defined by strictly drawn building lines and front gardens.

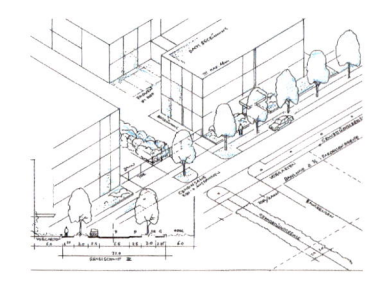

Umsetzung der städtebaulichen Ziele in einen rechtsverbindlichen Bebauungsplan für einen Teil des Gewerbegebiets

Implementation of the urban design goals through a statutory development plan for part of the commercial zone

Der Gestaltungsplan, Bebauungsplan 1998, zeigt die orthogonale Grundstruktur mit dem „Grünoval", der Zone der ehemaligen Flughafenbebauung.

The design/development plan, 1998, shows the orthogonal structure of the layout with the "green oval" – the zone of the former airport buildings.

Realisierungswettbewerb Park+Ride-Anlage

1998 wurde schließlich ein Ideen- und Realisierungswettbewerb für die Park+Ride-Anlage ausgelobt. Die außenliegenden Auf- und Abfahrtsrampen signalisieren dem Autofahrer bereits von weitem den Zweck des Gebäudes. Besonderer Wert wird auf gute Orientierung für Autofahrer und für Fußgänger gelegt. Mit der offenen und transparenten Gestaltung der Fassaden und mit dem Einbau der Lichthöfe ist eine natürliche Belichtung und Belüftung sichergestellt und eine benutzerfreundliche Übersichtlichkeit gegeben.

Competition for park-and-ride structure

Finally, in 1998, a competition was held in which ideas were expected for the construction of a parking complex as part of a park-and-ride concept. The external access and exit ramps indicate the function of this structure from afar. Special importance is attached to good orientation both for car drivers and pedestrians. The open, transparent design of the façades and the incorporation of light wells guarantee natural lighting and ventilation of the spaces and a user-friendly sense of clarity.

Die Stellung aller flankierenden Bauwerke und Anlagen weist auf den Messeeingang Ost hin.

The layout of the flanking structures and amenities indicates the direction of the eastern entrance to the trade fair site.

Busse, Frauen- und Behindertenparkplätze, Kiosk und Cafeteria sind durchweg mit kurzen Wegen der U-Bahn zugeordnet.

Bus facilities, parking areas for women and the disabled, the kiosk and the cafeteria are all connected with the underground railway via short routes.

Die außenliegenden Auf- und Abfahrtsrampen signalisieren die Zweckbestimmung des Gebäudes.

The external access and exit ramps indicate the function of the building.

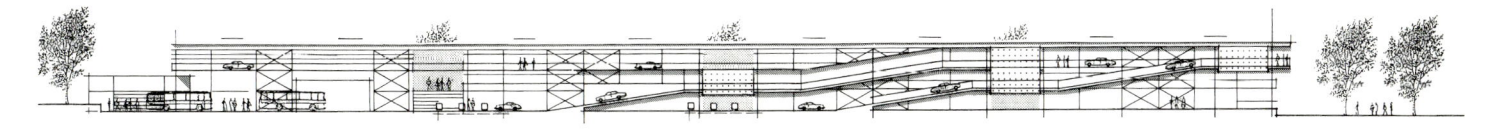

Was uns von Anfang an fasziniert hat, sind Aufgaben an der „Nahtstelle" zwischen Architektur und Städtebau. Wir verstehen ein Gebäude nicht als Solitär, nicht losgelöst von seiner Umgebung, sondern stets im Zusammenhang und im Austausch mit seinem Kontext. Nach unserer Auffassung füllt Architektur nicht Raum aus, sondern sie erzeugt einen Raum. Der Raum wiederum bestimmt die Determinanten der Architektur. Gerade die schöpferische Vorstellung über Architektur hinaus ist es, was die Spannweite unseres Berufs ausmacht.

Die Vieldeutigkeit moderner Lebenserfahrung, die Spiegelung der Lebensvielfalt darf und soll sich im Beziehungsgeflecht zwischen Architektur und Städtebau ausdrücken. Beispielhaft für dieses Gestaltungsprinzip ist unser Wettbewerbsentwurf für das Regierungsviertel Dresden aus dem Jahr 1993.

Der stadträumliche Lösungsansatz bezieht sich auf die historischen Strukturen, auf die Platz- und Straßenräume mit Sichtachsen und Fluchtpunkten und entwickelt diese weiter. Dabei spielt auch der Umgang mit Architektur aus der Zeit der DDR eine Rolle.

Unser Entwurf, das Vorhandene sensibel zurückzuübersetzen und die historischen Raumqualitäten für moderne, funktionale Objektarchitektur zu nutzen, das Raumgefüge zur Grundtextur für neue Ministerien, Wohn- und Gewerbebauten werden zu lassen, enthält somit auch die Chance für Vielfalt und Widerspruch. Eine stadträumliche Vision zu entwickeln ist gerade dann eine Herausforderung, wenn die Beseitigung mancher „Bausünde" aus der Zeit der DDR politisch nicht mehr durchsetzbar erscheint. Ungeachtet aller Schwierigkeiten ist es die Lust am Ort, die uns beflügelt.

***Bauen
im
städtischen Kontext***

***Building
in an urban context***

From the very beginning, we were fascinated by assignments at the "interface" between architecture and urban planning. We understand a building not as an isolated object, detached from its surroundings, but always in conjunction and conducting a dialogue with its context. To our mind, architecture is not something that fills space; it creates space. Space, on the other hand, determines the co-ordinates of architecture. What makes our profession so exciting is the creative faculty that extends beyond pure architecture.

The multivalency of modern human experience, the reflection of the rich variety of life can, and indeed should, find expression in the nexus between architecture and urban planning. Our competition scheme for the government district of Dresden dating from 1993 may serve as an example of this design principle.

There, our approach to urban space is based on historical structures: existing squares and streets, visual axes and points of alignment, which we proceed to extrapolate. In this respect, our attitude towards architecture dating from the era of the German Democratic Republic (GDR) also plays an important role.

Our scheme, which comprises a sensitive reinterpretation of existing elements and the use of historical spatial qualities to create modern, functional architecture, adopts the existing three-dimensional fabric as the basic structure for the new ministries, housing and commercial developments, thus providing scope for contrast and variety. Developing an urban spatial vision poses a challenge, especially when it would seem no longer feasible politically to remove some of the "constructional sins" of the GDR era. Regardless of the difficulties, it is the genius loci and the delight engendered by it that lends wing to our designs.

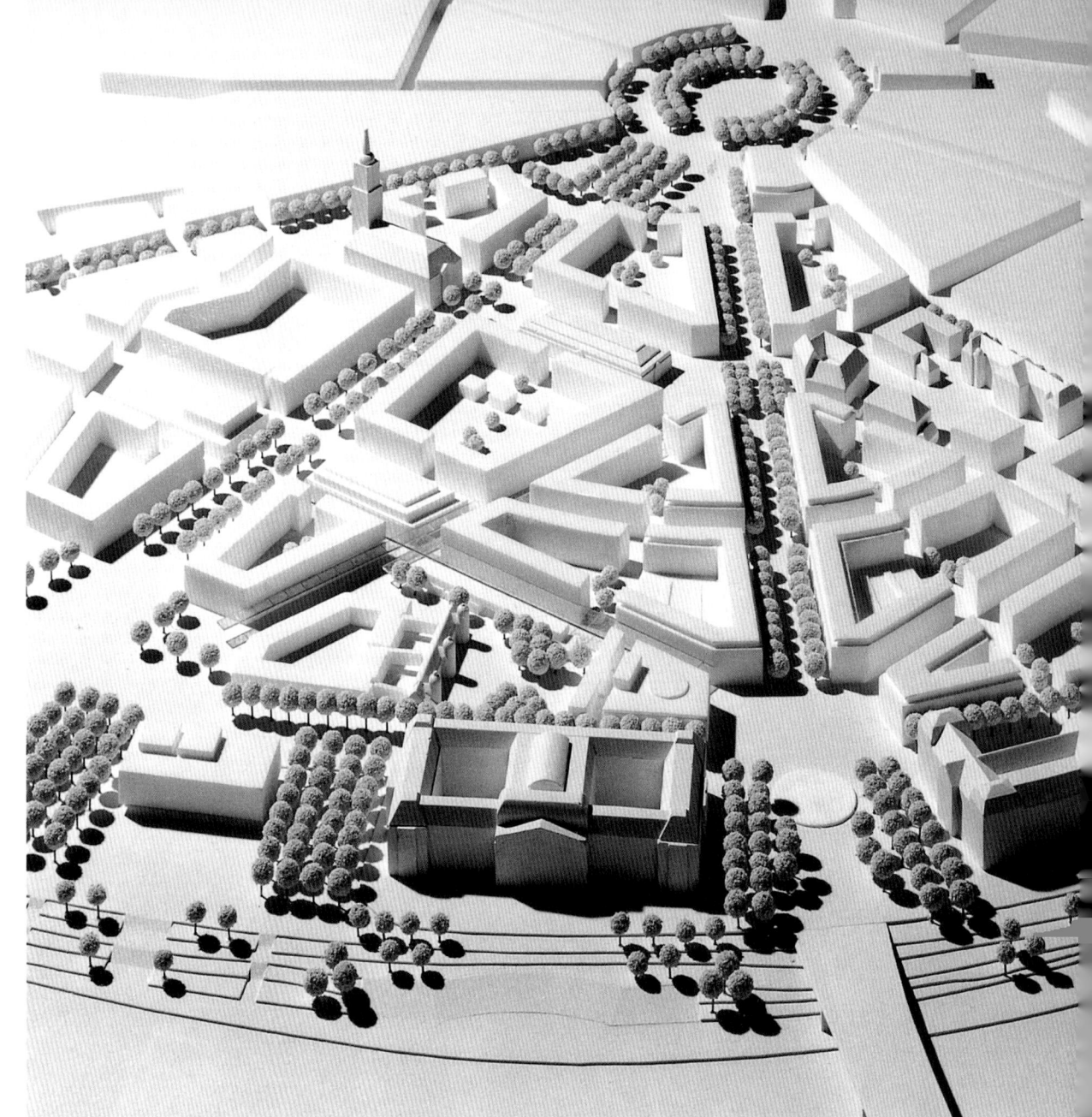

Auf den Spuren der historischen Stadtentwicklung wird eine Abfolge von Straßen- und Platzräumen gestaltet, die dem formalen Anspruch „Regierungsviertel" genügt, gleichzeitig zum Ausdruck einer neu gewonnenen demokratischen Gesellschaftsstruktur wird: Städtebaulicher Ideenwettbewerb, Modellaufnahme über die Elbe.

Tracing the lines of the historical urban development: a sequence of street spaces and squares designed to meet the formal requirements of a "government district"; and at the same time, an expression of regained democratic social structures; urban planning ideas competition; photo of model, looking across the River Elbe.

Carolaplatz: Der Maßstab der typischen Platzform (halbrund) des späten 19. Jahrhunderts wird in veränderter Form (Trapez) wieder aufgenommen.

Carolaplatz: the scale of the typical late-19th-century public open space (semicircular in shape) is adopted in modified form (trapezium).

Innere Neustadt Dresden – Regierungsviertel

Innere Neustadt, Dresden – Government District

5

1993 Wettbewerb Innere Neustadt/Regierungsviertel · 1. Preis
seit 1993 Städtebaulicher Rahmenplan Innere Neustadt
1994 Gutachten · Sanierung Teilgebiet Innere Neustadt
1995 – 1998 Bebauungsplan Regierungsviertel
1995 Wettbewerb Ministerialgebäude · 2. Preis

*1993 Competition for Innere Neustadt/Government District
of Dresden: first prize*
since 1993 Outline urban planning for Innere Neustadt
*1994 Planning study · Rehabilitation of part of
Innere Neustadt*
1995 – 1998 Development plan for Government District
1995 Competition for ministerial building: second prize

Behutsame Stadtreparatur auf historischem Grundriss in der Inneren Neustadt, einem Teil der Innenstadt Dresdens

Sensitive urban renewal of the Innere Neustadt in the centre of Dresden based on the historical layout

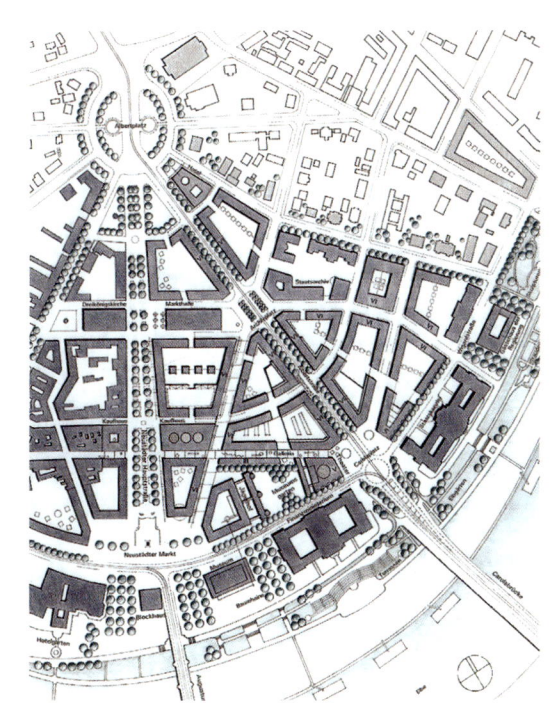

Spannungsvolle Abfolge aufeinander abgestimmter Sequenzen des öffentlichen Raumes: Städtebaulicher Ideenwettbewerb, Lageplan

An exciting sequence of coordinated public spaces; urban planning ideas competition, site plan

Innere Neustadt Dresden | 59

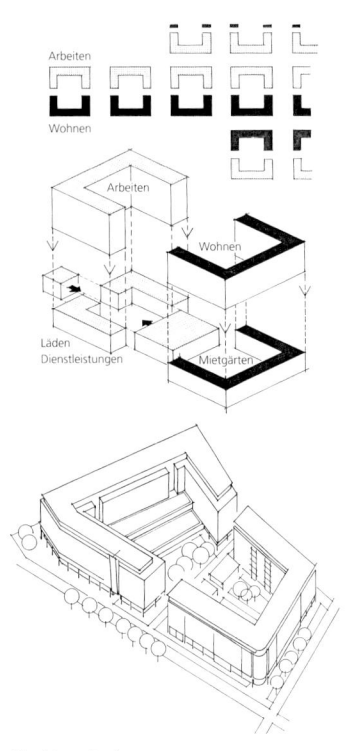

*Strukturprinzip:
Büro- und Wohngebäude bilden jeweils einen öffentlich zugänglichen, ruhigen Innenhof.*

Structural principle: office and housing tracts combined to form quiet internal court-yards accessible to the public.

Die Innere Neustadt, ein Teil der Innenstadt Dresdens, mit einem lebendigen Miteinander von Arbeiten, Wohnen, Handel, Dienstleistungen, Gastronomie, Kultur und Erholung. Modellaufnahme, Blick in Richtung Altstadt

The Innere Neustadt, part of the urban centre of Dresden, exhibits a lively mixture of working, living, trade, services, gastronomic, cultural and recreational facilities. Photo of model: view towards the old city centre

Städtebaulicher Rahmenplan

Das Ergebnis des städtebaulichen Ideenwettbewerbes wurde im Hinblick auf eine langfristige Realisierung als städtebaulicher Rahmenplan für die Innere Neustadt und für das Regierungsviertel Dresdens weiter entwickelt.

Grundlage war die Wiederaufnahme der historischen Stadtstrukturen, verbunden mit der Akzeptanz von Bauten des Wiederaufbaus nach 1945, soweit an geeigneter Stelle gelegen. Das strahlenförmig aufgebaute Platz- und Straßengefüge der Inneren Neustadt soll wiederhergestellt werden. Im gesamten Gebiet wird eine städtebauliche Differenzierung angestrebt: eine spannungsvolle Abfolge aufeinander abgestimmter Sequenzen des öffentlichen Raumes. Eine räumliche Fassung bzw. Rückgabe der Maßstäblichkeit und einer geeigneten Dimension der Plätze und Straßenräume, insbesondere der Brückenköpfe, ist das Ziel.

Es soll ein Stadtteil mit einer lebendigen Mischung der Funktionen Verwaltung, Wohnen, Versorgung, Kultur, Freizeit entstehen.

Damit kann das Regierungsviertel zum Ausdruck einer neu gewonnenen demokratischen Gesellschaftsstruktur werden. Diese Funktionsmischung soll durch eine vertikale und horizontale Verknüpfung mit folgendem Prinzip der Blockstruktur erreicht werden: die öffentlichen Einrichtungen wie Verwaltung/Ministerien (Obergeschosse) sowie Einzelhandel und publikumswirksame Dienstleistungen (Erdgeschosse) orientieren sich zu den Verkehrsstraßen, das Wohnen findet dagegen auf der ruhigeren Seite (Anliegerstraßen) statt.

Outline urban planning

The proposals submitted in the urban ideas competition for the Innere Neustadt (Central Neustadt) and the government district of Dresden were developed in the form of an outline urban plan conceived for long-term implementation.

The planning was based on a reinstatement of the historic urban structures and, wherever the location allowed, an acceptance of buildings erected during the period of post-war reconstruction. The radial layout of streets and squares in the Innere Neustadt is to be restored. A variety of urban situations is to be created through-out the area: an exciting sequence of public spaces co-ordinated with each other. The aim of the planning is to restore a sense of scale and proportion to the streets and squares, especially in the bridgehead areas.

The district will possess a lively mixture of functions, ranging from administration, housing and services to cultural and leisure amenities.

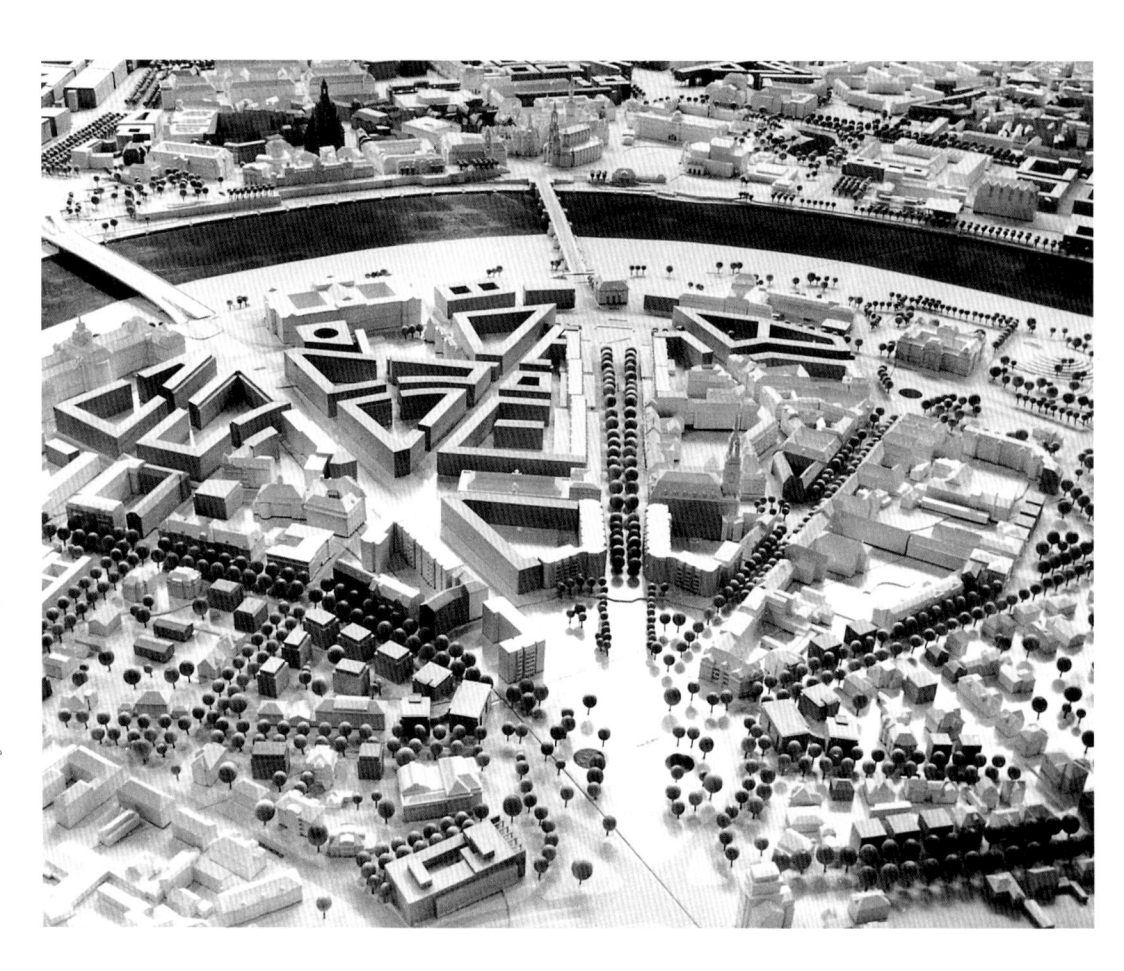

As a result of these measures, the government district should become

an expression of regained democratic social structures. The mixture of functions will be achieved by creating vertical and horizontal links between the various uses, which will, in turn, be laid out according to the following street-block principle. Public offices, such as those for the administration and ministries, will be located on the upper floors. Retail shopping facilities and services with close public links will be on the ground floor. Both will be oriented to roads with vehicular traffic. Housing functions, in contrast, will be situated on the quieter faces of the buildings, overlooking residential roads.

Machbarkeitsstudie

Gleichzeitig mit der Erstellung des städtebaulichen Rahmenplans wurden wir mit einer Machbarkeitsstudie für die Sanierung eines Teilgebietes der Inneren Neustadt beauftragt. Dieses Gebiet ist heute von massiven Nachkriegsbauten in Plattenbauweise der 60er und 70er Jahre geprägt. Die den Maßstab sprengenden zehngeschossigen Wohnbauten an der Sarrasanistraße stören das ehemals geschlossene und einheitliche Stadtbild der Inneren Neustadt.

Wir konnten zeigen, dass eine städtebauliche Neuordnung erreicht und in realisierbare Handlungsschritte umgesetzt werden kann, ohne wesentliche Abstriche von den Zielvorstellungen machen zu müssen. Abbruchmaßnahmen und Neubaumaßnahmen sollten so aufeinander abgestimmt sein, dass eine Umsiedlung der Bewohner innerhalb des Gebietes sukzessive erfolgen kann. Im Zuge der Nachverdichtung entsteht so ein Gewinn an Wohn-, Laden-, Dienstleistungs- sowie Büro- und Verwaltungsflächen von insgesamt 125 %.

Feasibility study

Parallel to the outline urban planning, we were commissioned to prepare a feasibility study for the rehabilitation of part of the Innere Neustadt. The area in question is marked today by massive post-war buildings in the panel construction system that was common in the 1960s and 70s. The ten-storey housing blocks in Sarrasanistrasse are not only completely out of scale; they destroy the cohesive, unified urban planning that was once a distinguishing feature of the Innere Neustadt.

We were able to demonstrate that an urban reorganization was feasible and that it could be implemented in a series of comprehensible stages, without compromising the overall goal. Demolition work and new construction should be coordinated with each other in such a way that it will be possible to resettle residents successively within the area. Through a higher density of development, an overall increase of 125 per cent in the areas of housing, shops, services, offices and administration could be achieved.

Die radialen Achsen des Albertplatzes überlagern sich mit dem dreistrahligen Achsensystem des Neustädter Marktes und mit dem des Carolaplatzes sowie mit den vier Strahlen des Archivplatzes; dadurch entstehen abwechslungsreiche Stadträume und Blickbeziehungen.

The axes radiating from Albertplatz intersect the three-part axial system of the Neustädter Markt and that of Carolaplatz, as well as the four axes extending from Archivplatz. The result is a richly varied network of urban spaces and visual links.

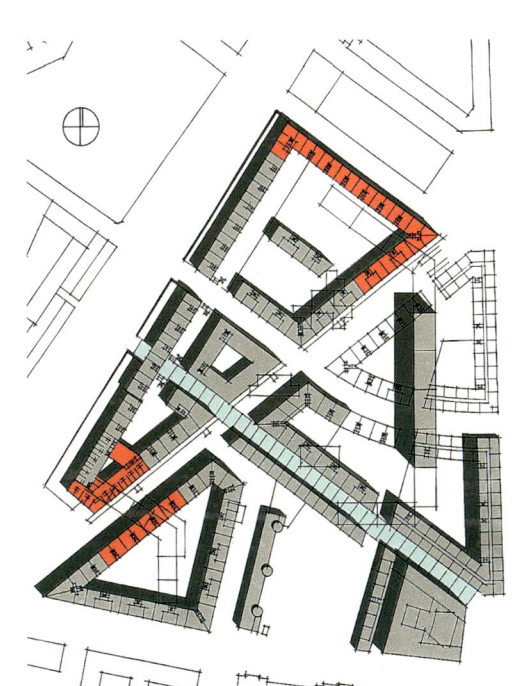

Bestand und Neuplanung überlagern sich. Der städtebauliche Entwurf soll in mehreren aufeinander abgestimmten Bauabschnitten umgesetzt werden (hier Baustufe 2).

New planning measures overlaid on the existing urban structure. The rehabilitation plan is to be implemented in a number of construction stages (here, stage 2).

Innere Neustadt Dresden | 61

Bebauungsplan

Auf Grundlage des städtebaulichen Wettbewerbs und dem daraus entwickelten Rahmenplanentwurf wurde für den östlichen Bereich der Inneren Neustadt ein Bebauungsplan erstellt.

Die Festsetzung der Nutzungsart trägt dem Ziel einer lebendigen Funktionsmischung Rechnung. Das Maß der Nutzung wird unter anderem durch zwingend festgesetzte Traufhöhen und durch die Höchstzahl der Geschosse bestimmt; damit kann eine genaue Höhenentwicklung vorgegeben und ein homogenes städtebauliches Erscheinungsbild des Stadtteils erreicht werden.

Das städtebauliche Grundprinzip des Wettbewerbs, die Innenhöfe zu öffnen und der Allgemeinheit zugänglich zu machen, wird durch entsprechende Festsetzung von Baulinien und Baugrenzen umgesetzt; zusätzlich entsteht so ein Sichtbezug zur Staatskanzlei.

Development plan

Based on the urban planning competition and the outline planning proposals to which this led, a development plan was drawn up for the eastern area of the Innere Neustadt.

In designating the various uses, a first step was taken towards creating the lively mixture of functions foreseen in the planning. The intensity of use will also be determined by establishing fixed eaves heights and the maximum number of storeys. This will ensure a precise control of the height of developments and help to achieve a homogeneous urban appearance within the district.

One of the basic principles of the urban planning in the competition was to open up the courtyards to the general public. This will be implemented by defining the appropriate building lines and the outer limits of developments. These measures will also create a visual link to the state chancellery building.

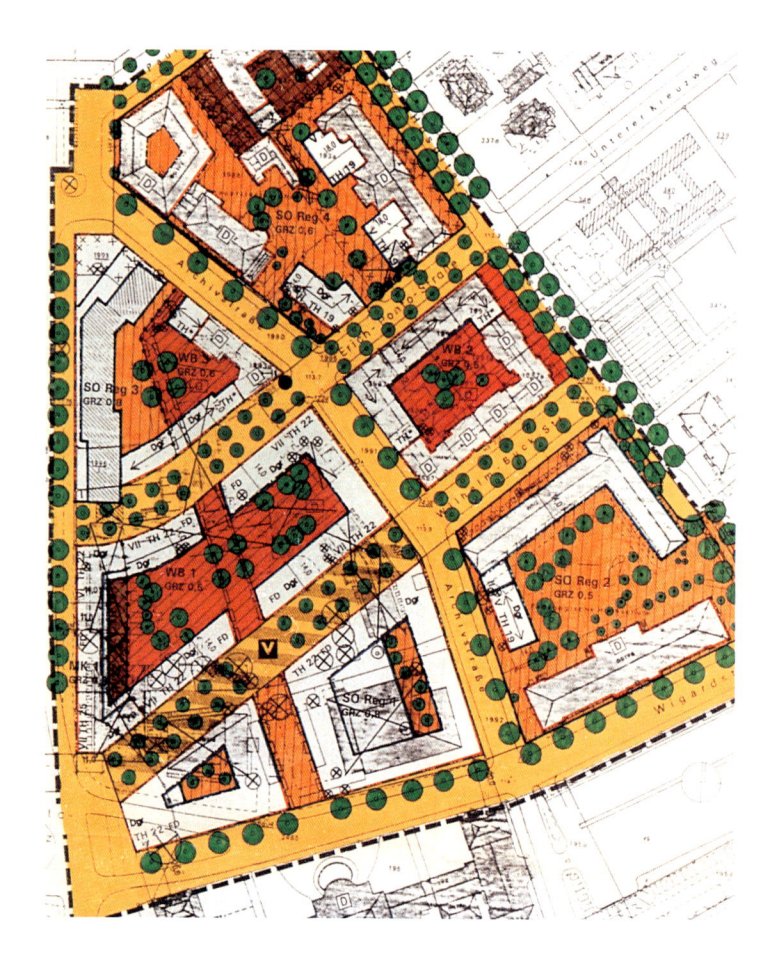

Umsetzung der städtebaulichen Ziele in einen rechtsverbindlichen Bebauungsplan

Translation of urban goals into a statutory development plan

Realisierungswettbewerb

Das Ministeriumsgebäude am Carolaplatz ist der erste Realisierungsbaustein des städtebaulichen Rahmenplanentwurfs. Der in seiner Grundgeometrie vorgegebene Baublock ist unter Beibehaltung der städtebaulichen Vorgaben – öffentlicher Durchgang – nunmehr entsprechend seiner Nutzung in drei Innenhöfe aufgelöst. Die Eingänge der drei im Gebäude untergebrachten Ministerien (Sächsische Staatsministerien des Inneren, für Wirtschaft und Arbeit, für Umwelt und Landesentwicklung) liegen in dem zentralen öffentlichen Innenhof, der achsial mit dem Mittelrisalit der Staatskanzlei korrespondiert und die Zusammengehörigkeit dieser Gebäude deutlich macht.

Realisation

The ministerial building in Carolaplatz will be the first object to be realized in the context of the outline urban planning proposals. The basic geometry of the development was determined in advance by the form of the street block. The complex is also articulated into three internal courtyards in accordance with its use and fulfils the planning requirements by providing public access across the site. The entrances to the three ministries housed in the block (the Saxon State Ministries of the Interior; Economics and Labour; and the Environment and Regional Development) are situated in the central projecting tract of the state chandellery opposite, thereby indicating the close relationship between the two buildings.

Öffentlicher Eingangshof mit Läden und Kantine

Public courtyard, containing entrances to ministries as well as shops and a canteen

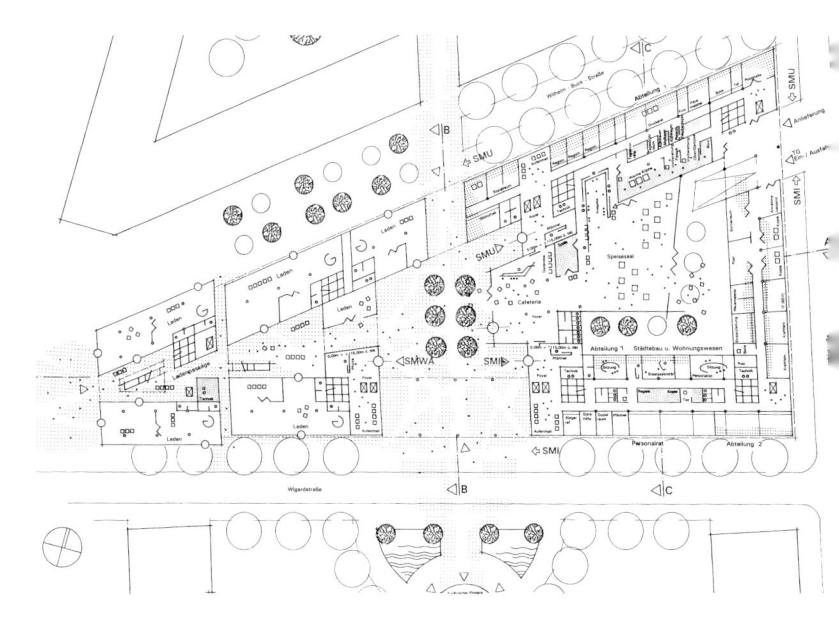

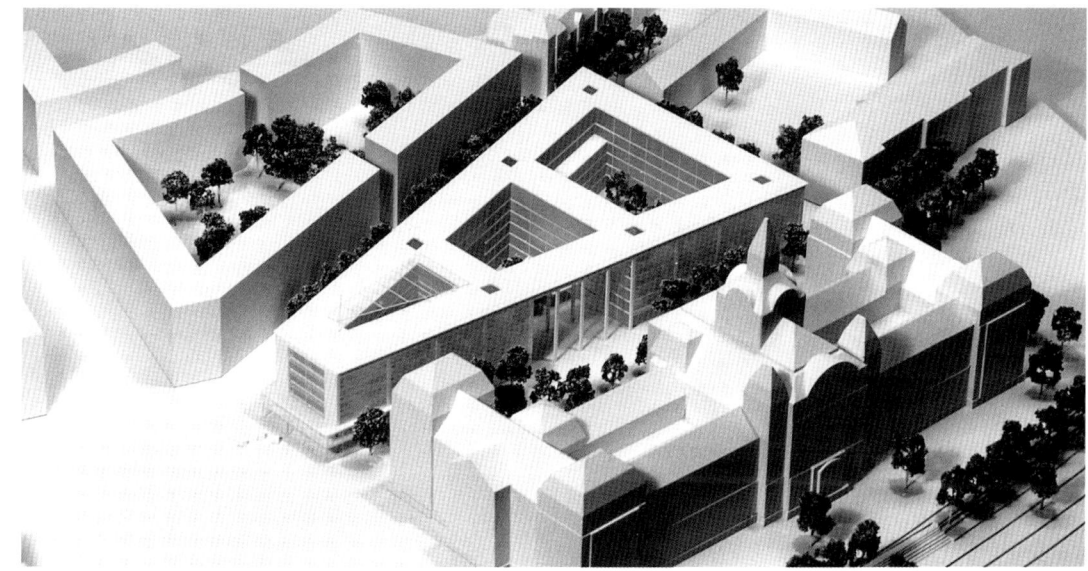

Ministeriumsblock mit den drei Innenhöfen und großer Öffnung zur Staatskanzlei

Ministerial block with the three courtyards and the large opening opposite the state chancellery

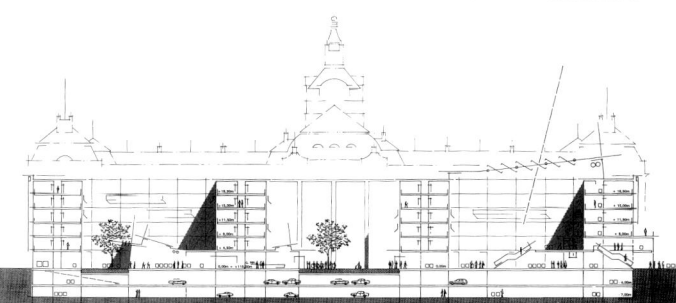

Ministeriumsblock: Der Schnitt zeigt die Situation der drei Höfe.

Section through ministerial block, showing the layout of the three courtyards

Innere Neustadt Dresden

Das Wettbewerbs-
modell zeigt deutlich
das heterogene städte-
bauliche Umfeld.

*The competition model
reveals the hetero-
geneous quality of the
urban surroundings.*

Universität Leipzig – Chemische Institute

6   **University of Leipzig – Institutes for Chemistry**

1994   *Wettbewerb Chemische Institute · 1. Preis*
1995 – 1999   *Chemische Institute · Neubau*
    Planung und Realisierung
1996 – 1999   *Studentenwohnheim*
    Sanierung und Umnutzung
    Planung und Realisierung

1994   *Competition for Institutes for Chemistry: first prize*
1995 – 1999   *New Institutes for Chemistry*
    planning and construction
1996 – 1999   *Rehabilitation and conversion of students' hostel:*
    planning and construction

Neubau und Ausbau der traditionsreichen Chemischen Institute zu einem Hightech-Studienzentrum im Park

New construction and conversion of the famous Institutes for Chemistry into a high-tech study centre in a park setting

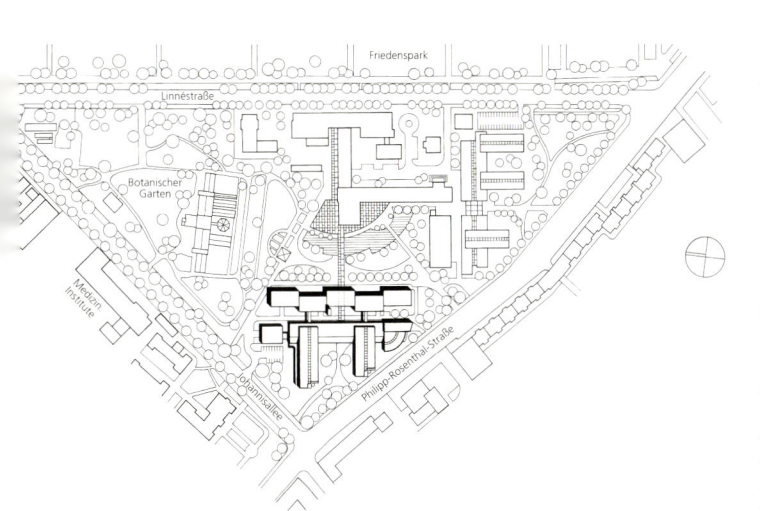

Das so genannte „Linné-Dreieck": links der Botanische Garten, oben vorhandene Universitätsbauten, unten das Studentenwohnheim im engen Zusammenhang mit unserem Neubau, rechts mögliche Erweiterungen

The so-called "Linne triangle": on the left, the Botanical Garden; at the top, the existing university buildings; at the bottom, the students' hostel closely related to the new chemistry buildings; on the right, possible extensions

Synthese aus Alt und Neu und großen Bäumen

Synthesis of old and new, with large mature trees

Realisierungswettbewerb

Der Lehrstuhl für Chemie besitzt an der Universität Leipzig eine über 300 Jahre zurückreichende Tradition, die Nobelpreisträger wie Ostwald, Bosch und Bergius hervorgebracht hat. Nach der Zerstörung im Krieg wurden die Institute nur teilweise wieder errichtet und entsprachen seit langem nicht mehr modernen Anforderungen. Mit dem Neubau Chemie, der Erweiterung der Physik, der Pharmazie und einer zentralen Bibliothek sollte auf dem „Linné-Dreieck" wieder ein naturwissenschaftliches Zentrum entstehen. 1994 lobte der Freistaat Sachsen hierzu einen offenen einstufigen städtebaulichen Ideen- und Realisierungswettbewerb aus. Als Träger des 1. Preises wurden wir mit der Planung beauftragt.

Das Grundstück ist geprägt durch seine drei „grünen Ecken": den Botanischen Garten, den wertvollen alten Baumbestand im Bereich der Philipp-Rosenthal-Straße/Johannisallee sowie im Bereich der Liebigstraße/Johannisallee. Kennzeichnend ist darüber hinaus das fragmentarisch wirkende Nebeneinander bestehender wissenschaftlicher Gebäude sowie des achtgeschossigen Plattenbau-Studentenwohnheimes. Die Umgebung ist gekennzeichnet durch eine sehr heterogene bauliche Struktur.

Um den wertvollen alten Baumbestand auf dem Grundstück weitgehend zu erhalten, bot es sich an, die gesamte städtebauliche Neuordnung am Bestand zu orientieren und möglichst kompakt als Kammstruktur von innen heraus zu entwickeln.

Das Studentenwohnheim, das sich als Querriegel dieser Absicht zunächst in den Weg stellte, wurde eng mit dem Institutsgebäude verknüpft und so in die Gesamtbebauung integriert. Dies ging nur, indem wir Teile der beiden unteren Geschosse des Wohnheims in Büros, Werkstätten und in eine Cafeteria für die Chemischen Institute umnutzten und einen großzügigen Durchbruch zwischen dem Neubau Chemie und der geplanten zentralen grünen Mitte, dem „Campus", als Ort der Begegnung und Erholung schufen.

Construction competition

The Department for Chemistry at the University of Leipzig can look back on a more than 300-year-old tradition that has produced Nobel prizewinners such as Ostwald, Bosch and Bergius. After their destruction during the war, the institutes were only partially rebuilt, and for a long time they failed to comply with modern standards. With the construction of a new chemistry department, the creation of a central library and the extension of the departments for physics and pharmacy, a centre of the natural sciences was to be established again within the "Linné triangle". In 1994, the Free State of Saxony held a single-stage open urban-planning ideas and construction competition. As winners of the first prize, we were entrusted with the planning.

The site is distinguished by its three "green corners": the Botanical Garden, and the corners of Philipp-Rosenthal-Strasse and Johannisallee, and Liebigstrasse and Johannisallee with their valuable stock of old trees. A further feature is the seemingly fragmentary arrangement of the

existing scientific buildings and the eight-storey students' hostel in prefabricated panel construction. The surroundings reveal an extremely heterogeneous built structure.

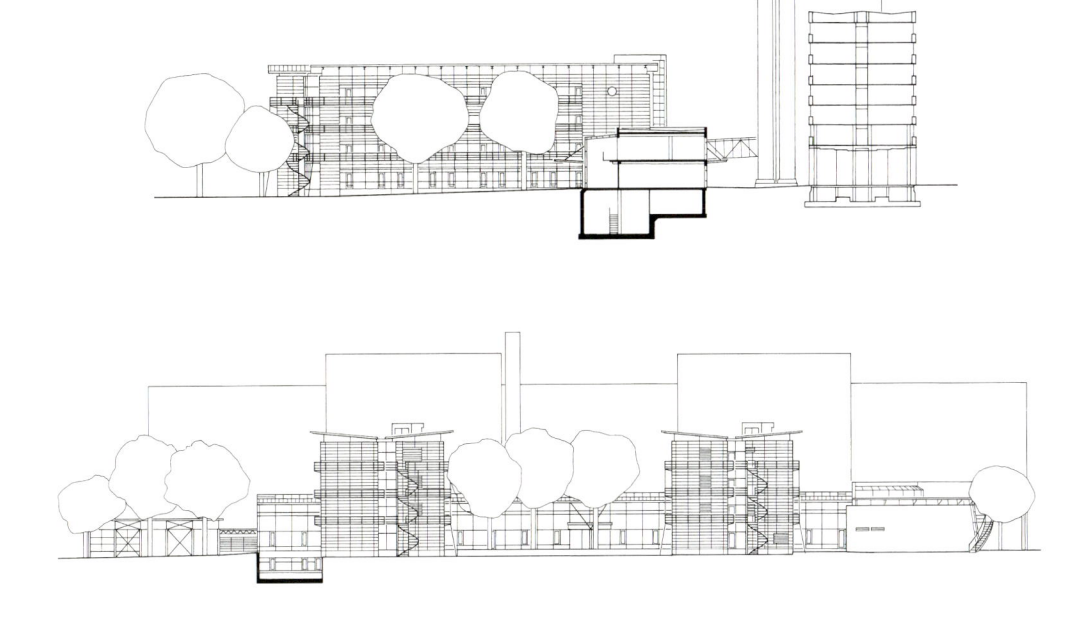

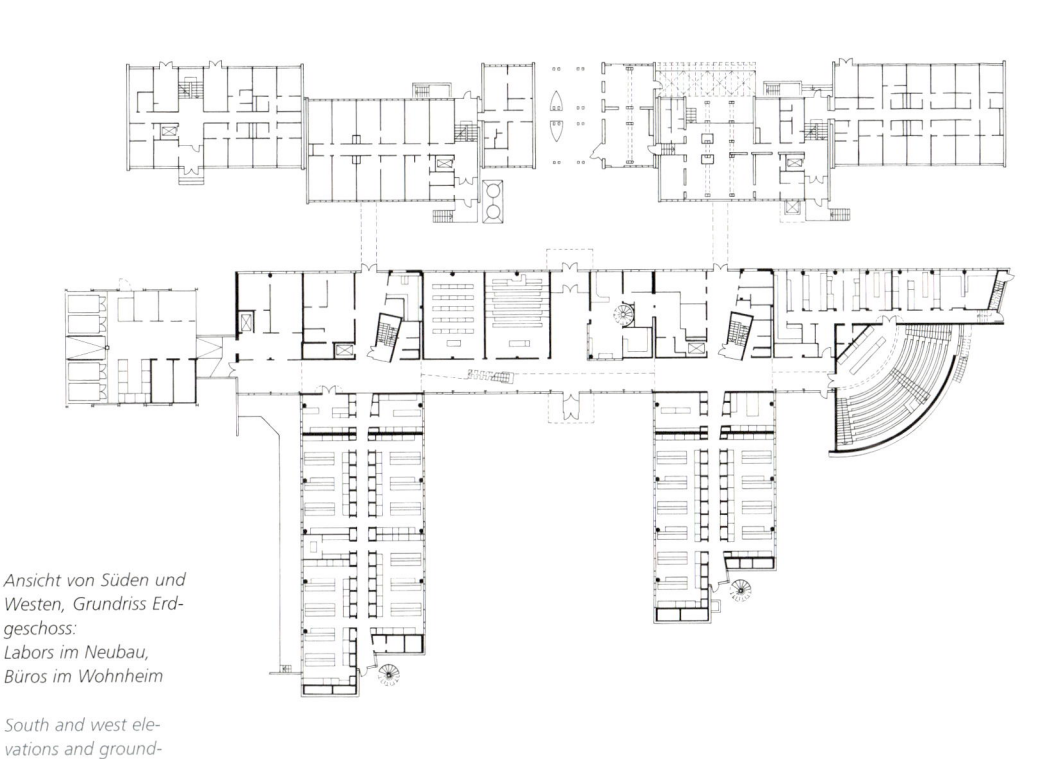

In order to retain as many of the mature trees on the site as possible, the entire urban restructuring was organized around the existing situation, and the new buildings were designed as compactly as possible in a comb-like layout from the inside outwards.

The students' hostel, in the form of a long transverse strip that was initially seen as an obstacle to these intentions, was tightly linked with the institute building and thus integrated into the overall development. This was possible only because we converted parts of the two lower storeys of the hostel into offices, workshops and a cafeteria for the Institutes of Chemistry and created a generous through-route from the new chemistry building to the planned landscaped centre of the site – the campus – which was to form a place of communication and recreation.

Ansicht von Süden und Westen, Grundriss Erdgeschoss:
Labors im Neubau,
Büros im Wohnheim

South and west elevations and ground-floor plan: laboratories in the new structure; offices in the hostel

Universität Leipzig

Neubau Institutsgebäude und Sanierung Studentenwohnheim

Der Neubau Chemie ist eine Lehr- und Forschungseinrichtung, die von ca. 1.000 jungen Menschen, Studenten und Doktoranden, genutzt wird. In einer zweigeschossigen Verbindungsspange sind die übergeordneten Bereiche wie Hörsäle, Seminarräume und Bibliothek untergebracht. Die hoch installierten Laborräume befinden sich, deutlich ablesbar, in den viergeschossigen Mittelflurbaukörpern, den „Kämmen". Bei Neuanforderungen an räumliche Zusammenhänge kann so flexibel reagiert werden. Im umgenutzten Teil des Studentenwohnheimes, angebunden über zwei Brücken, sind die Büros der Institute und eine Cafeteria untergebracht.

Für ein Laborgebäude mit vorwiegend präparativen Arbeiten bestand eine große Herausforderung in der Reduzierung der Gesamtluftmenge, um eine städtebaulich, architektonisch und wirtschaftlich überzeugende Lösung zu finden. Wichtigstes gestalterisches Ziel war es, die Baumasse auf dem parkartigen Grundstück optisch und technisch so weit wie möglich zu reduzieren und die Verknüpfung von Wohnheim und Neubau durch Ausbildung der gleichen Fassade bewußt zu betonen.

Die Fassade ist in den geschlossenen Bereichen eine filigran gebänderte Faserzement-Stülpschalung. Die großzügigen Fensterbereiche sind als Aluminium-Pfosten-Riegel-Konstruktion mit Holztüren, farbigen Brüstungen und Markisen ausgebildet. Die ebenfalls durch uns geplante Sanierung des verbleibenden Studentenwohnheims folgte mit einer darauf abgestimmten Putzfassade. Die Kämme erhielten ein Flügel-Blechdach.

New institute buildings and rehabilitation of students' hostel

The new buildings for the department of chemistry form a teaching and research facility used by roughly 1,000 young people, students and doctoral candidates. General areas such as lecture halls, seminar rooms and the library are housed in the two-storey linking tract. The highly equipped laboratories are legibly situated in the four-storey structures with a central corridor layout; i.e. in the teeth of the comb. This layout allows a flexible response in the event of new spatial relationships becoming necessary. Offices for the institutes and a cafeteria are now housed in the converted section of the students' hostel. The different tracts are connected via two bridges.

In the context of designing chemistry laboratories, a great challenge was posed by the need to reduce the overall cross-sections of the ventilation ducts to a minimum in order to achieve a convincing urban planning, architectural and economical solution. The most important design goals were to

Ein Steg zwischen Laborbau und den dazugehörigen Büros im ersten Obergeschoss des Wohnheims

Bridge between the laboratory tract and the ancillary offices that now occupy the first floor of the students' hostel

reduce the volume of the building as far as possible – both visually and technically – in this park-like situation, and to accentuate the links between the hostel and the new development by using the same façade construction for both.

The closed areas of the façade consist of narrow strips of shiplapped fibre-cement boarding. The generous areas of fenestration are in an aluminium post-and-rail construction with wood doors, coloured apron-wall panels and sunblinds. The rehabilitation of the rest of the students' hostel, for which we also did the planning, was executed with a matching rendered façade. The structures forming the teeth of the comb have shallow-pitched butterfly roofs with sheet metal coverings.

Universität Leipzig | 69

Farbe und Licht prägen die Atmosphäre eines Lehr- und Forschungsgebäudes.

The atmosphere of this building for teaching and research is characterized by colour and light.

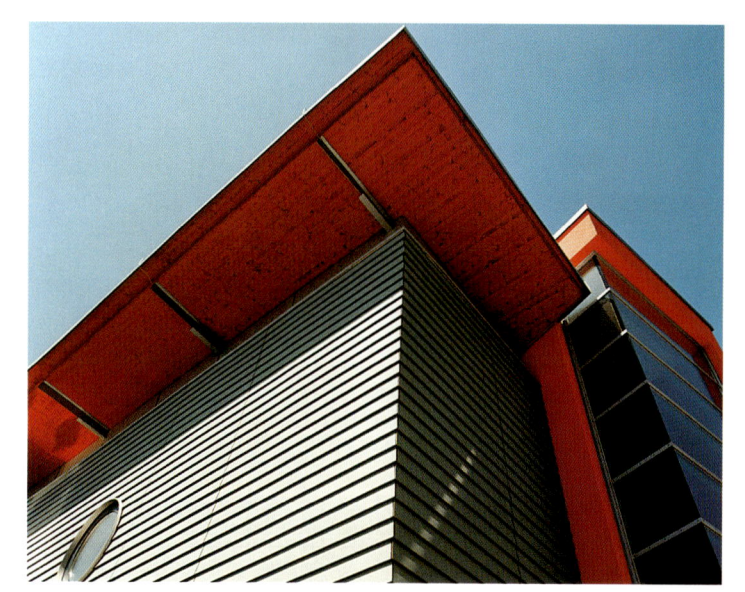

Holz und Faserzement an den Fassaden signalisieren Bescheidenheit und Kostenbewußtsein bei öffentlichen Bauvorhaben.

Timber and fibrecement in the façades signal restraint and cost consciousness in public construction.

Ein Glassteg schafft die Verbindung zum sanierten Studentenwohnheim.

A glass bridge forms a link to the refurbished students' hostel.

Bodenleuchten führen zum Haupteingang.

Recessed lighting in the paving marks the route to the main entrance.

Universität Leipzig | 71

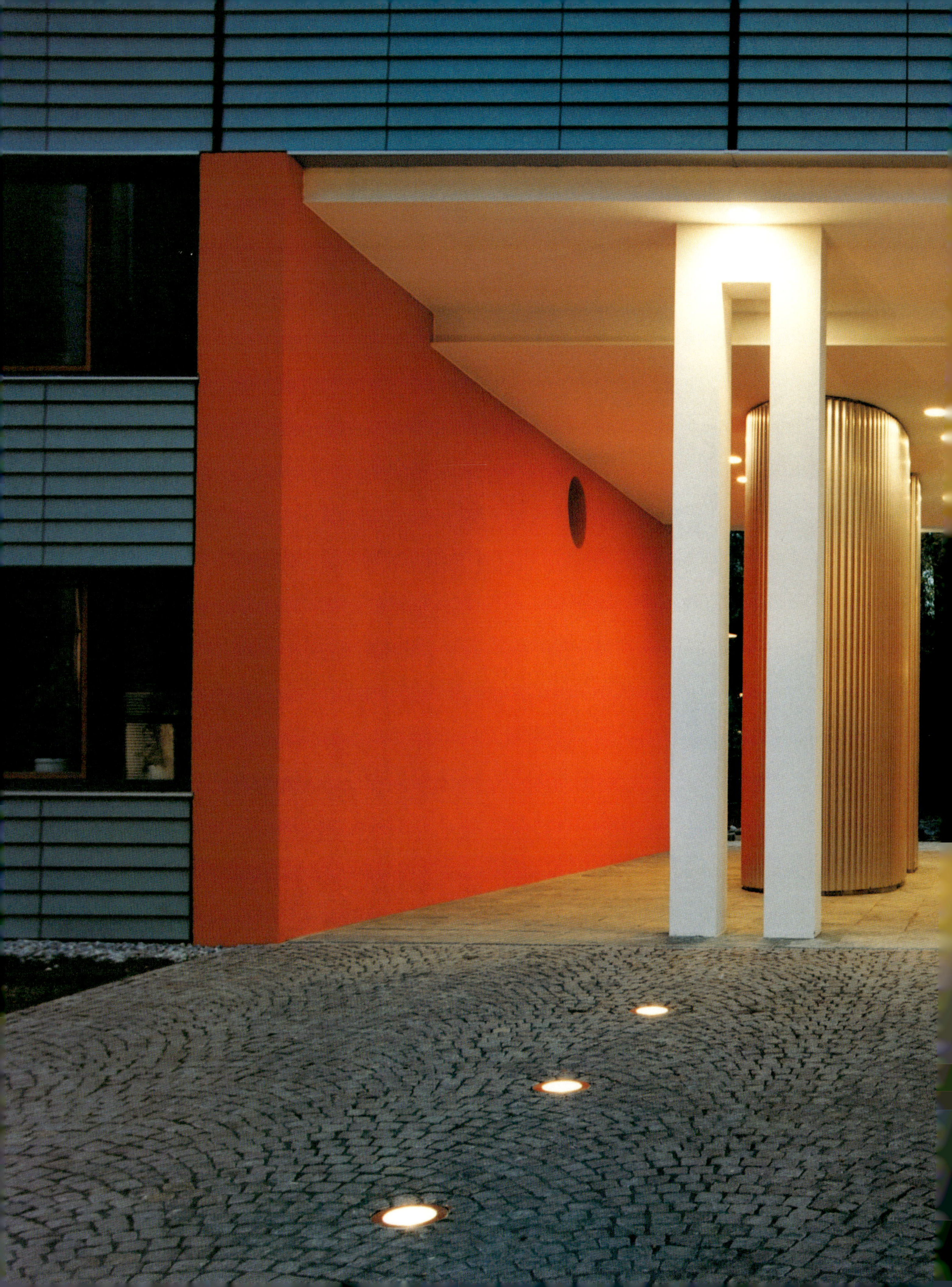

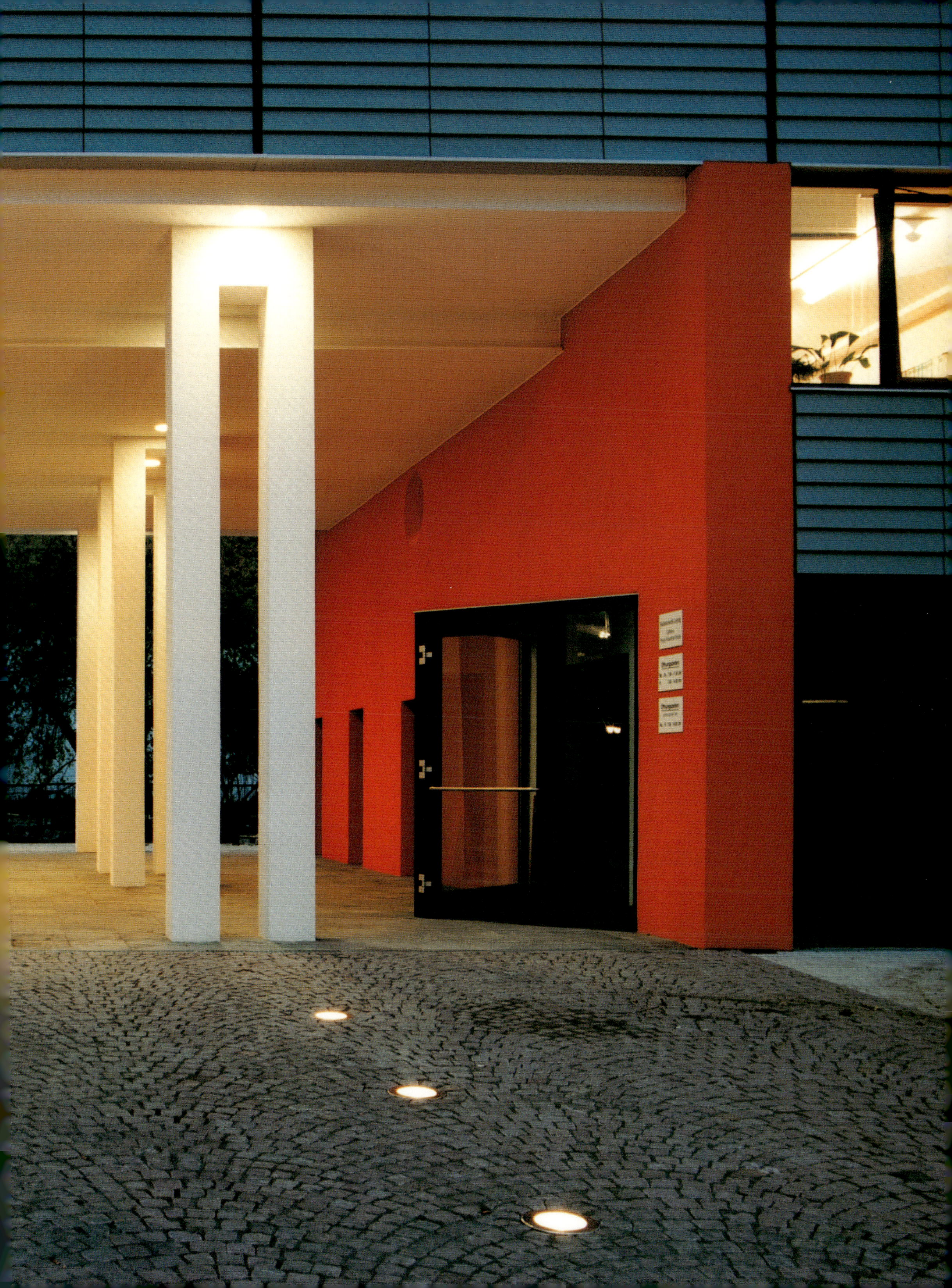

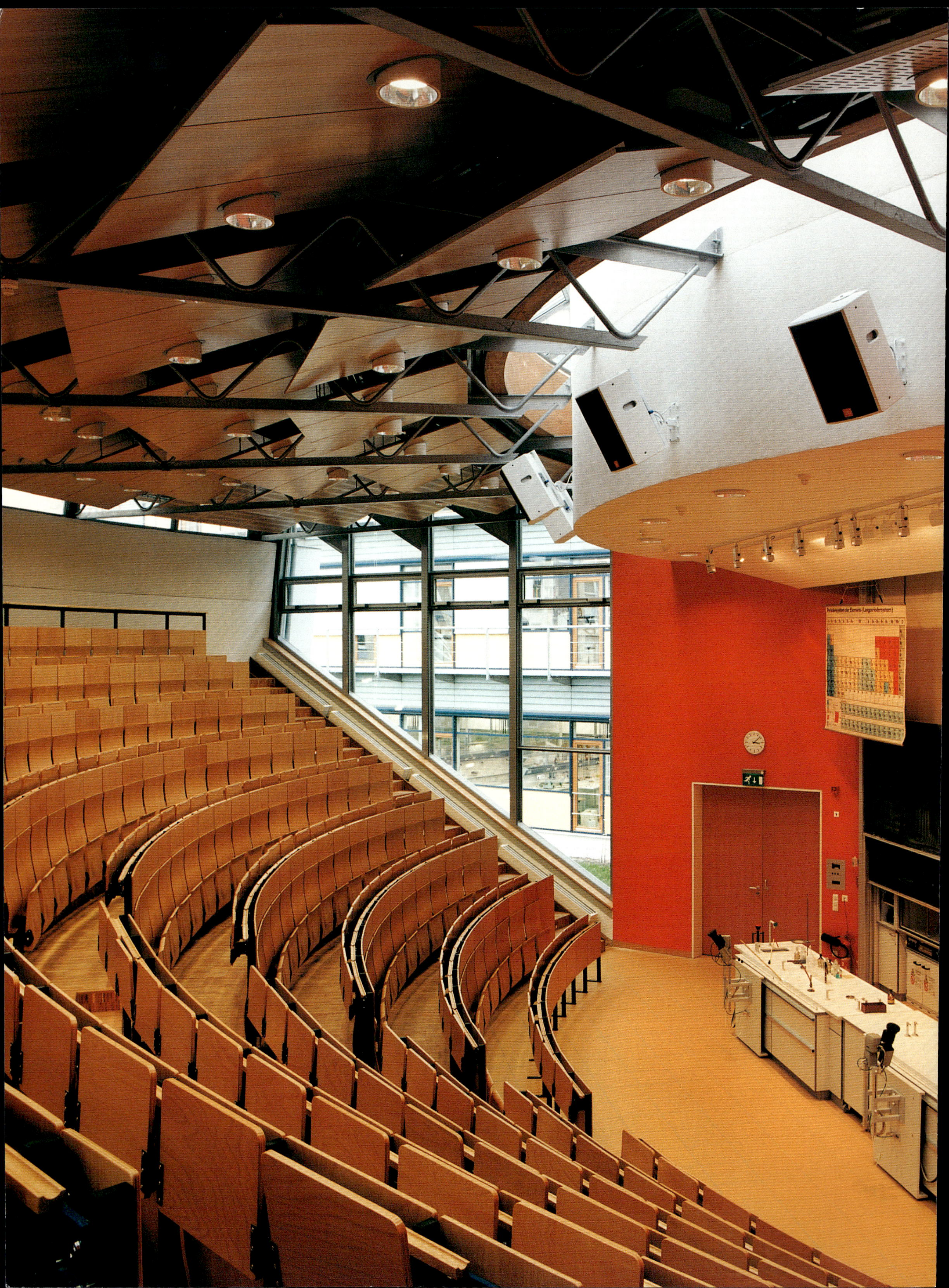

Das Besondere am Hörsaal ist die vielfältige und geschickte Einbeziehung des Tageslichts.

A special feature of the lecture hall is the subtle, varied exploitation of daylight.

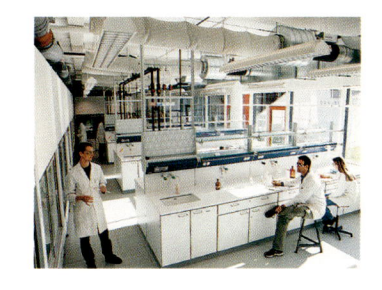

Innenausbau

Die zweigeschossige Verbindungsspange, als Erschließungsmagistrale, öffnet sich im Westen mit einer raumhohen Stahl-Glaskonstruktion zum alten Baumbestand. Der große Experimentalhörsaal mit einem Stahl-Blechdach bildet als verputzte Viertelkreis-Sonderform deren Abschluss.

Wichtiges Ziel war auch die Wechselwirkung von Außen- und Innenraum. Großzügige, wenn möglich raumhohe Glasflächen sollen den Baumbestand auch von innen sichtbar machen und das Gebäude entmaterialisieren. Oberlichter, nachts erleuchtet, unterstreichen die Wegeführung und schaffen helle Stimmungen und Raumakzente auch bei tiefen Räumen.

Besondere Bedeutung kommt der Verwendung von Materialien in ihrer spezifischen Erscheinung und dem Einsatz von Farbe und Holz in ausgewählten Bereichen zu, wie z. B. Brüstungen, Treppenhäuser, Hörsäle, Cafeteria und vor allem dem „Durchbruch".

Kunst und Architektur verbinden sich im wichtigen Durchgangsbereich und an der Hörsaalwand.

Die Objekte des Leipziger Künstlers Hael Yggs, Lichtquadrate, gestaltete Glasflächen und eine Ziffernfolge der Eulerschen Zahl, sollen eine spezielle Verbindung zur Thematik der Forschung und praktischen Anwendung herstellen, ohne eine vordergründige Verknüpfung mit einzelnen Erscheinungen darzustellen.

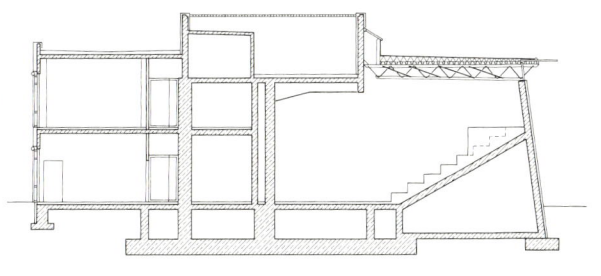

Querschnitt durch Hörsaal und Verbindungsspange

Cross-section through lecture hall and linking tract

Internal finishings

The two-storey linking tract, in the form of an access thoroughfare, opens towards the west into a tall steel-and-glass structure that affords views of the old trees outside. The large lecture hall for experimental work marks the termination of this route. It is in the form of a quadrant with rendered walls and a sheet-steel roof.

An important aspect of the design was to establish a reciprocal relationship between indoors and outdoors. Generous areas of glazing – extending over the full room height wherever possible – were designed to allow broad views of the trees from the internal spaces and to dematerialize the building. Roof lights, illuminated at night, accentuate the line of circulation and create spatial accents and a bright mood even in the deeper rooms.

Special importance was also attached to the use of materials in their essential forms and to the exploitation of colours and timber surfaces in selected areas; for example, in upstand walls, staircases, lecture halls, the cafeteria and especially in the cross-route created through the building tracts.

Art and architecture are united in this important through-route and on the external wall of the lecture hall.

The objects created by the Leipzig artist Hael Yggs – illuminated squares, specially designed areas of glass and a series of numerals based on Euler's constant – seek to establish special links with the research conducted here and its practical application, without superficially describing specific phenomena.

Universität Leipzig

7 6 2 7 7 2 4 0 7 6

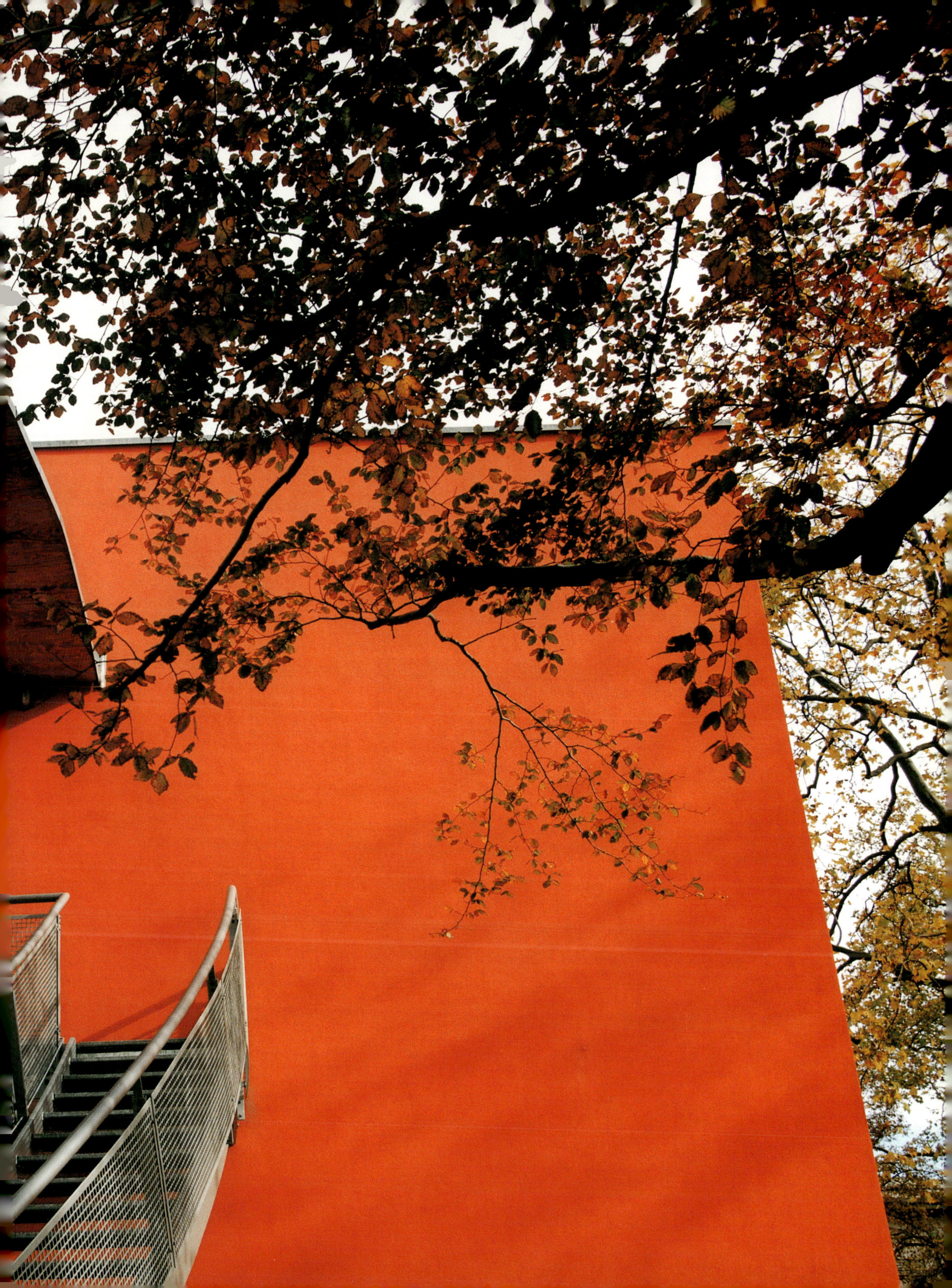

Städtebauliche Situation im Luftbild

Aerial view of urban context

Das gläserne Treppenhaus als Mittelpunkt der Anlage – Dächer ohne Installationsaufbauten

The glazed staircase forms the centre of the development. The roofscape was designed without service structures.

Frankona Rückversicherungs AG München

7 **Frankona Reinsurance Building, Munich**

1982   Wettbewerb erster Erweiterungsbau · 1. Preis
1982 – 1985 Planung und Realisierung
            erster Erweiterungsbau
1996 – 1998 Planung und Realisierung
            zweiter Erweiterungsbau

1982   Competition for first extension: first prize
1982 – 1985 Planning and construction of first extension
1996 – 1998 Planning and construction of
            second extension

Ein begrüntes Terrassengebäude
in einem grünen Hof
in einem grünen Stadtviertel

A verdant, terraced building set in a
landscaped courtyard in a garden-like
district of Munich

Lageplan mit Hauptgebäude (A) und Erweiterung an der Törringstraße (B)

Site plan, showing the main building (A) and the extension in Törringstrasse (B)

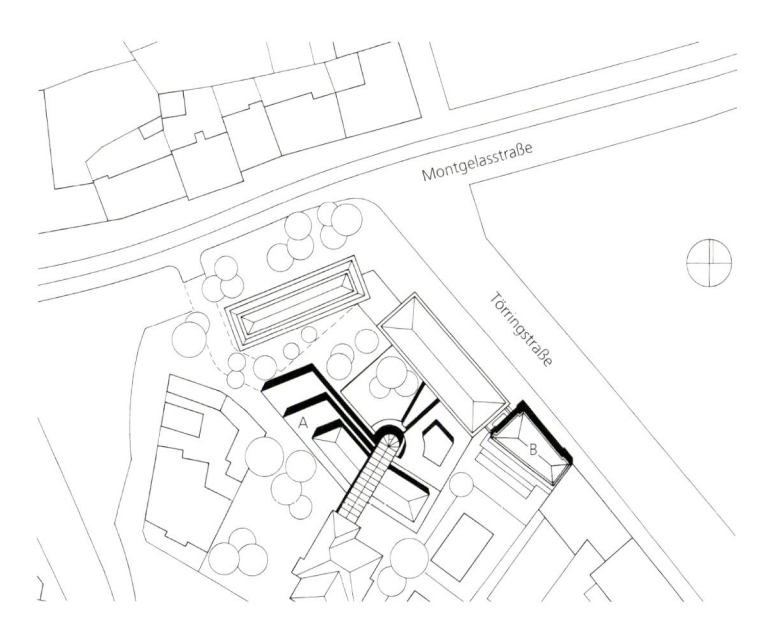

Ost-West-Schnitt A-A, von Norden

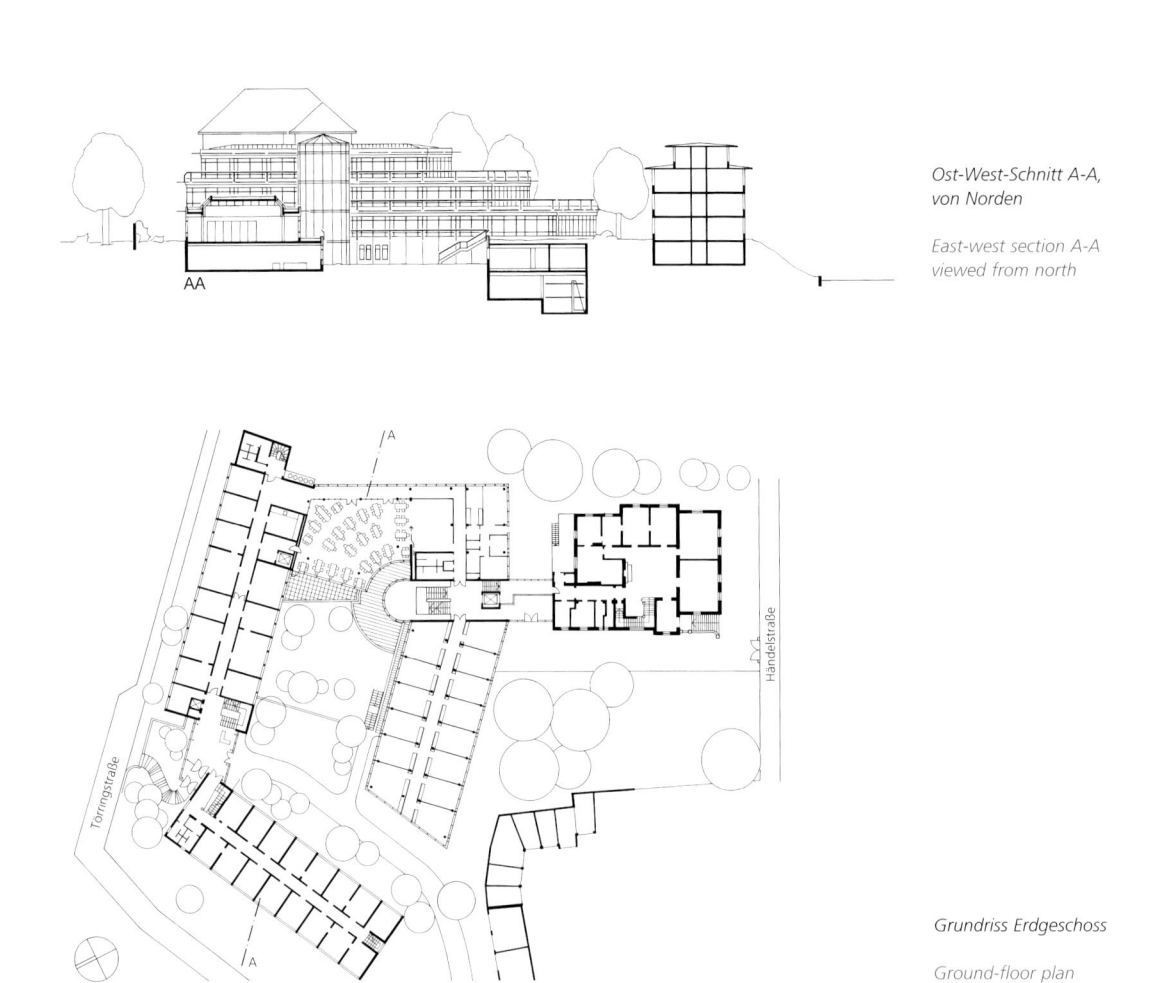

East-west section A-A viewed from north

Grundriss Erdgeschoss

Ground-floor plan

Erster Erweiterungsbau

Das Areal liegt im Verlauf der Hangkante des ehemaligen Isarhochufers, im Schnittpunkt mehrerer Grünanlagen und Parks. Dies und die auf dem Grundstück bereits reichlich vorhandene Vegetation legten es nahe, die Verknüpfung der genannten Grünzüge durch eine starke Betonung der Außenanlagen und der Grüngestaltung zum stadtgestalterischen Entwurfskriterium zu machen. Aus diesem Grund, und auch weil die räumliche Situation zwischen den bestehenden Gebäuden sehr beengt ist, ist der Baukörper des Neubaus so weit wie möglich zurückhaltend entwickelt. Der Innenhof wurde um ein Geschoss abgesenkt: so ist die relativ große Baumasse vertretbar, die sicherheitsempfindlichen Bereiche (Rechenzentrum) erhalten Tageslicht.

Geplant wurde ein terrassierter, leichter und möglichst niedriger Baukörper, der gegenüber der Vegetation sehr stark in den Hintergrund tritt. Das Zurückstaffeln der Stockwerksebenen verbessert die Belichtungs- und Sichtverhältnisse in der Gesamtsituation.

Die Dachflächen sind extensiv begrünt: Der Grünzug soll sich durch das gesamte Grundstück über das Gebäude hinweg bis in den Herzogpark fortsetzen.

Der Schnittpunkt der Baugrenzen sowie der Erschließungsachse zu dem bestehenden Gebäude in der Händelstraße ist im Entwurf durch ein wichtiges Gestaltungselement markiert: das intensiv bepflanzte gläserne Treppenhaus, welches in einem kleinen Teich steht. Es soll als optischer Anziehungspunkt in jedem Geschoss des Neubaus, besonders im Speisesaal, wirksam werden und das Grün der Außenanlagen ins Gebäudeinnere fortsetzen. Gleichzeitig ist es Haupterschließung und Mittelpunkt sowohl des Neubaus wie auch der bestehenden Bauten.

First extension

The site lies on the edge of a slope – once the upper embankment of the River Isar – in an area with a number of parks and landscaped gardens. These and the fact that the site itself was covered with rich vegetation led to the idea of linking up the existing green areas by placing special emphasis on the external works and landscaping of the present scheme, making this a central aspect of the urban design. In view of this, and because the spaces between the existing buildings are relatively confined, the visible structure of the new development is restrained in appearance as far as possible. By sinking the level of the internal courtyard by one storey, the relatively large volume of the building is reduced to acceptable proportions. In addition, this layout allows the high-security areas (computer centre) to receive natural light. The building was planned as a light, terraced structure of restricted height, so that, set amidst the rich vegetation of the site, it seems to recede into the background. Daylighting, views and visual links were also optimized by stepping back the various storeys.

The roof areas are extensively planted. The aim was to draw the park-like surroundings over the entire site, including the building, and to link them with the open landscape areas of nearby Herzogpark.

The point of intersection of the outer limits of building development and the line of access to the existing building in Händelstrasse is marked by an important design element: an intensively planted glazed staircase which stands in a small pool of water. The aim was to create an effective visual attraction on every floor of the new structure, especially in the dining hall, and to continue the external landscape into the interior. The staircase is also the main line of access and the focal point of the new and existing buildings.

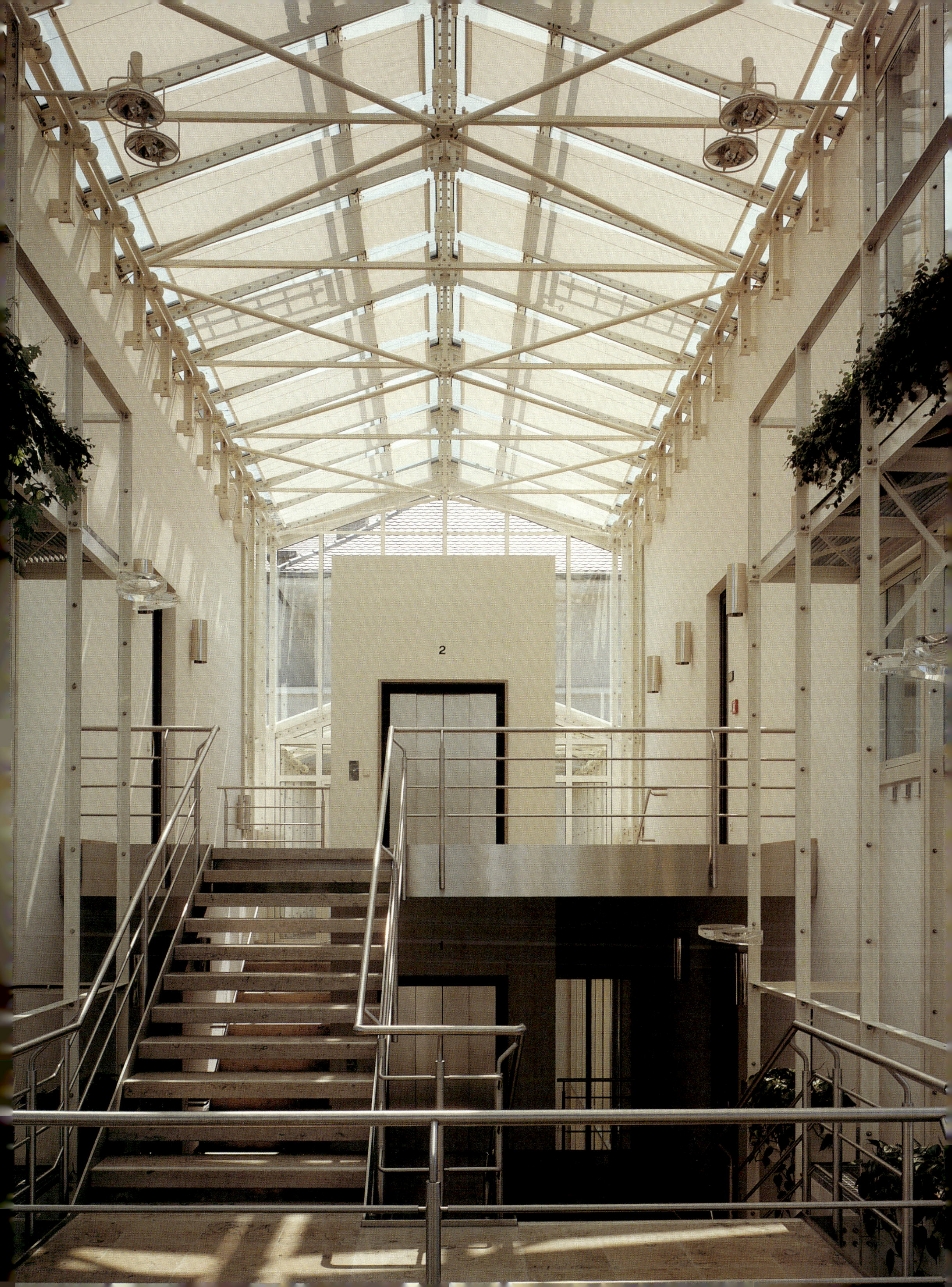
2
1

Das gläserne Treppenhaus ist Haupterschließung und Mittelpunkt des Ensembles.

The glazed staircase structure forms the main access route and the centrepiece of the ensemble.

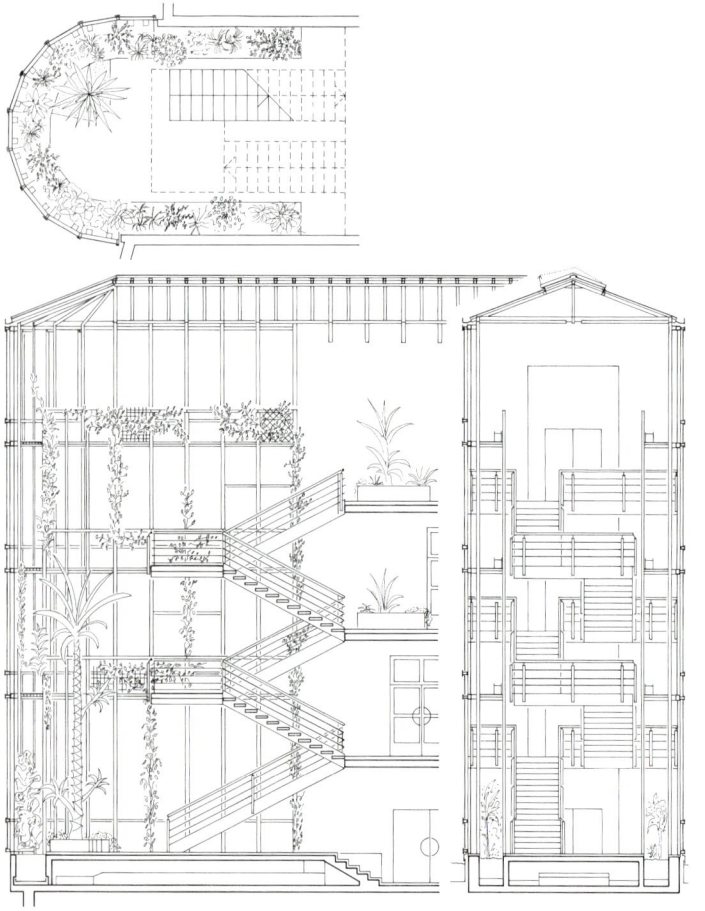

Intensive Bepflanzung des gläsernen Treppenhauses

Glazed staircase with intensive planting

Detailansicht der Hoffassade – im Hintergrund der Sep-Ruf-Bau

Part of the courtyard façade, with the building by Sep Ruf in the background

Staßenansicht Törringstraße

Street face in Törringstrasse

Zweiter Erweiterungsbau

1996 konnte die Frankona Rückversicherungs AG das Grundstück Törringstraße 10 erwerben, um das eigene Ensemble zu erweitern und eine Baulücke zwischen dem Gebäude des Architekten Sep Ruf und dem Togalwerk zu schließen. Die Straßenfassade nimmt die Trauf- und Geschosshöhen sowie den Fassadenrhythmus des benachbarten Sep-Ruf-Baues auf. Die Hofseite dagegen ist terrassiert ausgebildet. Dadurch werden die Abstandsflächen optimal ausgenutzt und eine Beziehung zum ersten Erweiterungsbau von 1982 hergestellt.

Second extension

In 1996, the Frankona reinsurance company was able to acquire the site at Törringstrasse 10 for a further extension of its complex. In the process, the gap was closed between the adjoining building by the architect Sep Ruf and the Togal block. Along the street face, the extension adopts the eaves and storey heights of the building by Sep Ruf as well as the rhythm of its facade. On the courtyard face, the new structure was designed with a series of terraces. This allowed the statutory regulations relating to spaces between buildings to be exploited in an optimum form and also established a relationship to the first extension dating from 1982.

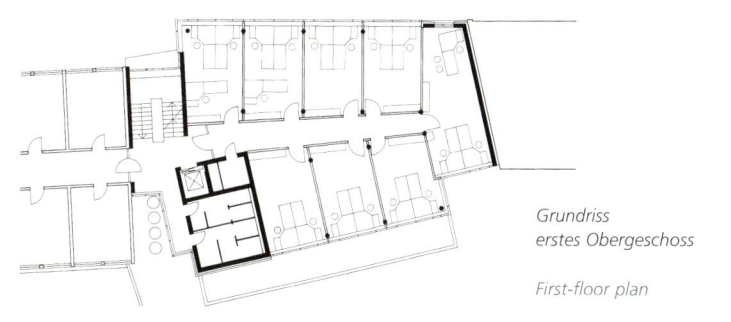

Grundriss erstes Obergeschoss

First-floor plan

Entwurfsskizze der Fassade

Design sketch of façade

Frankona Rückversicherungs AG

Im Verlauf von dreißig Jahren haben wir 151 Architektenwettbewerbe bearbeitet und abgegeben, von Kulmbach bis Köln und von Bozen bis Helsinki, also im Durchschnitt fünf Wettbewerbe pro Jahr, 44 Mal erfolgreich, wenn man auch einen Ankauf als Erfolg bezeichnen kann. 107 Mal sind wir „durchgefallen", ein volks- und betriebswirtschaftlicher Unsinn?

Bei den 44 erfolgreichen Wettbewerben waren wir 13 Mal auf dem ersten Platz, also seltener als jedes zweite Jahr. Aus den Erstplatzierungen entstanden elf Planungsaufträge direkt und einige indirekt in Folge.

Das ist kein Aufsehen erregendes, wahrscheinlich kaum ein überdurchschnittliches Ergebnis – aber dennoch: die aus den Wettbewerben entstandenen Aufträge waren die für uns weitaus wichtigsten, was die Planungsaufgaben und das gebaute Ergebnis betraf.

Wir meinen,
- *Architektur- und Städtebau-Wettbewerbe sind ein ganz wesentliches Element, in der Vergangenheit wie heute, zur Verbesserung der Gestaltung unserer Umwelt, es gibt kein besseres!*
- *Wettbewerbe sind immer noch die beste Chance, besonders auch für unsere jungen Kollegen, auf faire Weise spannende, große, besonders öffentliche Aufträge zu erhalten.*
- *Das Wettbewerbsverfahren zwingt den Bauherrn, vor Beginn der Architektenarbeit durch die Erarbeitung eines Raumprogrammes genau zu formulieren, was er eigentlich bauen will.*
- *Eine von einer unabhängigen Jury anonym ausgewählte Arbeit hat von sich aus ein gewisses Gewicht, eine „Autorität", die es dem Architekten leichter macht, das Ergebnis planend umzusetzen.*

***Aufträge
aus
Wettbewerben***

***Commissions
resulting
from competitions***

Over a period of 30 years, we have prepared and submitted 151 schemes for architectural competitions, from Kulmbach to Cologne, from Bolzano to Helsinki; in other words, an average of five competitions a year. On 44 occasions, we were successful, if one counts the purchase of a scheme as a success. That also means we "failed" on 107 occasions – a managerial and economic absurdity?

In the 44 cases in which we were successful, we won first prize 13 times – less than once every two years. Of the 13 schemes for which we won first prize, 11 led to direct planning commissions and some to an indirect assignment.

That is nothing very sensational; probably not even an above-average performance. Nevertheless, the commissions we gained from these competitions were by far the most important projects for our office in terms of the planning content and the built results.

We believe that

- *architectural and urban planning competitions are a major factor, now as in the past, in improving the design quality of our environment; there is no better way;*
- *competitions still provide the best opportunity, especially for younger colleagues, to gain exciting, large-scale contracts by fair means – and especially public commissions;*
- *by forcing clients to formulate a spatial programme, the competition process makes them define precisely what they want to build before the architectural work begins;*
- *a scheme selected anonymously by an independent jury bears a certain weight, a stamp of authority, which makes it easier for the architect to translate the result into reality through the planning process.*

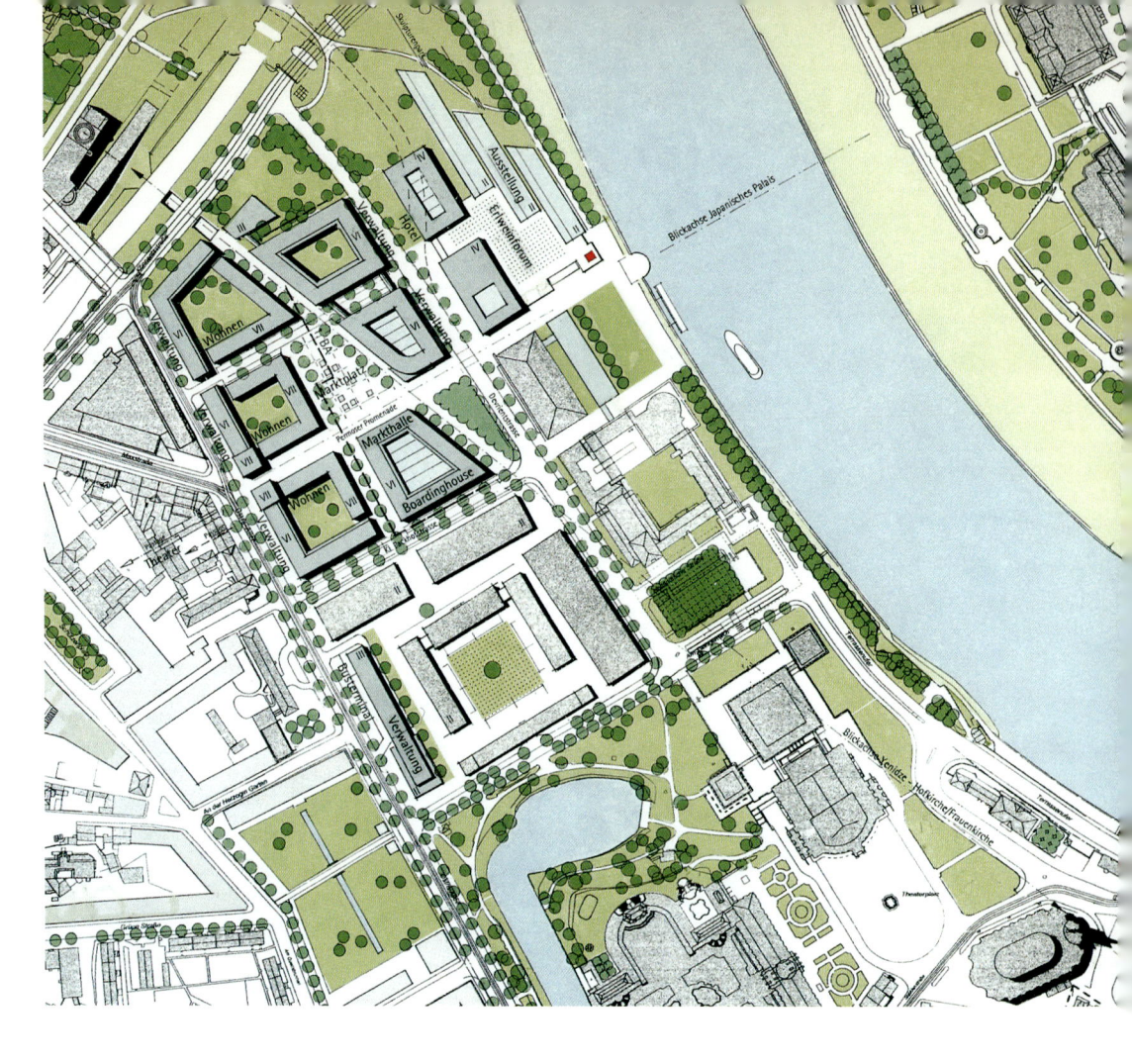

Städtebaulicher Wettbewerb Neue Terrasse – Ostra-Allee

Die Elbe mit ihren naturnahen Uferzonen ist ein wichtiges Landschaftspotenzial der Stadt Dresden; gleichzeitig ist sie malerischer Vordergrund der einzigartigen Stadtsilhouette, wie sie sich auf der Altstädter Seite über der Brühlschen Terrasse und um den Theaterplatz erhebt und das berühmte Panorama von Dresden bildet. So ist die Gestaltung der historischen Elbuferbereiche im Zentrum der Stadt geprägt von der Forderung nach harmonischer Beziehung zwischen Bebauung und Uferzone sowie nach flussübergreifenden Achs- und Sichtbeziehungen („Canalettoblick").

Das innerstädtische Terrassenufer besteht aber nicht nur aus den Ensembles auf der Brühlschen Terrasse und dem Theaterplatz, sondern reicht im Osten bis zur Albertbrücke und im Westen bis zur Marienbrücke. Gerade dieses westliche Terrassenufer verlangt nach einem qualitätvollen Abschluss.

Als Bindeglied zwischen den noch nicht verbundenen Grünzügen des Großen Gartens und des Großen Ostrageheges kann an der Neuen Terrasse mit einer die Bebauung begleitenden Grünverbindung der Übergang in die Elblandschaft wieder aufgenommen werden.

Grundgedanke unserer städtebaulichen Konzeption war es, die in diesem Gebiet Dresdens vergleichsweise nur rudimentär vorhandenen historischen Bezüge aufzugreifen und zu einer städtebaulichen Neuordnung weiter zu entwickeln, die sich in erster Linie durch Anpassungsfähigkeit an heute erkennbare, aber auch künftige Nutzungswünsche beschreibt.

Urban planning competition New Terrace – Ostra-Allee

The River Elbe and the natural areas along its banks form an important part of the landscape potential of the city of Dresden. At the same time, they constitute the scenic foreground to the unique urban silhouette – the famous panorama of the city – which rises above the Brühl Terrace on the side of the river where the historical centre and the Theaterplatz are situated. Any design measures in these areas along the banks of the Elbe at the centre of the city are, therefore, governed by the need to maintain a harmonious relationship between the existing building fabric and the riverside zone, and the obligation to respect axial and visual links that extend across the river (the so-called "Canaletto view").

The riverside terraces in the city centre consist not only of the ensembles along the Brühl Terrace and around Theaterplatz, however. They extend eastwards as far as Albert Bridge and to the west as far as St Mary's Bridge. This western section of the river bank in particular calls for a qualitative termination.

The transition to the Elbe landscape along the New Terrace can be extended by creating a linking green zone parallel to the building development, thus connecting the landscape spaces of the Grosser Garten and the Grosses Ostragehege, which are as yet still separate areas.

The underlying idea of our urban planning concept was to adopt historical references, which in this area of Dresden are comparatively rudimentary, and to extrapolate them as the basis of a process of urban restructuring that would be distinguished by its adaptability to user needs – those recognizable today and those that may manifest themselves in the future.

Neue Terrasse – Ostra-Allee, Dresden
8 New Terrace – Ostra-Allee, Dresden

1997 Wettbewerb · 1. Preis
1997 Städtebaulicher Rahmenplan
1997 Städtebauliche Leitlinien Kongresszentrum
1999 Wettbewerb Kongresszentrum

1997 Competition: first prize
1997 Outline urban planning
1997 Urban guidelines for Congress Centre
1999 Competition for Congress Centre

Aktivieren von vorhandenen Sicht- und Bezugsachsen und Schaffen neuer Sichtbeziehungen im wertvollen Bestand

The activation of existing visual axes and links and the creation of new sets of relationships in a unique existing urban situation

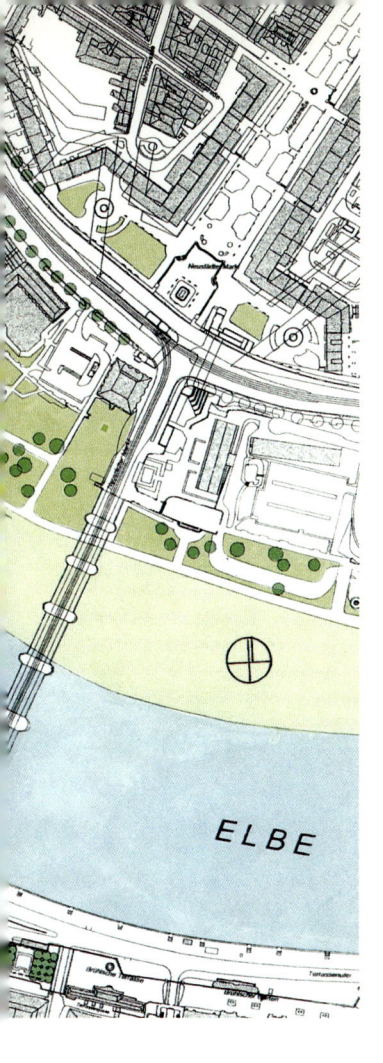

Historische Bezüge werden aufgenommen und zu einer städtebaulichen Neuordnung weiter entwickelt.

Historical points of reference are adopted and elaborated to create a new urban structure.

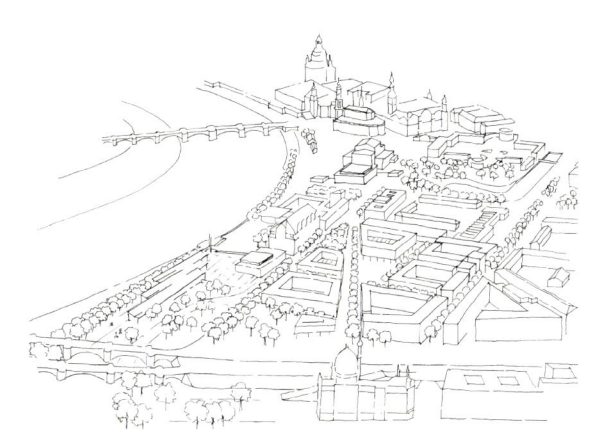

Neue spannungsvolle Sichtbeziehung von der früheren Zigarettenfabrik Yenidze zum historischen Altstadtkern: Yenidze, Hofkirche und Frauenkirche liegen in einer Achse.

Exciting new visual links from the former Yenidze cigar factory to the historic city centre: Yenidze, Hofkirche and Frauenkirche are situated along a single axis.

Städtebaulicher Rahmenplan Neue Terrasse – Ostra-Allee

Der städtebauliche Rahmenplan konnte aufzeigen, dass unser „idealisiertes" Wettbewerbsergebnis ohne Abstriche von den ursprünglichen Zielvorstellungen in realisierbare Einzelschritte umsetzbar ist.

Das Schwergewicht der städtebaulichen Gestaltung lag auf dem Herausarbeiten von Bezügen zu Objekten und Situationen in der näheren und weiteren Umgebung des eigentlichen Wettbewerbsgebietes (ehemalige Zigarettenfabrik Yenidze, Japanisches Palais, Großes Ostragehege, Schützenplatz, historischer Altstadtkern).

Hier meinen wir das Aktivieren vorhandener und Schaffen neuer Sichtbeziehungen, aber auch ein funktionales Verknüpfen zugunsten des Bürgers und des Besuchers der Stadt als Fußgänger, Radfahrer oder Autofahrer. Die vorgeschlagenen Blockgrößen definieren die angemessene „Körnigkeit" einer künftigen Bebauung, ermöglichen eine gute Durchlässigkeit durch das Quartier und bilden Straßenräume.

Ein wichtiges Element städtebaulichen Gestaltens ist das Herstellen einer neuen, spannungsvollen Sichtbeziehung: Yenidze – Hofkirche – Frauenkirche. Die frühere Zigarettenfabrik Yenidze ist ein Merk- und Wahrzeichen der Stadt Dresden. Es erscheint möglich und wünschenswert, sie optisch stärker an das historische Stadtzentrum anzubinden und ihre „Abseitslage" hinter Könneritzstraße und Bahnlinie zu verbessern.

Die vorhandene und bedeutsame Sichtachse Permoserstraße – Japanisches Palais sollte – räumlich differenziert – aufgewertet werden und nach Süden durch Passagen zum „Theater im Hof" und zum Schützenplatz ergänzt werden.

Outline urban planning New Terrace – Ostra-Allee

The outline urban planning demonstrated that it would be possible to implement our "idealized" competition proposals in a series of steps without diluting the original goals.

The main emphasis of the urban design lay in forging links to objects and situations around the competition area: the former Yenidze cigar factory, the Japanese Palace, the Grosses Ostragehege, Schützenplatz and the historical city centre itself.

This implied activating existing visual links, creating new ones, and establishing functional connections that would benefit citizens and visitors alike, whether as pedestrians, cyclists or car drivers. The proposed dimensions of the street blocks determine the appropriate "grain" or consistency of the future building development; they also facilitate a high degree of permeability through the neighbourhood; and they form a network of street spaces.

A major element of the urban design is the creation of a new and exciting sequence of visual links: Yenidze – Court Church (Hofkirche) – Church of Our Lady (Frauenkirche). The former Yenidze cigar factory is a monument and landmark of the city, and it would seem to be possible, indeed desirable, to link it in a visually more immediate manner with the historical city centre, thus enhancing its somewhat out-of-the-way position behind Könneritzstrasse and the railway line.

The important existing visual axis between Permoserstrasse and the Japanese Palace should also be revitalized in a spatially varied form and augmented to the south by arcades to the Theater im Hof and to Schützenplatz.

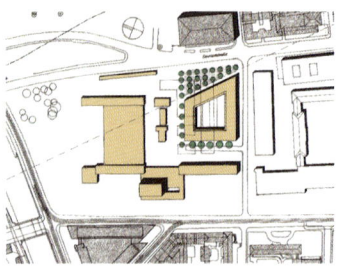

1. Bauabschnitt
1st stage of construction

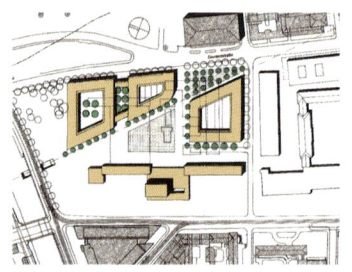

2. Bauabschnitt
2nd stage of construction

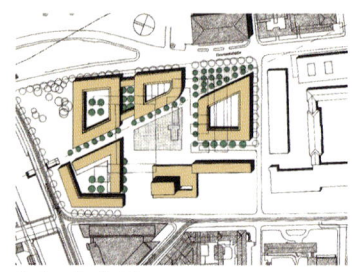

3. Bauabschnitt
3rd stage of construction

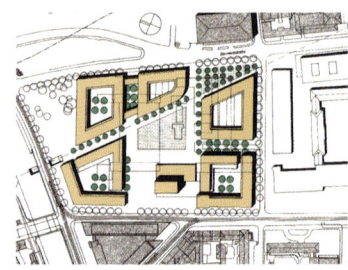

4. Bauabschnitt
4th stage of construction

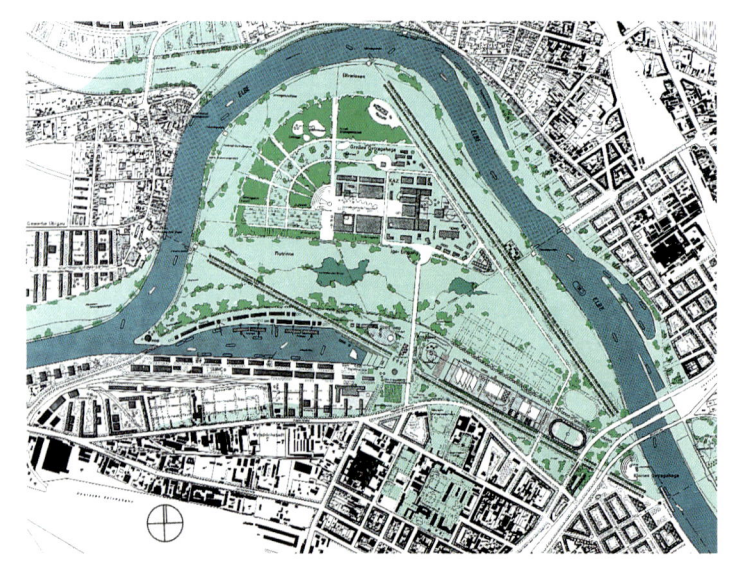

Bereits beim Wettbewerb Großes Ostragehege 1995 war ein Kerngedanke die Bindegliedfunktion des Kleinen Ostrageheges zwischen Großem Ostragehege und Innenstadt.

As early as the competition for the Grosses Ostragehege in 1995, one of the key ideas was to use the Kleines Ostragehege to form a link between the Grosses Ostragehege and the city centre.

Realisierungswettbewerb Kongresszentrum

Das Kongresszentrum in exponierter Lage am Elbufer steht im Schnittpunkt von wichtigen städtebaulichen Sicht- und Bezugsachsen Dresdens, die durch die „städtebaulichen Leitlinien für das Kongresszentrum" formuliert waren. Hierdurch erhält das Kongresszentrum seine prägende räumliche Ausformung in einzelne Gebäudevolumina, die sich durch ihre Maßstäblichkeit in die vorhandene städtebauliche Struktur einfügen.

Das Kongresszentrum hat drei Hauptebenen und eine Aussichtskanzel mit Café im obersten Geschoss. Das Herzstück des Gebäudes bildet die gläserne Foyerhalle, die sich zur Elbe hin öffnet. Von der erhöht liegenden „Beletage" genießt man den Blick auf die Elbauen und auf die vielen umliegenden historischen Gebäude. Im Gegensatz zur transparenten Foyerhülle stehen die metallverkleideten „Erdkörper", die Kongresssäle, Konferenz-, Seminar- und Verwaltungsbereiche beinhalten, also architektonisch „auf der Erde" fixiert sind.

Competition for construction of Congress Centre

The Congress Centre, occupying a prominent position on the bank of the Elbe, lies at the intersection of a number of important urban axes – both visual and referential – which were formulated in the "Urban Planning Guidelines for the Congress Centre"; hence the striking spatial form of the centre. It consists of a number of distinct volumes, the scale of which helps to integrate them into the existing urban fabric.

The Congress Centre is laid out on three main levels and has an elevated viewing area with a café at the top. The heart of the building is the glazed foyer hall, which opens on to the River Elbe. From the raised bel-etage, visitors can enjoy views over the river meadows and to the many historic buildings in the area. In contrast to the foyer with its transparent skin, the metal-clad "earth volumes", housing the congress halls and conference, seminar and administration spaces, are architecturally focused "on the ground".

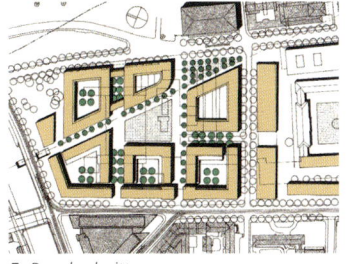

5. Bauabschnitt
5th stage of construction

Das Kongresszentrum mit dem großen gläsernen Foyer und den festen „Erdkörpern" an der Elbe

The Congress Centre with its large glazed foyer and solid "earth volumes" on the Elbe

Neue Terrasse – Ostra-Allee, Dresden

Formale und funktionale Klarheit der Architektur prägt das neue Erscheinungsbild des Klärwerks München I.

The new image of the Munich I Sewage Treatment Plant is distinguished by the formal and functional clarity of the architecture.

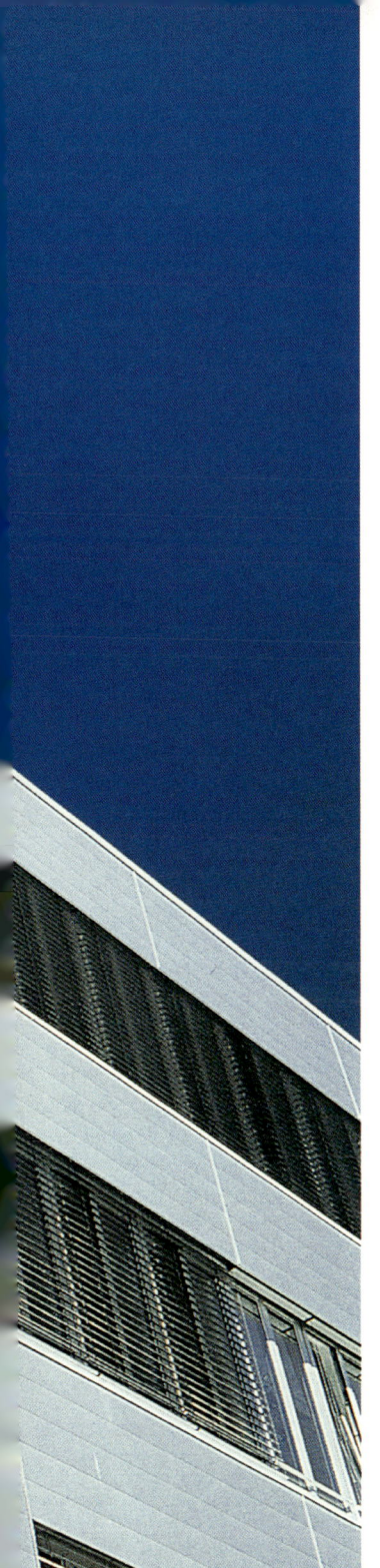

Klärwerk München I Gut Großlappen

Sewage Treatment Plant Munich I, Grosslappen Estate

*1986 – 1993 Maschinenhaus 2
 Planung und Realisierung
1987 – 1988 Zweite Biologische Reinigungsstufe
 Konzept und Gestaltung
1987 – 1989 Sanierung Faulbehälter · Konzeptstudien
1990 – 1994 Entwicklung von Leitdetails für das
 Gestaltungshandbuch
1991 – 1996 Verwaltung und Labor
 Planung und Realisierung*

*1986 – 1993 Hall 2 for mechanical plant:
 planning and construction
1987 – 1988 Second stage biological purification:
 concept and design
1987 – 1989 Refurbishment of sapropel chambers:
 conceptual studies
1990 – 1994 Development of standard details for
 design manual
1991 – 1996 Administration and laboratory tracts:
 planning and construction*

Erhalten und Verbessern der Wasserqualität ist eine wichtige Herausforderung unserer Zeit. Hierfür sind Um- und Neubauten erforderlich – eine verantwortungsvolle Bauaufgabe.

The maintenance and improvement of water quality represent a great challenge to modern society. The conversion of existing structures and the construction of new buildings for this purpose are, therefore, assignments of great responsibility.

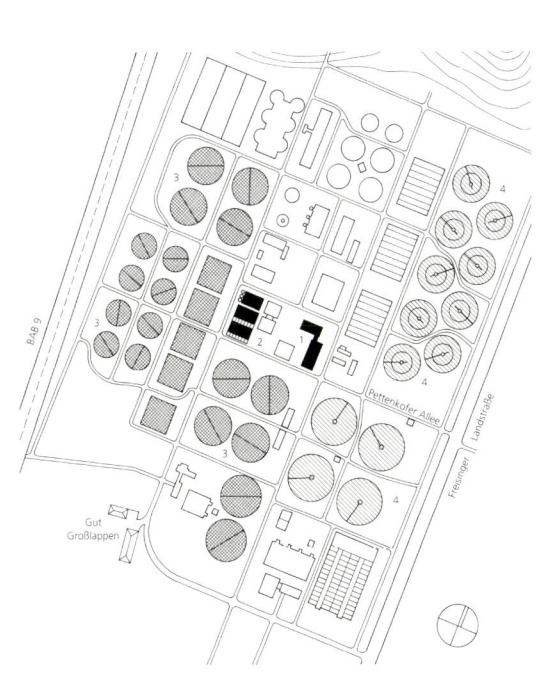

*Lageplan
Klärwerk München I
1 Verwaltungs-
 und Laborgebäude
2 Maschinenhaus
 mit Gerätehalle
3 Zweite biologische
 Reinigungsstufe
4 Erste Reinigungsstufe*

*Site plan of Munich I
Sewage Treatment Plant
1 Administration and
 laboratory tracts
2 Hall for mechanical
 plant and equipment
3 Second stage bio-
 logical purification
4 First stage purification*

Klärwerk München Großlappen | 91

Der im Zentrum der Gesamtanlage gelegene gläserne Treppenturm erschließt das Verwaltungsgebäude und ermöglicht einen attraktiven Aufgang zur Besucherterrasse.

The glazed staircase tower at the centre of the complex provides general access to the administration building and an attractive route to the visitors' terrace on the roof.

Bauten für Kläranlagen haben in erster Linie funktionale Aufgaben zu erfüllen. Dass darüber hinaus gestalterische Aspekte Berücksichtigung finden müssen, zeigen die in den letzten Jahren realisierten Klärwerksanlagen für die Landeshauptstadt München.

Über einen Zeitraum von 13 Jahren (1986 bis 1999) haben wir das neue Gesicht des alten Klärwerks München I gestaltet: Planung und Bauleitung der Neubauten sowie Detailgestaltung der Ingenieurbauwerke. Im einzelnen bearbeiteten wir hierbei folgende Aufgaben:
- Baukünstlerische Beratung zu allen Ingenieurbauwerken des Neubaus der zweiten Biologischen Reinigungsanlage
- Neubau Maschinenhaus mit Kfz- und Gerätehalle
- Neubau Verwaltungs- und Laborgebäude
- Neubau Wärmezentrale
- Neubau Geräte- und Elektrowerkstatt
- Baukünstlerische Beratung für den Neubau Energiezentrale und die Neubauten des Betriebshofes Nord
- Fassadensanierung Klärwasserpumpwerk.

Neubau Verwaltungs- und Laborgebäude

Die beiden drei- und viergeschossigen Neubauten für die Verwaltung und das Labor sind im rechten Winkel zueinander angeordnet und durch eine verglaste Stahlbrücke im ersten Obergeschoss verbunden. In der Blickachse der Haupteinfahrt liegt der Treppenturm des Verwaltungsgebäudes, der durch seine bauliche Ausformung zum Mittelpunkt der Gesamtanlage wird. Das gesamte Erdgeschoss ist als öffentlicher Bereich transparent gestaltet. Im Foyer werden Ausstellungen über das Klärwerk gezeigt, ein großer Vortragssaal mit Multimediaausstattung dient ebenfalls der Öffentlichkeitsarbeit.

Sewage treatment structures have, first and foremost, to meet functional needs. Nevertheless, a number of treatment plants built in recent years for the city of Munich demonstrate that design considerations can also play an important role.

Over a period of 13 years, from 1986 to 1999, we have helped to give the old Munich I sewage treatment plant a new face. The project comprised the planning and construction management of the new buildings, as well as the detailed design of the engineering structures. The work included:
- Artistic and architectural consultancy in respect of the new engineering structures forming the second biological purification plant
- Construction of a new building for mechanical plant with a hall for vehicles and equipment
- Construction of administration buildings and laboratories
- Construction of a heating plant
- Construction of a workshop for equipment and electrical installations
- Artistic and architectural consultancy in respect of the hall for mechanical plant and the new buildings for the northern works yard
- Façade refurbishment of the water purification pumping house.

Construction of administration and laboratory tracts

The laboratories and the administration are housed in two new structures, three and four storeys high respectively. These are laid out at right angles to each other and linked by a glazed steel bridge at first floor level. The staircase tower serving the administration tract is set on the visual axis of the main line of approach. The constructional form of the tower makes it the focal point of the whole complex.

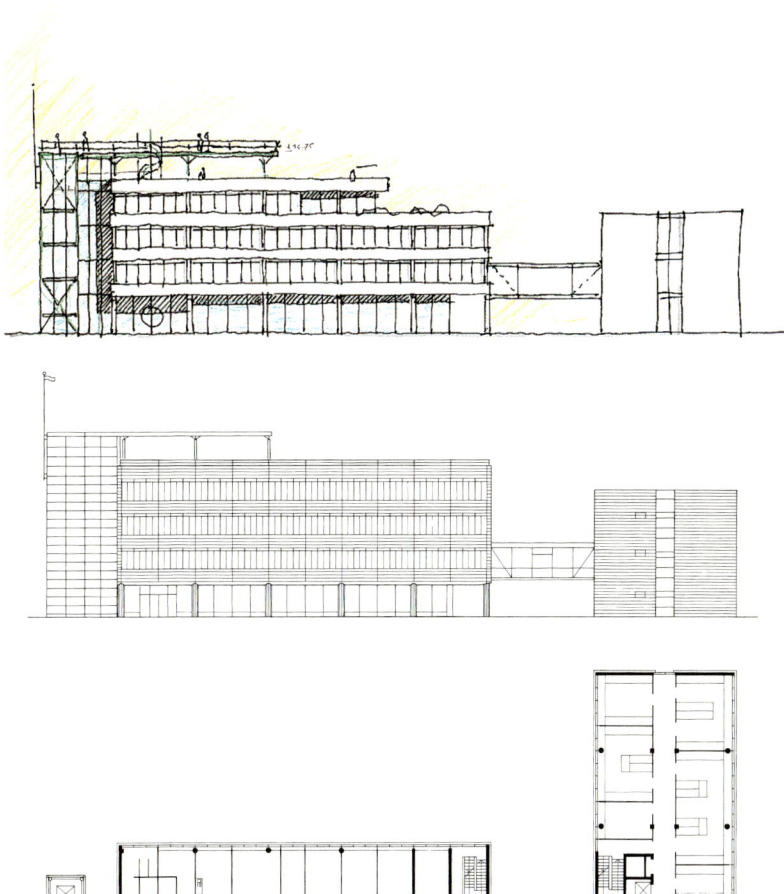

Entwurfsskizze, Ansicht Ost, Grundriss erstes Obergeschoss Die beiden rechtwinklig zueinander stehenden Gebäudetrakte für Verwaltung und Labor sind im ersten Obergeschoss durch einen Glassteg verbunden.

Design sketch, east elevation, first-floor plan. The two tracts of the building, housing the administration and laboratories, are set at right angles to each other and are linked by a glazed bridge at first-floor level.

Schnitt Maschinenhaus: Die technischen Betriebsabläufe werden zu bestimmenden Entwurfsmerkmalen, wie hier die Zuluftführung zu den Turboverdichtern.

Section through the hall for mechanical plant: the technical operations taking place in the hall had a great influence on the design; here, for example, the air supply ducts to the compressed-air turbines are clearly visible.

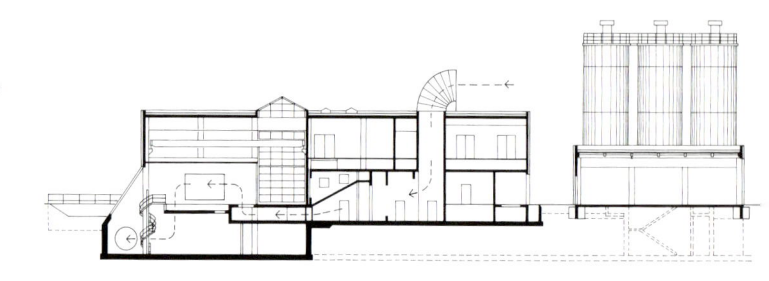

Integration der Neubauten in die vorhandene Anlage

Integration of the new structures into the existing complex

Grundriss Maschinenhaus
1 Lufterzeugung
2 Elektroversorgung
3 Kalkmilchaufbereitung
4 Kfz- und Gerätehalle

Plan of hall for mechanical plant
1 Air generation
2 Electrical supply
3 Milk of lime processing
4 Vehicle and equipment hall

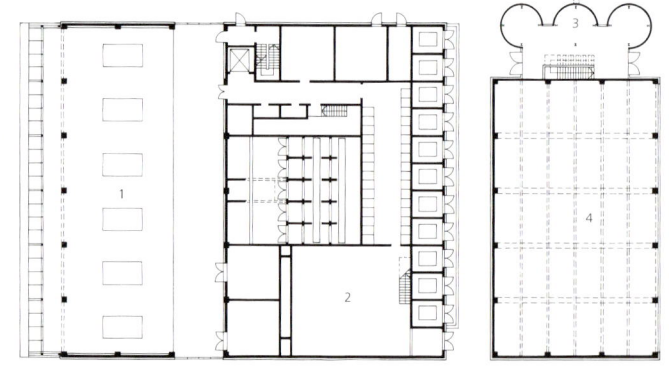

Die Besuchergruppen erreichen über den Treppenturm die Dachterrasse, von der man einen Überblick über das gesamte Klärwerksgelände hat. Die Büros in den Obergeschossen bestehen vorwiegend aus konventionellen Zweipersonenräumen. Im dritten Obergeschoss befindet sich die Klärwerksleitung sowie ein großer Besprechungsraum. Im Laborgebäude sind die für den Klärwerksbetrieb erforderlichen Labor- und Analyse-Räume untergebracht.

Neubau Maschinenhaus mit Kfz- und Gerätehalle
Dem Maschinenhaus kommt eine zentrale Bedeutung beim Ausbau der zweiten Biologischen Reinigungsanlage zu. Die Aufgaben sind:
- Drucklufterzeugung zur Belebung des biologischen Abbauprozesses in den Belebungsbecken
- Elektrotechnische Versorgung der gesamten zweiten biologischen Reinigungsanlage
- Kalkmilchaufbereitungsanlage zur Erhöhung der Alkalität des Abwassers und zur Verbesserung der Absetzfähigkeit des Belebtschlammes, Vorhalten des erforderlichen Kalkpulvers
- Unterstellhalle für Fahrzeuge und Geräte des Betriebs.

Die Planung des Maschinenhauses erforderte eine intensive Zusammenarbeit mit den Fachplanern für Betriebstechnik. So wurde bereits in den ersten Entwurfskonzepten die das Gebäude wesentlich bestimmende Luftführung entwickelt.

Ziel der Gestaltung war es, durch klare geometrische Bauformen die Funktionseinheiten des Maschinenhauses zu zeigen und durch geeignete Material- und Farbauswahl den technischen Charakter der Anlage zum Ausdruck zu bringen. Vertikal gegliederte, ruhige Leichtmetall-Fassaden aus stranggepressten Aluprofilen sowie großflächige Glaselemente bestimmen das architektonische Erscheinungsbild.

The entire ground floor is a public area and is designed accordingly as a transparent zone. Exhibitions portraying the work of the sewage plant are held in the foyer. A large lecture hall with multimedia equipment is also used for public-relations work. Visiting groups have access, via the staircase tower, to the roof garden, from where there is a view over the entire sewage treatment site. The offices on the upper floors are mainly divided into conventional two-person spaces. Situated on the third floor are the areas for the works management and a large conference room. The laboratory tract houses the requisite lab facilities and analysis rooms for the operation of the sewage treatment plant.

New hall for mechanical plant, vehicles and equipment
The hall housing mechanical equipment plays a key role in the development of the second biological purification plant.

The design of this hall necessitated a close collaboration with specialist planners in various fields of engineering technology. The air circulation system was determined at an early stage as part of the initial design concept and had a major influence on the form of the building.

The design aimed to show the various functional elements of the power station in a series of clear geometric forms and to express the technical character of the complex through an appropriate coloration and choice of materials. The overall architectural appearance is distinguished by restrained, vertically articulated lightweight metal façades, consisting of extruded aluminium sections and large-area panes of glass.

Durch klare geometrische Bauformen sind die Funktionseinheiten des Maschinenhauses ablesbar: Montagestraße (oben), Verglasung der Turbohalle (unten).

The different functional elements of the hall for mechanical plant are legible in the clear geometric forms of the building: assembly and maintenance strip (top); glazing to the turbine hall (bottom).

Rankende Pflanzen bestimmen das Bild der Hoffassade.

Climbing plants transform the appearance of the rear facade.

1993 stand in Leipzig-Reudnitz, der so genannten Medienstadt, eine „Baulücke" zwischen zwei sanierungsbedürftigen Gründerzeitbauten zum Verkauf. Auf diesem Trümmergrundstück entstand ein siebengeschossiges Wohn- und Bürogebäude. Die Büros befinden sich im Souterrain, im erhöhten Erdgeschoss und teilweise im Dachgeschoss.

Selbstverständlich mussten bei dieser Bebauung inmitten denkmalgeschützter Gründerzeithäuser Baufluchten und Traufhöhen eingehalten werden: die Fassaden sind hinsichtlich Fensterteilung und Materialwahl auf die umliegende Bebauung abgestimmt.

Da die Erschließungstreppe auf der Straßenseite liegt, entstanden helle südorientierte Wohnungen mit überdachten Balkonen oder Loggien und im Dachgeschoss eine Terrasse.

Als Blickfang im Innenhof wirkt die begrünte Fassade. Dort wuchs der Knöterich bereits im ersten Jahr bis zum Dachgeschoss. Im Hof, der über eine Durchfahrt zu erreichen ist, befinden sich vier Stellplätze, zwei Garagen und Fahrradabstellplätze. Der Plan, den gesamten Innenhof von Stellplätzen zu befreien und mit einer Tiefgarage für das gesamte Quartier zu unterbauen, bleibt zunächst eine Idee.

In 1993, this vacant site in the Reudnitz district of Leipzig – the so-called "Media City" – came up for sale. It is situated between two buildings dating from the Gründerzeit (the period of economic growth in Germany at the end of the 19th century), both of which were in need of rehabilitation. On this bomb site, we erected a seven-storey housing and office block. The offices are at lower and upper ground floor level and in the attic storey.

Since the development is situated in the midst of listed 19th-century structures, it was necessary to observe existing building lines and eaves heights. The façade design also reflects the window divisions and use of materials of the surrounding developments.

By locating the access staircase on the street side, it was possible to create brightly lit south-facing dwellings with covered balconies or loggias, and a roof garden at the top.

The planted rear face forms an attractive visual feature of the courtyard. Within a year of the completion of the building, the knotgrass already grew up to the roof. In the courtyard, which is reached via a driveway through the building, there are four parking spaces, two garages, and bicycle stands. The plan to build a basement garage for the entire neighbourhood and thus keep the rear garden area free of parking spaces remains no more than an idea for the time being.

Büro- und Wohnhaus Wittstockstraße Leipzig

Office and Housing Block in Wittstockstrasse, Leipzig

1992 – 1995 Planung und Realisierung

1992 – 1995 Planning and construction

In diesem Gebäude befindet sich unsere Niederlassung Leipzig, in einem schönen Büro im Dachgeschoss mit Galerie und mit Blick über die Dächer von Reudnitz bis zum „Uniturm".

The building houses the Leipzig branch of our practice – a lovely office in the attic with a gallery and a view over the rooftops from Reudnitz to the university tower.

oben:
Straßenfassade mit dunkelgrün gestrichenen Holzfenstern

top:
street face with wood casements painted dark-green

unten:
Lichtdurchflutete Büroräume im Dachgeschoss

bottom:
offices filled with light in the attic storey

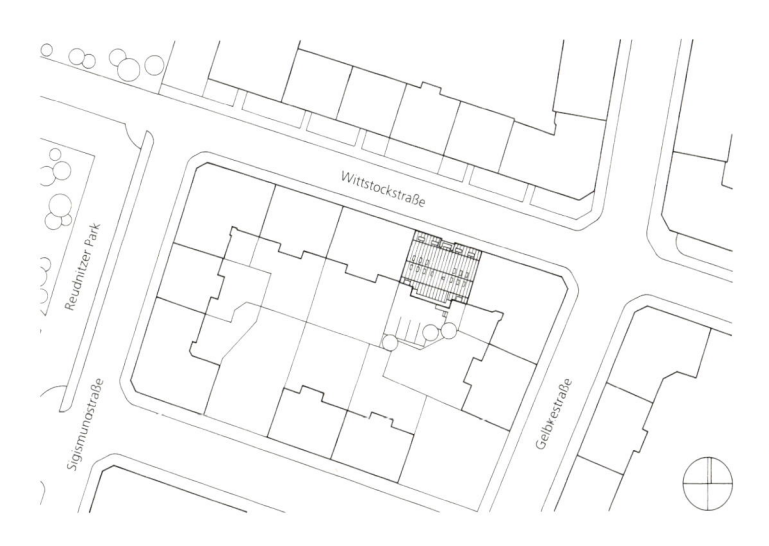

Lageplan

Site plan

Kreativität heißt nicht, sich das Ungewöhnliche einfallen zu lassen, das Noch-nicht-Dagewesene. Kreativität heißt nicht, etwas neu Erfundenes oder die eigene Idee durchsetzen zu wollen. Unsere Auftraggeber glauben häufig, Architekten entwerfen mehr für sich als für den Kunden, seien in erster Linie an der Durchsetzung eigener Gestaltungsabsichten interessiert, wollten sich „ein Denkmal setzen" . . .

Kreativität ist in unseren Augen viel mehr: Wir sehen uns als Dienstleister, die sich an den Kundenwünschen zu orientieren haben, die Gesetze, Vorschriften, Normen, besonders die Bauphysik, ökologische Ziele berücksichtigen müssen und vorgegebene Kosten und Termine einzuhalten haben. Bis hierher können das auch andere leisten, vielfach tun sie es besser als die Architekten.

Kreativität ist: diese Parameter als selbstverständlich zu erfüllende Grundvoraussetzung zu sehen für den Entwurfsprozess und das „Gestalten".

Was wir damit meinen: Ein Museum etwa ist ein Ort der Kontemplation, der Konzentration auf das dort Ausgestellte – die Akustik des Raumes ist deshalb von besonderer Bedeutung. Aus formalen Gründen ausschließlich Beton, Glas, Naturstein im Innenraum zu verwenden und damit einen „lauten" Raum zu bauen, ist nicht „kreativ". Oder einen Gymnastikraum für Feuerwehrleute zu den Nachbarhäusern hin bis zum Boden zu verglasen, weil die Gestaltung des Innenraumes dies verlangt, in unseren Augen ebensowenig.

Kreativität heißt also: Erst jenseits dieser vorgegebenen Zwänge und Aufgaben beginnt die größere Freiheit des Architekten, die stadtplanende, bau- und raumgestaltende Herausforderung, die zugleich Verpflichtung ist – eine zusätzliche Verantwortung der Öffentlichkeit gegenüber, die weit über die Forderungen des Bauherrn hinausgeht.

Kreativität

Creativity

Creativity does not mean coming up with unusual concepts or doing something that has never been done before. Creativity does not imply implementing a new invention or one's own ideas, either. The people who award us commissions often believe that architects design for themselves rather than for their clients, that they are more interested in the realization of their own design goals, that they want "to erect monuments to themselves".

In our eyes, creativity is much more than that. We regard ourselves as service providers who have to respect the wishes of their clients, who have to comply with laws, regulations and standards – especially those relating to constructional physics and the environment – and who have to adhere to fixed cost estimates and deadlines. Up to this point, these are tasks that others can perform, and perhaps even better than architects.

Creativity means accepting these parameters as fundamental conditions of the design process which have to be fulfilled as a matter of course.

The following examples will perhaps clarify what we mean by this. A museum is a place of contemplation, where people concentrate on the things exhibited. The spatial acoustics are particularly important, therefore. To use only concrete, glass and stone in the interior for purely formal reasons, thereby creating a "loud" space, is not being creative. Similarly, to build a fitness room for members of a fire brigade with full-height glazing facing neighbouring buildings, simply because the interior design calls for this, is not being creative either to our mind.

Creativity, then, means that the architect's greater design freedom lies beyond these constraints and obligations – in the challenges posed by urban planning, construction and spatial design; and these impose a further obligation: the additional responsibility towards the public at large, which far outweighs the needs of the client.

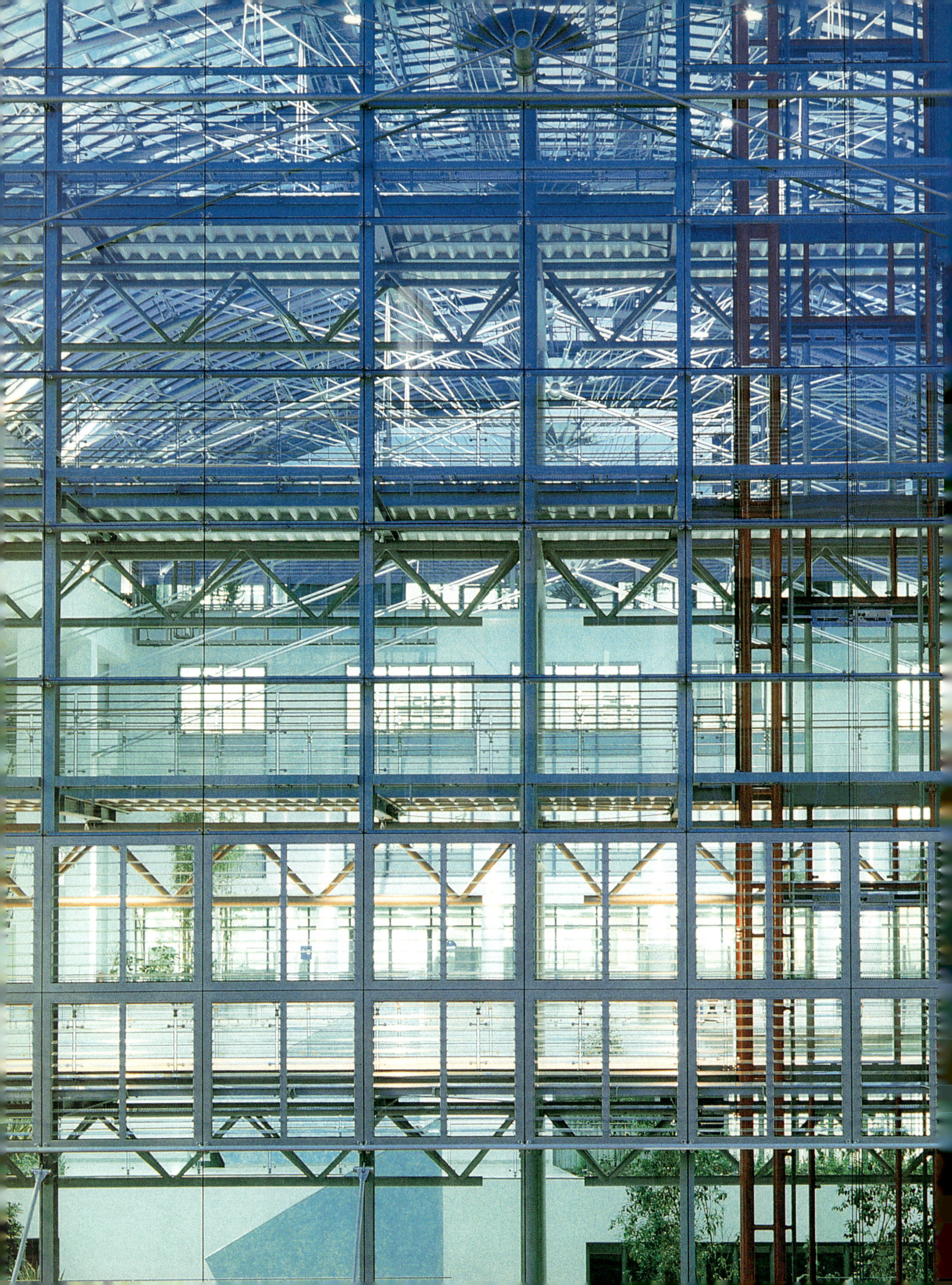

*Lichtstimmung
in der Glashalle*

*Lighting mood in
the glazed hall*

Postbank Leipzig

11 | **Post Office Bank, Leipzig**

1991 – 1995 Planung und Realisierung

1991 – 1995 Planning and construction

Das Gebäude steht im Spannungsfeld von Tradition und Moderne. Nach außen fügt es sich mit seiner Architektur in den städtebaulichen Kontext ein – innen schlägt ein gläsernes Herz.

The building is distinguished by the vibrant interplay between traditionalism and modernism in its design. Outwardly, the architecture is integrated into the urban context; internally, there beats a heart of glass.

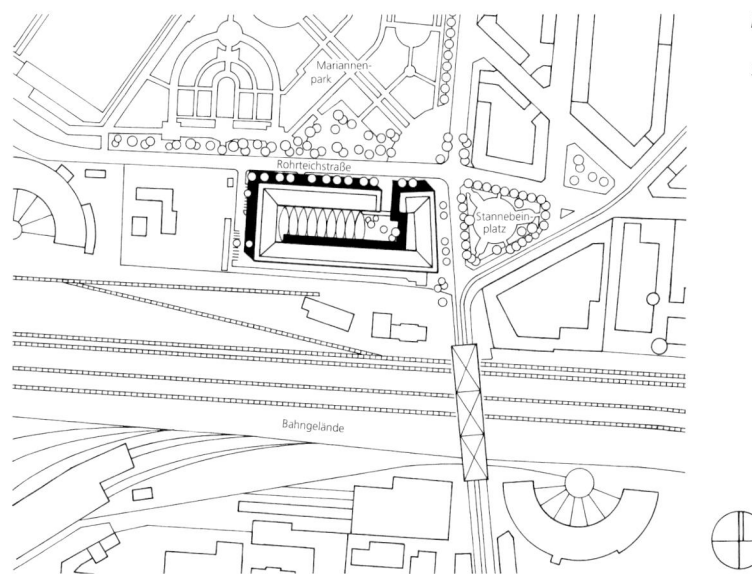

Lageplan

Site plan

Terracotta und Alu-Glaselemente prägen die Fassade.

Terracotta tile cladding and glazed aluminium elements determine the appearance of the façade.

Kontrast von Glashalle und Massivbauteilen

Contrast between glazed hall and solid structure

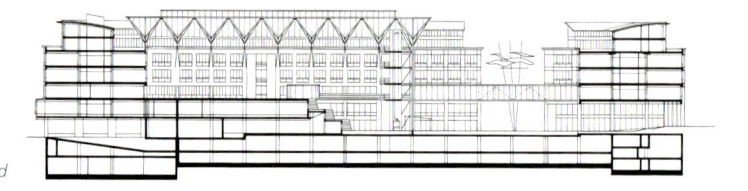

Entwurfsidee

Design idea

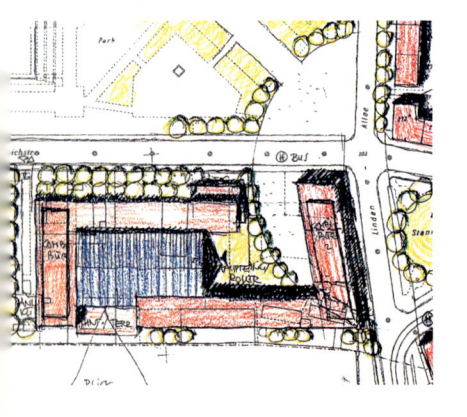

Die Stadtstruktur von Leipzig ist geprägt vom großen Bevölkerungswachstum um die Jahrhundertwende. So stieg die Zahl der Einwohner zwischen 1891 und 1941 von 106.000 auf 600.000. Diese Expansion hatte einen enormen Bauboom zur Folge. Die Blockstrukturen der Gründerzeitbebauung, die sich um den historischen Stadtkern entwickelten, machen noch heute das Stadtbild Leipzigs aus.

Das Grundstück für den Neubau der Postbank Leipzig – eine der ersten öffentlichen Baumaßnahmen nach der Wende – liegt im nordöstlichen Randbereich der Innenstadt von Leipzig an der Rohrteichstraße zwischen dem Mariannenpark im Norden und Bahnanlagen mit der S-Bahnhaltestelle Volkmarsdorf im Süden. Im Westen grenzt ein teilweise bebautes Grundstück der Bahn an, im Osten der Stannebeinplatz mit vier- und fünfgeschossiger Randbebauung. Leipzigs große Bahntradition mit Fern- und S-Bahngleisen, mit Werkstätten und Schuppen, ebenso Wohnbebauung und gewerbliche Strukturen prägen die unmittelbare Nachbarschaft: städtebaulich eine reizvolle Aufgabe.

Aus diesen Zusammenhängen entstand eine an der Nord-Ost-Ecke aufgebrochene Blockrandbebauung. Der mit Terracotta verkleidete Hauptbaukörper nimmt die Traufhöhen der umliegenden Gebäude am Stannebeinplatz auf. Zwei zusätzliche, zurückgesetzte Dachgeschosse erhöhen die zulässige Ausnutzung und setzen sich mit ihrer Aluminium-Glas-Fassade von den umliegenden Dächern ab.

Der Innenhof mit dem Haupteingang wird durch die Blocköffnung nach Norden und Passagen nach Osten von außen erkennbar und zieht so den Mariannenpark unmittelbar ins Blockinnere hinein. Hier steht auch ein von Herbert Peters gestalteter Brunnen. Im Hof und entlang der Straßen finden sich Mietflächen für Läden und ein Restaurant. Die zentrale, begrünte Halle mit Glasdach verbindet als Kommunikationsbereich alle Funktionen im Haus: Haupteingang, Büroflächen, Besprechungsräume und Betriebsrestaurant.

Längsschnitt durch die Glashalle mit dem abgestuften Hof

Longitudinal section through glazed hall with terraced courtyard

Grundriss zweites Obergeschoss: Haupterschließungsebene

Second-floor plan: main circulation level

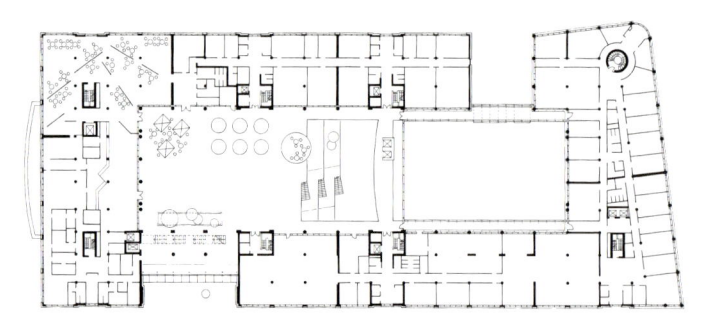

Die Tragkonstruktion des gewölbten Hallendachs erinnert an das Bauprinzip des Rades: Nabe, Speichen und Felgen.

The load-bearing structure of the curved hall roof is reminiscent of a wheel, consisting of a hub, spokes and a rim.

Die gläserne Haut der Halle ist außen glatt und leicht zu reinigen – der Dachaufbau im Scheitel dient der permanenten Durchlüftung.

The smooth glazed skin over the hall is easy to clean. The raised lantern at the crest is designed to support a permanent process of ventilation.

Die Stirnfassade der Halle bestimmt mit der gläsernen Auskragung das Erscheinungsbild.

The end face of the hall is dominated by the broad glazed cantilevered roof.

The rapid population growth that took place in Leipzig at the end of the 19th and the beginning of the 20th centuries had a decisive influence on the urban structure of the city. The population rose from 106,000 in 1891 to 600,000 in 1941. This expansion resulted in an enormous construction boom. The townscape of Leipzig is still characterized by the street-block structure that developed around the historic city centre during the Gründerzeit, the period of industrial growth in Germany at the end of the 19th century.

The new Post Office Bank in Leipzig was one of the first public buildings to be erected in the city after the reunification of Germany. The site is located in Rohrteichstrasse on the north-eastern edge of the city centre between Mariannenpark to the north and the railway lines with the Volkmarsdorf rapid sub-urban railway (S-Bahn) station to the south. The site is bounded to the west by a partly developed area belonging to the railways. To the east is Stannebeinplatz, a public open space surrounded by four- and five-storey buildings. The city's important railway tradition, as an interchange for long-distance and S-Bahn trains, is reflected in the workshops and locomotive sheds – together with housing and commercial structures – in the immediate neighbourhood. The assignment was, therefore, an attractive one, especially in terms of the urban planning.

In response to the existing situation, a closed street-block development was designed with an opening near the north-east corner. The main volumes of the complex, which are clad with terracotta tiles, adopt the eaves heights of the neighbouring buildings in Stannebeinplatz. A maximum exploitation of the site was achieved by adding two set-back storeys on the roof. These are contrasted with the roof structures of the surrounding buildings through their glass and aluminium façade construction.

The internal courtyard, in which the main entrance is situated, is visible from outside through the opening in the northern tract of the block and through arcades to the east. In this way, the landscaped space of Mariannenpark is drawn directly into the interior of the block, where a fountain designed by Herbert Peters also stands. Within the courtyard and along the street faces are leasable areas for shops and a restaurant. The central planted, glass-roofed hall forms a communications area that links all functional realms within the complex: the main entrance, the office areas, the conference rooms and the staff restaurant.

Postbank Leipzig | 103

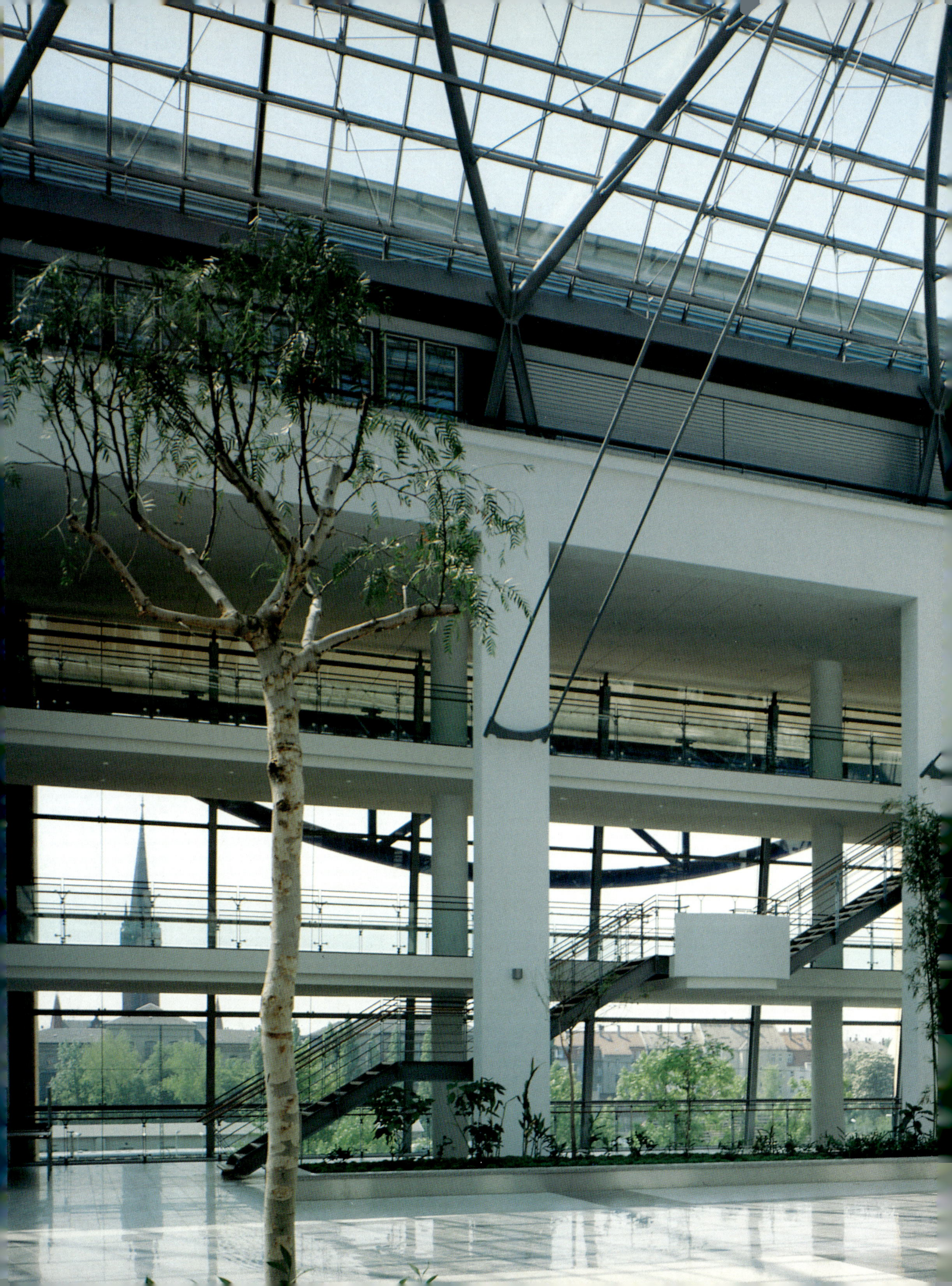

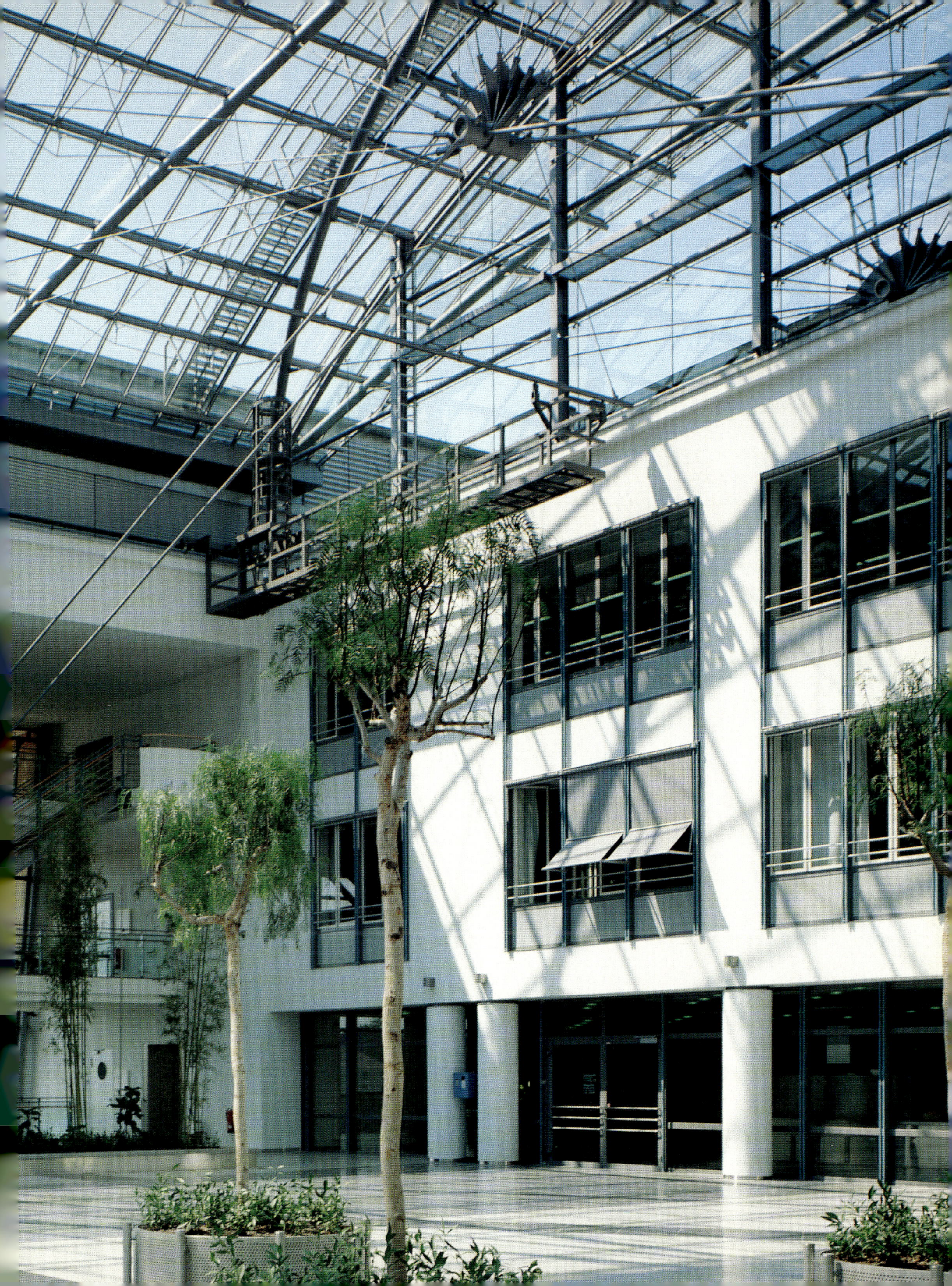

Eine begehbare „Laterne" im Scheitel der Glastonne mit senkrechter, offener Verglasung sorgt für die permanente Durchlüftung der Halle.

Along the crest of the glazed arched roof is a lantern capable of bearing foot traffic. Opening lights in the vertical sides facilitate constant ventilation of the hall.

Die Haupterschließungsebene für die Büroflure liegt im zweiten Obergeschoss der Halle und verhindert so den Kontakt der Besucher mit sicherheitsempfindlichen Bereichen.

Die Terracotta-Verkleidung in einem gelblich-warmen Ziegelton nimmt das Farbspektrum der Nachbargebäude auf. Als vorgehängte Fassade ist das traditionelle Baumaterial zeitgerecht verwendet.

Im Gegensatz zum Hauptgebäude mit seiner traditionellen Fassadengliederung steht die filigrane Stahl-Glashalle im Zentrum der Gesamtanlage. Sie überspannt eine Grundfläche von ca. 30 x 60 m bei einer Firsthöhe von 29 m. Verglast ist die Ostseite der Halle mit einer rahmenlosen, geschraubten Nurglasfassade. Eine große, schräge, verglaste Öffnung der Halle über fünf Geschosse gibt den Blick frei nach Süden über die Bahngleise in Richtung Leipziger Innenstadt.

Die Anlieferung erfolgt im Erdgeschoss von Westen in einen großen, traditionell postüblichen Ladehof.

In einer mehrgeschossigen Tiefgarage werden ca. 460 Stellplätze angeboten.

Abendstimmung im Eingangshof

Evening atmosphere within the entrance courtyard

Querschnitt durch die Halle mit Schrägverglasung nach Süden

Cross-section through the hall, showing the raking glazed wall to the south

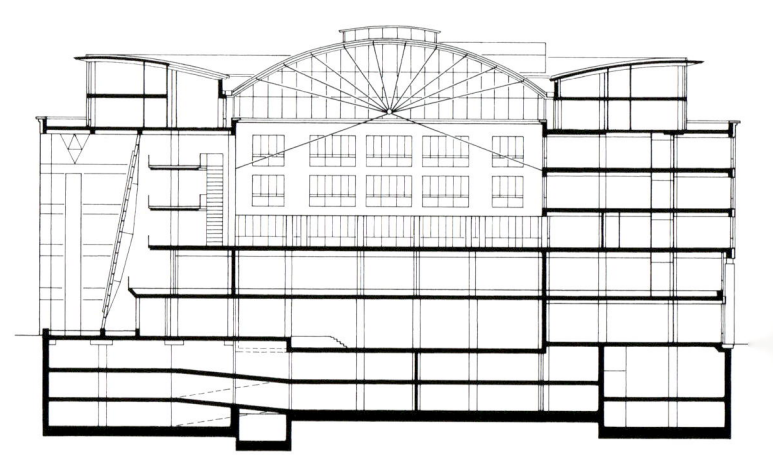

Blick in die glasüberdeckte Halle mit Aufgang vom Haupteingang in das zweite Obergeschoss; darunter liegt das Rechenzentrum.

View of glass-covered hall, with stairs leading up from the main entrance to second-floor level and with the computer centre beneath.

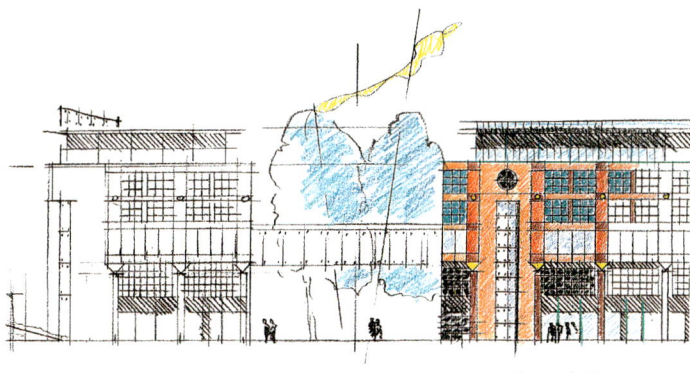

Entwurfsskizze der Fassade

Design sketch of façade

The principal circulation level for access to the offices is on the second floor of the hall, thereby effectively separating visitors from sensitive security areas.

The terracotta tile cladding in a warm yellowish tone echoes the coloration of the surrounding buildings. Designed as a curtain-wall façade, the cladding is an example of the use of traditional materials in a modern form.

The slenderly dimensioned steel and glass hall at the centre of the complex forms a striking contrast to the main structure with its traditional façade divisions. The hall covers an area roughly 30 metres wide and 60 metres long and is 29 metres high at the crest of the roof. At its eastern end, the hall is closed by a frameless, all-glass façade with bolted fixings. On the south side is a large opening with a raking glass front that extends over five storeys. It affords a view out of the hall over the railway lines towards the city centre of Leipzig.

At ground-floor level at the western end is a large, traditional post office freight yard for deliveries. The multi-storey basement garage provides parking space for roughly 460 vehicles.

Seite 104/105:
Die 1.800 m² große Halle ist ausschließlich natürlich belüftet. Eine permanente, thermisch wirksame Durchlüftung Glasfassade-Dach sorgt an heißen Tagen für ein angenehmes, pflanzenfreundliches Raumklima, eine Fußbodenheizung an kalten Tagen für 6 °C Minimaltemperatur. Die innenliegenden Büroräume sind daher nur einfach verglast mit zu öffnenden Fenstern, außenliegendem Sonnenschutz und ohne künstliche Belüftung.

pp. 104/105:
The great hall, covering an area of 1,800 square metres, is ventilated entirely by natural means. A permanent through-flow of air from the glazed façade to the roof ensures a pleasant internal atmosphere – conducive to plants – even on hot days. On cold days, an under-floor heating installation ensures a minimum temperature of 6 °C. The internal offices are, therefore, singly glazed, have opening casements with external sunblinds and require no artificial ventilation.

Postbank Leipzig | 107

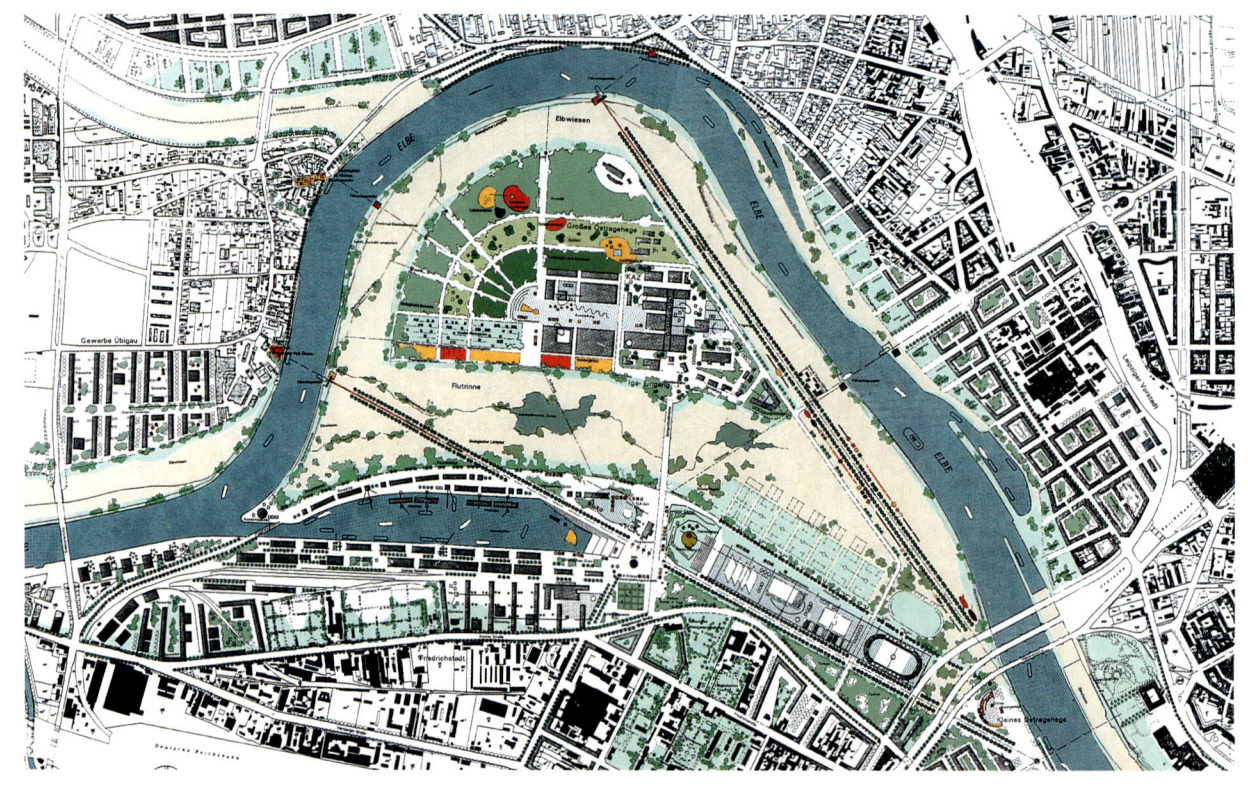

Das Große Ostragehege wird über zwei Grünachsen an die Elbterrasse angebunden.

The Grosses Ostragehege, a protected landscape area, is linked to the Elbe terraces by two planted axes.

Die sächsische Landeshauptstadt Dresden entwickelte nach der Wiedervereinigung neue Planungsleitbilder und Stadtentwicklungsstrategien. So hat die Stadt 1995 beschlossen, im Jahre 2003 eine Internationale Gartenbauausstellung im sogenannten „Großen Ostragehege" als Katalysator für eine langfristige Stadtentwicklung auszurichten.

Das Gelände, unmittelbar westlich des Zentrums am Elbbogen gelegen, historisch für Dresden von hoher Bedeutung als Fasanerie und Tiergarten aus dem 17. Jahrhundert, Teil einer barocken Parkanlage und einer denkmalgeschützten Schlachthofanlage aus den Jahren 1906 bis 1910 (Architekt Hans Erlwein), bot hierfür eine einmalige Chance.

Dresden ist eine der wenigen Städte in Europa, die nicht neben, sondern mit ihrem Fluß leben; eine einmalige, stadtbildprägende Symbiose aus Elbe, weiten Flussauen und historischer Silhouette hat sich gebildet. Sie gilt es zu pflegen und zu erhalten. Die Tradition Dresdner Bau- und Gartenkultur (Gartenstadt Dresden-Hellerau) war deshalb eine wesentliche Vorgabe für das Wettbewerbskonzept im Sinne einer „Landschaftsstadt Dresden".

Diese stadträumlichen Qualitäten zu erhalten und zur tragenden Idee einer langfristigen Stadtentwicklung im Nordwesten auszubauen, war unser Ziel: Auf den Spuren der historischen Entwicklung sollte langfristig ein Erholungs-, Ausstellungs- und Aktivitätsfeld an der Schnittstelle von Stadt und Elblandschaftsraum entstehen.

Die denkmalgeschützten Gebäude der Schlachthofanlage werden in ein Ausstellungs- und Kongresszentrum einbezogen und um eine große Mehrzweckhalle, einen Konferenzbereich und ein Hotel ergänzt.

Das Preisgericht befand denn auch, dass die besondere Qualität unserer Arbeit darin liegt, ihre städtebaulichen und landschaftsplanerischen Ideen in hohem Maße aus dem Bestand heraus zu entwickeln. Prägende Ausgangspunkte hierfür sind die beiden Alleen und die Figur des Elbbogens mit der Schlachthofinsel selbst, die deutlich akzentuiert wird. Die Großzügigkeit der Elbauen bleibt erhalten, und das Ostragehege wird in die landschaftliche Umgebung eingebunden.

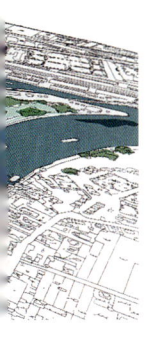

Das Große Ostragehege aus der Vogelperspektive, Blick über den Elbbogen

Bird's-eye view of the Grosses Ostragehege across the bend in the Elbe

Großes Ostragehege – IGA Dresden 2003

Grosses Ostragehege – International Horticultural Show (IGA), Dresden, 2003

12

1995 Wettbewerb IGA 2003 · 3. Preis

1995 Competition for International Horticultural Show (IGA), 2003: third prize

Das Große Ostragehege: zur IGA 2003 im Bestand neu strukturiert und an die Dresdner Altstadt städtebaulich angebunden

The Grosses Ostragehege is to be restructured and linked to the old city centre of Dresden

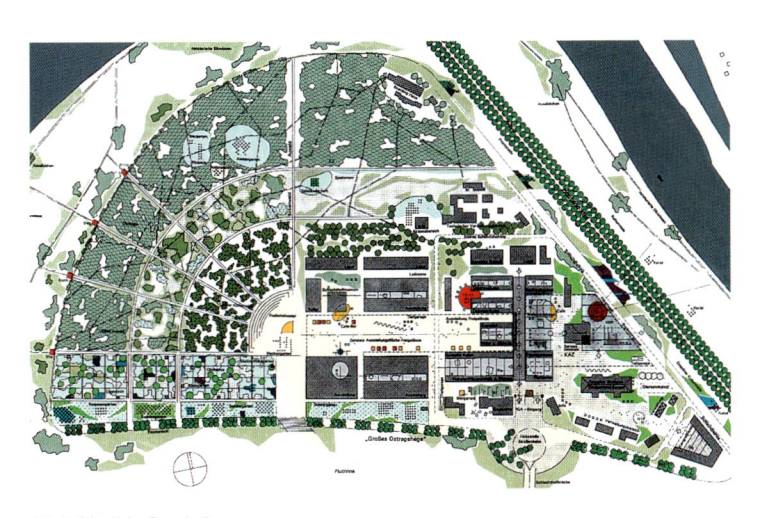

Die Schlachthofinsel als Zentrum der IGA mit dem Kongresszentrum

The abattoir area at the heart of the IGA with the new congress centre

Since the reunification of Germany, Dresden, the capital of the Free State of Saxony, has drawn up new urban planning goals and strategies. In 1995, for example, the city decided to stage an International Horticultural Show in the Grosses Ostragehege in 2003. The project is to be a catalyst for a long-term process of urban development.

The site, immediately west of the city centre in the bend of the River Elbe, enjoyed historical importance in Dresden as a pheasantry and game park dating from the 17th century. It also forms part of a Baroque park and includes a listed abattoir built between 1906 and 1910 by the architect Hans Erlwein. The area is, therefore, ideally suited to staging a horticultural show.

Dresden is one of the few European cities to live in a reciprocal relationship with its river rather than just alongside it. A unique urban symbiosis has developed here, consisting of the Elbe, the extensive river meadows and the historical urban silhouette – a heritage that has to be preserved and cultivated. Dresden's architectural and horticultural tradition (the garden city of Hellerau is an example of this) was, therefore, a major factor in drawing up the competition concept, which had as its motto "Dresden, the landscape city".

Our aim was to preserve these urban spatial qualities and to extrapolate them to form the basis of a long-term development in the northwest of the city. Continuing Dresden's historical path of evolution, the ultimate goal is to create an area for recreation, exhibitions and other activities at the interface between the city and the landscape space of the River Elbe.

The listed buildings forming the abattoir complex will be incorporated into the horticultural exhibition and congress centre and will be complemented by a large multi-purpose hall, conference facilities and a hotel.

The competition jury also recognized the special quality of our scheme: the way the urban and landscape planning concept was developed to a large extent from the existing situation. The salient features in this respect are the two avenues of trees and the curve of the Elbe with the abattoir island itself. The line of the river is clearly accentuated. The generous expanse of the Elbe meadows is retained; and the Ostragehege is tightly integrated into the surrounding landscape.

Blick nach Nordosten: rechts vorne das Reichstagsgebäude, im Hintergrund die im Wettbewerb vorgesehene Erweiterungsfläche

View to north-east: bottom right, the Reichstag building; top left, the additional site offered for the competition

Der Alsenblock, nördlich des Reichstagsgebäudes gelegen, ist einer der Bausteine des städtebaulichen Gesamtkonzeptes „Band des Bundes" nach dem Entwurf der Architekten Axel Schultes und Charlotte Frank, Berlin. Entscheidend für eine angemessene Einfügung in das Spreebogenkonzept war die Bildung von wahrnehmbaren Raumkanten mit einer Höhe von 22 m auf der Nord- und Südseite.

Das äußere Erscheinungsbild ordnet sich der nachbarschaftlichen Dominanz des Reichstagsgebäudes unter und präsentiert sich angenehm zurückhaltend, so das Preisgericht.

Die Anordnung der beiden Längsbaukörper, die durch drei Spangen verbunden sind, ermöglicht öffentlich zugängliche „Entrée-Höfe" im Westen zum zukünftigen Forum und im Osten zum Spreebogen. An diesen Höfen liegen die Haupteingänge und wichtige Einrichtungen wie Besuchersäle, Anhörungssaal und Restaurant.

Die funktionale Gliederung des Gebäudes in eine Sockelzone, in die Beletage mit dem Ausschussbereich und in die Bürogeschosse ist nach außen sichtbar gemacht. Die Lobby- und Foyerzone des Ausschussbereiches sollte als wichtiger Kommunikationsbereich und als „Schaufenster der Demokratie" mit entsprechender Wirkung nach innen und außen verstanden werden. Die Abgeordnetenbüros ermöglichen in dreibündiger Anordnung flexible Einheiten und gute Nebenflächen für Kommunikation und Technik.

Eine besondere Schwierigkeit zeigte sich beim Bearbeiten des Wettbewerbs: das geforderte Raumprogramm war für das vorgesehene Grundstück innerhalb des „Bandes des Bundes" und westlich der Spree offensichtlich zu umfangreich. Ein nördlich dieses „Bandes" vom Auslober zusätzlich angebotenes Grundstück widersprach den städtebaulichen Vorstellungen des Schultes-Entwurfs und wurde deshalb von allen Verfassern preisgekrönter Arbeiten auch nicht in Anspruch genommen. Bei der Realisierung des 1. Preises (Stephan Braunfels, München) stand glücklicherweise dann doch noch das Grundstück östlich der Spree zur Verfügung.

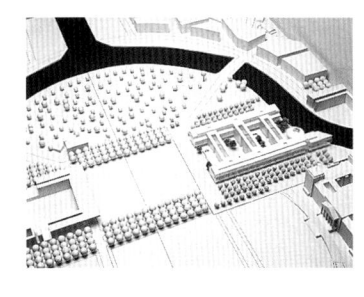

The Alsen Block, situated to the north of the Reichstag building in Berlin, is one of the elements that go to make up the large-scale urban concept known as the "Band des Bundes" or federal mile, a strip containing government and parliamentary buildings. The concept is based on proposals made by the architects Axel Schultes and Charlotte Frank, Berlin.

In order to integrate the new development satisfactorily into the concept for the area in the bend of the River Spree, it was important that it should form a perceptible spatial demarcation. This was achieved by designing it to a height of 22 metres along its northern and southern edges.

According to the competition jury, the development subordinates itself in its outward appearance to the dominant Reichstag building opposite and has an agreeably restrained form.

The layout, consisting of two longitudinal tracts linked by three cross-strips, allows the creation of public "access courtyards" at the ends. These courtyards open, at the western end, to the future Forum, and at the eastern end, to the curve of the Spree. Situated around these spaces are the main entrances and other important amenities, such as a restaurant and halls for visitors and political hearings.

The functional division of the building into a plinth zone, a beletage containing committee rooms, and the office levels is legible on the outside. The lobby and foyer zone to the committee rooms should be regarded as an important area for communication and as a "showcase of democracy", the effects of which may be felt both internally and externally. The three-bay layout of the offices for members of the Bundestag allows the creation of flexible units with ample ancillary spaces for communication and services.

A special difficulty arose while we were developing the competition scheme. The spatial programme specified in the brief was evidently too large for the designated site within the federal mile west of the Spree. The client offered an additional area north of the strip, but this was contrary to Schultes concept, and none of the prize-winning architects availed themselves of it. In realizing his scheme, which won first prize in the competition, Stephan Braunfels, Munich, was fortunate to be able to use a site east of the Spree.

Deutscher Bundestag Berlin, Alsenblock

13   **German Bundestag, Berlin: Alsen Block**

Heute Paul-Löbe-Haus
1994   Wettbewerb · 2. Preis

Now the Paul Löbe Building
1994   Competition: second prize

Verwaltungs- und Kommunikationsgebäude für die Abgeordneten des Deutschen Bundestags, unmittelbar neben dem Reichstagsgebäude

Administration and communications building for members of the German Bundestag; situated immediately next to the Reichstag

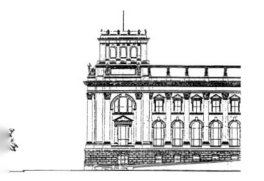

Der Reichstag (oben) und der Alsenblock (links) mit seinem „Entrée-Hof" zum Forum

The Reichstag (above) and the Alsen Block (left) with its public "access courtyard" opposite the Forum

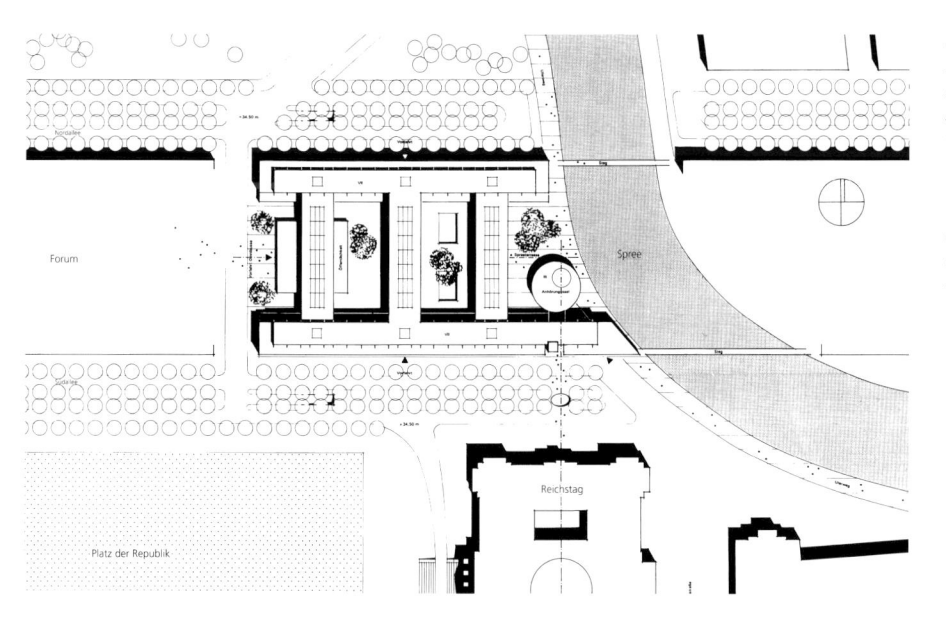

Der Alsenblock im „Band des Bundes" mit seiner Beziehung zur Spree, zum Reichstag und zum Forum

The Alsen Block within the "Band des Bundes" and in relation to the Spree, the Reichstag building and the Forum

Bundestag Berlin, Alsenblock | 111

Vor 16 Jahren haben wir unseren ersten CAD-Arbeitsplatz erworben – eine HP-Work-Station für DM 165.000 – und begonnen, die Entwurfs- und Ausführungsplanung für ein großes Projekt, Postsparkassenamt München, damit zu bearbeiten. Wir waren wohl eines der ersten Büros in Deutschland, das ein so großes, unter Termindruck stehendes Projekt „unwiderruflich" mit CAD bearbeitete. Die Vorentwurfspläne waren noch konventionell erstellt worden.

Heute haben wir – selbstverständlich – exakt so viele CAD-Arbeitsplätze wie Architekten und Bauzeichner im Büro. Wir arbeiten mit CAD in allen Leistungsphasen. Rapidographen, wenn es denn noch welche gibt, sind ausgetrocknet. Auch Wettbewerbe werden seit einigen Jahren fast ausschließlich mit CAD präsentiert.

Vieles entwerfen wir auch bereits am Computer, nicht alles. Denn das eigentliche Werk des Architekten ist nicht die Zeichnung, sondern der Entwurf, d. h. das, was zwischen den ersten Skizzen und der eigentlichen zeichnerischen Darstellung entsteht.

Das neue Werkzeug stellt uns hierfür hervorragende Tools zur Verfügung, die gut – immer besser – geeignet sind, Lösungen zu einzelnen Aspekten zu erarbeiten oder Varianten einer ersten Idee zu visualisieren und so den Entwurfsgedanken zu optimieren. Dennoch arbeiten wir auch mehr denn je mit anderen Werkzeugen, z. B. Arbeitsmodellen zum Überprüfen von räumlichen Vorstellungen im Gesamten und im Detail.

Der Copy-Befehl des Computers führt zu einer neuen Perfektion der Darstellung, aber nicht unbedingt zum optimalen Entwurfsergebnis. Innovation kommt eher aus dem Imperfekten, das Perfekte lässt vergleichsweise wenig Raum für Neues.

Das Fatale ist: der schier unglaubliche Geschwindigkeitszuwachs, den wir durch die neuen Werkzeuge in der Produktion von Plänen und beim Austausch von Daten mit Dritten gewonnen haben, führt zu einem simultanen Zuwachs von Erwartungen unserer Partner und Auftraggeber an unsere Leistungsfähigkeit. Das gilt übrigens in gleicher Weise für alle anderen EDV-Anwendungen, wie Ausschreibungen, Datenbankanwendungen, Tabellenkalkulation oder Terminplanung.

Es ist wie in der Fabel vom Hasen und Igel: je schneller wir uns zu rennen bemühen, desto früher steht der Bauherr-Igel im Ziel und erwartet die neuesten Index-Pläne.

Beim Wettbewerb für den neuen Terminal des Flughafens München sollten die drei ersten Preisträger ihre Entwürfe intensiv überarbeiten und hatten dafür 6 Wochen Zeit – wenig für ein so komplexes Projekt. Nach dieser Überarbeitung fiel jedoch nur eine Vorentscheidung. Die beiden im Rennen verbliebenen Teilnehmer sollten – nunmehr binnen einer Woche – nochmals überarbeiten, und zwar die wesentlichen Entwurfsgrundlagen – Durchfahrts-Vorfahrtslösung, Passagierführung, grundlegende Nutzungsverteilungen auf den diversen Ebenen ändern, „Skizzenform würde genügen".

Es gelang uns in dieser extrem kurzen Zeit, nicht nur den Entwurf in diesen Punkten grundsätzlich zu überarbeiten, sondern dank CAD waren wir auch in der Lage, eine perfekte Darstellung einschließlich Perspektiven, computerentwickeltem Modellfoto etc. zu präsentieren – vor nur drei Jahren wäre dies völlig undenkbar gewesen.

Künftig, nein heute schon, ist auch das Skizzieren am Computer möglich. Entwurfsarbeit wird zunehmend unabhängiger von den Werkzeugen, die ihrerseits zunehmend intelligenter werden. Wir bedienen uns schon heute mit großer Selbstverständlichkeit Darstellungs-, Präsentations- und Datenaustauschmethoden, die vor kurzem kaum vorstellbar waren.

Unsere große Sorge ist aber, dass trotzdem, vielleicht sogar deswegen, die Qualität unserer gebauten Umwelt nicht besser wird: Ein wesentlicher Faktor für Qualität heißt nämlich „reifen lassen". Das gute Produkt, zunächst als Idee, als Konzept entstanden, in einem oder wenigen Köpfen, muss vor der Produktionsreife immer wieder auf den Prüfstand. Viele leisten Beiträge auf dem Wege zur Qualität – sie können zeitlich aber nur nacheinander auf dem vorher Erarbeiteten aufbauen.

CAD als Arbeitsmittel

CAD as a working tool

Sixteen years ago, we acquired our first CAD workplace – an HP workstation – at a cost of DM 165,000. With this equipment, we began the design and construction planning for a large-scale project: the Post Office Savings Bank in Munich. We were probably one of the first offices in Germany to commit ourselves "irrevocably" to using CAD for a major scheme of this kind, which was also subject to strict deadlines. The preliminary design had been prepared by conventional means.

Today, of course, we have as many CAD workplaces as we have architects and construction draughtsmen in the office. We use CAD in all the work stages of a project. The drawing pens, if any still exist, have long since dried out. For some years now, we have also presented our competition schemes almost exclusively by means of CAD.

We do a lot of the design work – not everything – on the computer, too; for the essential discipline of an architect lies not in the act of drawing, but in design: in other words, in those things that are produced between the initial sketches and the drawn representation.

The new equipment provides excellent tools for this purpose. It lends itself increasingly to developing solutions to individual aspects of a project, or to visualizing variations on an initial concept, thereby optimizing design ideas. Despite this, we use other tools, such as working models, more than ever in our work to test spatial concepts on an overall scale and in detail.

The "copy" instruction given to the computer leads to a new perfection in the representation of things, but not necessarily to an ideal design solution. Innovation is more likely to emerge from imperfection. Perfection leaves little latitude for new developments.

The fatal aspect of all this is the incredible increase in speed these new tools have given us in the production of plans and in exchanging information with others. As a result, our partners and clients come to expect ever greater efficiency from us. The same, of course, applies to all other applications of electronic data processing, such as preparing specifications and bills of quantities, databank use, drawing up tables and calculations, or time scheduling.

One is reminded of the fable of the hare and the tortoise: the faster we try to run, the sooner the tortoise-client will be standing on the finishing line waiting for the latest revised plans.

In future – no, already today, it is possible to sketch on the computer as well. Design work will become increasingly independent of the tools used, which will, in turn, become more and more intelligent. We already take it more or less for granted to use methods of depiction, presentation and data exchange that would have been scarcely conceivable only a short time ago.

Our great concern, however, is that in spite this – or perhaps because of it – there will be no improvement in the quality of our built environment. A major factor in achieving quality is namely to "let things mature". A good product, resulting initially from the idea or concept of a single person or a small group of people, needs to be tested over and over again before it is fit for production. Many people contribute to this process of achieving quality, but they can only add, one after another, to what has gone before over a period of time.

Der lärmgeschützte Innenhof: großzügig verglaste Fassaden, nach oben zurückgestaffelte Terrassen, eine versteckte grüne Oase in der Innenstadt

Screened from street noise, the internal courtyard is distinguished by broad areas of glazing to the façades and by a series of terraced levels; a secluded oasis at the heart of the city.

Weitgehend geschlossene äußere Putzfassaden ergänzen den städtischen Straßenraum.

The largely closed and rendered outer faces of the block complement the structure of the existing street space.

Die Übergangszone zwischen Innenhof und Straßenraum entlang der Paul-Heyse-Straße wird über die ganze Blocklänge mit einer doppelten Baumreihe bereichert.

Along Paul-Heyse-Strasse, the transitional zone between the courtyard and the street space is enhanced by a row of trees extending over the entire length of the block.

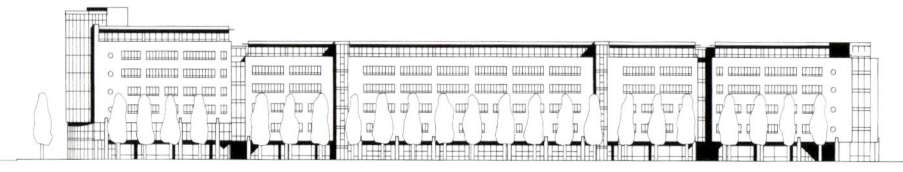

14 Postsparkassenamt München
Post Office Savings Bank, Munich

Heute Postbank München
1983   Wettbewerb · 1. Preis
1986 – 1993 Planung und Realisierung
Architekten: Koch · Benedek + Partner

Today, the Post Office Bank, Munich
1983   Competition: first prize
1986 – 1993 Planning and construction
Architects: Koch · Benedek + Partner

Ein Gebäude mit „dualistischem" Fassadenprinzip: außen verputzte, weitgehend geschlossene Lochfassaden, innen Höfe mit üppig begrünten Terrassen; großzügig geöffnete, mit tiefliegenden Brüstungen raumhoch verglaste Bürofassaden

A building based on a "dual" façade principle: mainly closed rendered walls with rectangular openings along the external street faces; internally, profusely planted terraced courtyards and open office façades with full-height glazing and low apron panels

Der im Krieg zerstörte städtische Straßenraum wird durch nachbartypische Traufhöhen wiederhergestellt.

The urban street space, which was destroyed during the war, has been reinstated by adopting the eaves heights of neighbouring buildings.

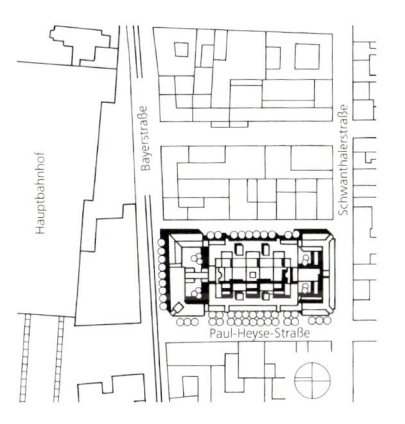

Lageplan: Das städtebauliche Ziel war die Ergänzung der innerstädtischen Blockstruktur.

Site plan: the aim of the urban planning was to extend and close the inner-city block structure.

Die intensiv begrünten Innenhöfe prägen mit ihrer dichten Vegetation das Erscheinungsbild des Blockinneren.

The interior of the block is dominated by the dense vegetation of the landscaped courtyards.

Bereits im Jahr der Fertigstellung nahm die Clematis „montana rubens" die Innenhoffassaden in Besitz.

Within a year of the completion of the development, the internal courtyard façades were covered with montana rubens clematis.

Die Wettbewerbsaufgabe 1983 bestand darin, für das posteigene Grundstück südlich des Münchner Hauptbahnhofs, seit Kriegsende als Parkplatz für Postfahrzeuge genutzt und entlang der Bayerstraße mit desolaten eingeschossigen Nachkriegsprovisorien bebaut, ein Verwaltungsgebäude für etwa 1.500 Mitarbeiter mit Schalterhalle, Kantine und Schulungsbereich, Rechenzentrum, Post-Ärztezentrum, Anlieferhof und Tiefgarage zu entwerfen.

Entwurfsziel war einerseits, den städtischen Straßenraum durch Übernahme der nachbartypischen Traufhöhe und Ausbildung einer verputzten Lochfassade zu komplettieren. Andererseits war eine Vielzahl von Einzelbüros unterzubringen, die – gemäß Postrichtlinien – auch bei starken Immissionen nicht klimatisiert werden durften. Wegen der sehr lärmintensiven Umgebungsstraßen war es daher von entscheidender Bedeutung, einen möglichst großen Anteil dieser Einzelräume in das ruhigere Blockinnere zu orientieren, um so optimale Arbeitsbedingungen zu gewährleisten. Dagegen konnten die ohnehin lüftungstechnisch zu behandelnden Gruppen- und Großräume, wie etwa EDV und Karteiräume, den lauten Straßenseiten zugeordnet werden. Dies führte zum Konzept der terrassierten, nach oben zurückgestaffelten und intensiv begrünten Innenhöfe. Durch ein geschossweises Versetzen der Erschließungsflure, ermöglicht durch die unterschiedlichen Raumtiefen der Sondernutzflächen an den Straßen, ist eine besonders große Abwicklungslänge für die Innenhoffassaden mit Einzelraumtiefe erreicht. So konnten über 70 % der Einzelräume zu den Höfen orientiert werden.

Dem folgt konsequent auch die Ausbildung der Fassaden. Nach außen zum öffentlichen Straßenraum hin bleibt die verputzte Lochfassade weitgehend geschlossen. Im Gegensatz dazu sind die Innenhoffassaden großzügig geöffnet, um den Blick auf die üppig begrünten Terrassen und Fassaden freizugeben.

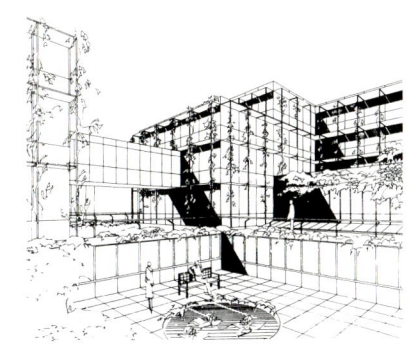

Entwurfsskizze der terrassierten Innenhöfe mit raumhoch verglasten Fassaden

Design sketch of courtyard terraces with room-height façade glazing

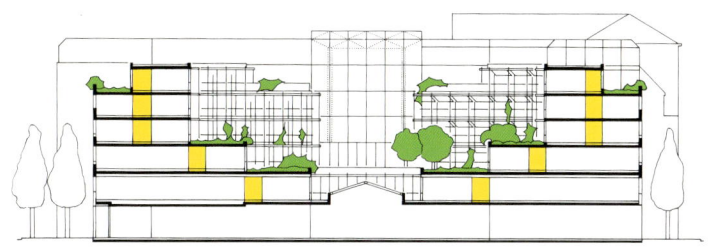

After the war, the post office used this site south of the main station in Munich as a parking area for its vehicles. In the post-war years, a number of dreary, temporary single-storey structures were also erected along Bayerstrasse. In 1983, a competition was held for the development of the site. The brief required the creation of an administration building for a staff of approximately 1,500, with a banking hall, a canteen and training areas, a computer centre, a staff medical centre, a delivery yard and a basement garage.

On the one hand, the design sought to conform with the existing urban street space by adopting the eaves height of the neighbouring buildings and a closed, rendered façade construction with rectangular openings. On the other hand, a large number of single office spaces had to be accommodated in the complex; and, in accordance with post-office guidelines, these were not to be air-conditioned, even where subject to heavy external pollution or noise. In view of the high noise levels in the surrounding streets, it was essential to orient as many of the single offices as possible towards the quieter internal spaces within the block development, where optimum working conditions could be guaranteed. The group offices and open-plan spaces – computer and card-filing areas, for example – where it was anyway necessary to provide air-conditioning, could be located along the noisy street faces. This led to a concept of profusely planted internal courtyards, stepped back in a series of terraces towards the top. The varying depths of the spaces for special purposes along the street front resulted in a layout in which the position of the access corridors is staggered from floor to floor. This, in turn, allowed a maximum linear arrangement of offices of standard depth along the internal courtyard faces.

Querschnitt und Terrassenaufsicht zeigen die dichte Bebauung des Grundstücks (die Geschossflächenzahl beträgt 3,8) und die unterschiedlichen Begrünungsebenen über alle Geschosse.

Cross-section and plan of terraces, showing the high-density development of the site (floor area / site area factor = 3.8) and the landscaped areas on top of the various floors.

Postsparkassenamt München | 117

Tageslichtdurchflutete Schalterhalle in der Symmetrieachse der Gesamtanlage

Main banking hall flooded with daylight: view along central axis of the development

Symmetrische Sichtachse durch die Haupttreppenhäuser und den Innenhof

View along central axis of development through the main staircases and the courtyard

In diesem „dualistischen" Gestaltungsprinzip der Innen- und Außenfassaden zeigt sich eine Vielzahl von Gegensatzpaaren:
- außen – innen
- Straße – Hof
- Putzfassade – begrünte Metall-Glasfassade
- geschlossen – offen
- laut – leise
- Straßenlärm – Vogelstimmen
- Großräume – Einzelräume.

Im Gegensatz zur Wettbewerbsanforderung, die aus Sicherheitsgründen eigentlich keine öffentlichen Durchgänge durch das Grundstück zuließ, schlugen wir zwei öffentliche Höfe vor, den sogenannten Bayer- und den Schwanthalerhof. Diese tragen mit Geschäften und mit der Schalterhalle der Postbank zur Aufwertung und Belebung des gesamten Komplexes bei und erhöhen den Erlebniswert für Mitarbeiter und Besucher. Lediglich der in der Mitte liegende Verwaltungsbereich, der wenig Publikumsverkehr verursacht, ist für die Öffentlichkeit nicht zugänglich.

Unsere wesentlichen Entwurfsziele konnten vom Vorentwurf bis zur Ausführung konsequent verfolgt werden. Ziel der äußeren Gestaltung der Bankfassade war es, ein zurückhaltendes, unaufdringliches und dennoch elegantes Erscheinungsbild zu erhalten, das unmittelbar an die Tradition der Münchner Postbauten der 20er und 30er Jahre anknüpft. Die Straßenräume der Mitterer- und Paul-Heyse-Straße sind durch Rücksprünge der Mittelteile verbreitert. Mit zusätzlich gepflanzten Bäumen entlang der 145 Meter langen Längsfassade ist eine weitere optische Gliederung erreicht und die Übergangszone zwischen Straßenraum und Innenhof bereichert.

In Zusammenarbeit mit dem Landschaftsarchitekten Peter Kluska wurden alle terrassierten Flächen intensiv, alle Dachflächen extensiv begrünt. Bereits im Jahr der Fertigstellung nahm die Clematis „montana rubens" die Innenhoffassade in Besitz. Seither prägt sie mit ihrer dichten Vegetation das grüne Erscheinungsbild des Blockinneren.

Zusammen mit dem Lichtplanungsbüro Christian Bartenbach wurde für die Schalterhalle ein Lichtkonzept entwickelt, das durch Kunstlichtreflexion und Tageslichtnutzung den unterschiedlichen Anforderungen der variablen Möblierung und der fixen Einbauten entspricht.

It was, therefore, possible to orient more than 70 per cent of the single office units towards the courtyards. This layout is clearly legible in the design of the façades.

Those on the outside overlooking the public street spaces consist largely of closed rendered walls punctuated by rectangular openings. The courtyard faces, in contrast, are generously open, affording views of the landscaped terraces and other façades.

The dual design principle on which the internal and external façades are based results in a large number of antitheses:
- outside and inside
- street and courtyard
- rendered façades and planted metal-and-glass façades
- closed and open spaces
- noisy and quiet zones
- street sounds and bird call
- open-plan spaces and single office units.

For security reasons, no public access routes across the site were foreseen in the competition brief. We nevertheless proposed the creation of two public courtyards: the Bayerhof and the Schwanthalerhof, which contain shops and businesses and from where access is provided to the main hall of the Post Office Bank. The courtyards upgrade and enliven the entire complex, increasing the leisure value for employees and visitors alike. Only the central administration tract is not open to the general public.

We were able to pursue our main goals consistently from the preliminary design to the construction stage. Our concept for the outer façade of the bank was to achieve a restrained, unobtrusive, yet elegant appearance that would directly reflect the strong tradition of post office building in Munich in the 1920s and 30s. Two of the flanking street spaces – Mittererstrasse and Paul-Heyse-Strasse – were broadened by setting back the central sections of the complex. A further visual articulation was achieved by planting additional trees along the 145-metre-long face of the development in Paul-Heyse-Strasse. At the same time, these plantings enrich the transitional zone between the street space and the courtyard.

In collaboration with the landscape architect Peter Kluska, all the terraced areas were intensively planted; and all the roof areas were extensively planted. Within a year of the completion of the development, the montana rubens clematis had taken possession of the courtyard façades, and since then, its dense vegetation has come to dominate the appearance of the landscaped interior of the block.

A lighting concept for the main banking hall was developed in collaboration with the Christian Bartenbach office. It is based on reflected artificial light and the exploitation of daylight to meet the needs of different layouts: some with variable furnishings, others with permanent fittings.

Haupttreppenhaus mit Blick in den begrünten Innenhof

Main staircase with view to landscaped courtyard beyond

Blick vom Wertach-brucker Tor auf die geschwungene Ostfassade am Senkelbach

View of curved east face along Senkel stream from Wertachbrucker Gate

Lageplan: rechts der realisierte 1. Bauabschnitt, links die Erweiterungsmöglichkeit

Site plan: on the right, the first stage of construction, already completed; left, the potential extension

Arbeitsamt Augsburg

15 **Jobcentre, Augsburg**

1981 Wettbewerb · 1. Preis
1984 – 1989 Planung und Realisierung

1981 Competition: first prize
1984 – 1989 Planning and construction

Das Gebäude schafft ein positives Milieu mit einer sachlichen, zugleich offenen, transparenten Grundstimmung. Es soll dem Besucher entgegenkommen, nicht sich ihm verschließen.

The building establishes a positive environment with a sober, yet open, transparent atmosphere. It is designed to welcome visitors and not to be off-putting.

Die gläserne Eingangsspange im Licht- und Reflexionsspiel bei Tag und bei Nacht

Glazed entrance tract: reflections and play of light by day and at night

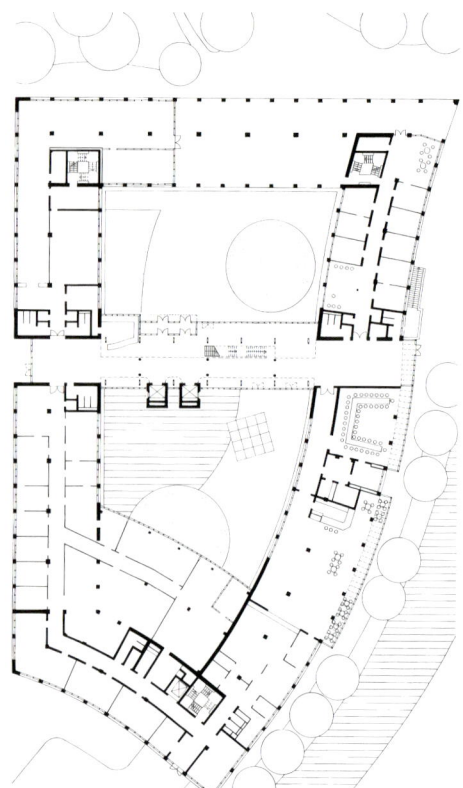

Grundriss Erdgeschoss mit Außenanlagen und dem gestalteten Innenhof

Ground floor plan with external works and courtyard design

Am Rand der blockartig geschlossenen Bebauung der Augsburger Altstadt war es angemessen, einen gleichfalls geschlossenen „Baublock" mit Innenhöfen vorzusehen, um dem Charakter und der Maßstäblichkeit der Altstadt zu entsprechen.

Der gekrümmte Verlauf des Senkelbaches und die gebogene Fassade der Wohnbauzeile in der Friedrich-Chur-Straße waren die Vorgabe für die an zwei Seiten geschwungene Ausbildung der Fassaden dieses Baublocks. So entstand ein geschlossener Baukörper, der seine räumliche Wirkung aus dem Gegensatz rechtwinkliger und geschwungener Bauteile bezieht. Besonderer Wert wurde auf die städtebauliche Eigenständigkeit des realisierten ersten Bauabschnittes gelegt.

Eine große, alle Geschosse erreichende gläserne Spange bildet im Erdgeschoss den Haupteingang und führt den Besucher mit Treppen und Aufzügen auf kurzen Wegen durch alle Ebenen in die einzelnen Abteilungen. Diese Eingangshalle erschließt alle publikumsintensiven Bereiche, die sich vorwiegend im Erdgeschoss, aber auch im ersten und zweiten Obergeschoss befinden. Sie dient der Besucherverteilung, erleichtert die Orientierung im Gebäude und bietet vielfältige Ausblickmöglichkeiten. Dies ist angesichts des hohen täglichen Besucheraufkommens – bis zu 2.000 – von besonderer Bedeutung.

In view of the location of the site on the edge of a continuous, closed street-block development that forms part of the inner city of Augsburg, it seemed appropriate to create a further closed building block with internal courtyards, thereby reflecting the character and scale of the historic city centre.

The bend of the Senkel stream and the curved face of the housing strip in Friedrich-Chur-Strasse were points of reference for the façade lines of the new development, which is also curved on two sides. The outcome was a closed street block, the spatial character of which is based on the contrast between rectilinear and curved elements. Special importance was attached to giving the first stage of the scheme an urban identity of its own.

The main entrance is situated on the ground floor of the large glazed tract that extends over all storeys. From here, visitors have direct access via stairs and lifts to all levels and to the various departments of the centre. The entrance hall forms the point of access to those parts of the development where close contact with the public is foreseen. These areas are located primarily on the ground floor, but also at first and second-floor levels. The hall serves to distribute the flow of visitors; it also facilitates orientation within the complex and affords a wide range of views out of the building. Great importance was attached to these aspects of the design in view of the large volume of visitors to be expected – up to 2,000 a day.

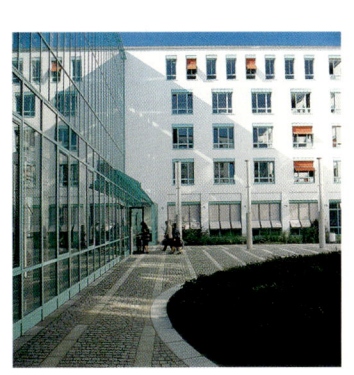

Die beiden Innnenhöfe mit Wasserbecken und Lichtstelen von Manfred Mayerle und Florian Lechner

The two internal courtyards with pools of water and illuminated stelae by Manfred Mayerle and Florian Lechner

Der Hauptbaukörper ist massives, verputztes Mauerwerk, mit Stahlbeton-Decken und -Innenstützen; die Einzelfenster sind in Holz/Alu-Konstruktion ausgeführt. Als spannungsvoller Gegensatz hierzu ist die zentrale Erschließungsspange von oben bis unten durchsichtig und voll verglast. Die beiden durch diese Glasspange entstehenden Innenhöfe sind damit erkennbar und erlebbar.

Das Gebäude ist kein Behördenpalast, in dem sich der Rat und Hilfe suchende Bürger als Bittsteller und Untertan fühlen und orientierungslos umherirren muss.

Es gibt hier keine Zäune; jeder kann überall hingehen. Baukörperform und damit korrespondierende Flure, im Wechsel geschwungen, rechtwinklig und gerade, und die Transparenz der gläsernen Erschließungsspange ermöglichen jedem Besucher wie von selbst Übersicht und Orientierung.

Das Gebäude knüpft an die Tradition der Architektursprache der 20er und 50er Jahre an und führt sie mit zeitgemäßen Mitteln fort.

Westliches Ende der Glasspange: hier kann ein 2. Bauabschnitt angebunden werden.

Western end of glazed tract; a second stage of the development can be attached here.

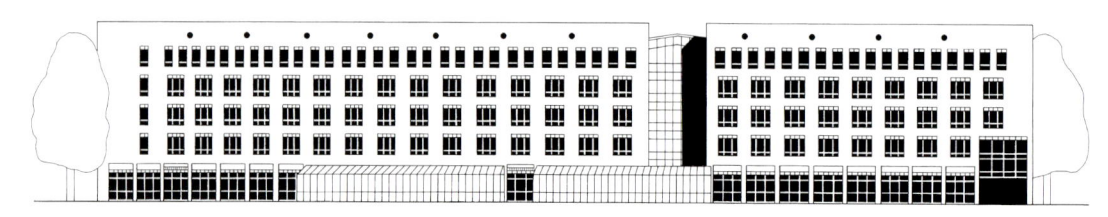

Geschwungene Ostansicht als Lochfassade

View and elevation of curved east face with rectangular window openings

Blick in den Luftraum

Interior of glazed tract

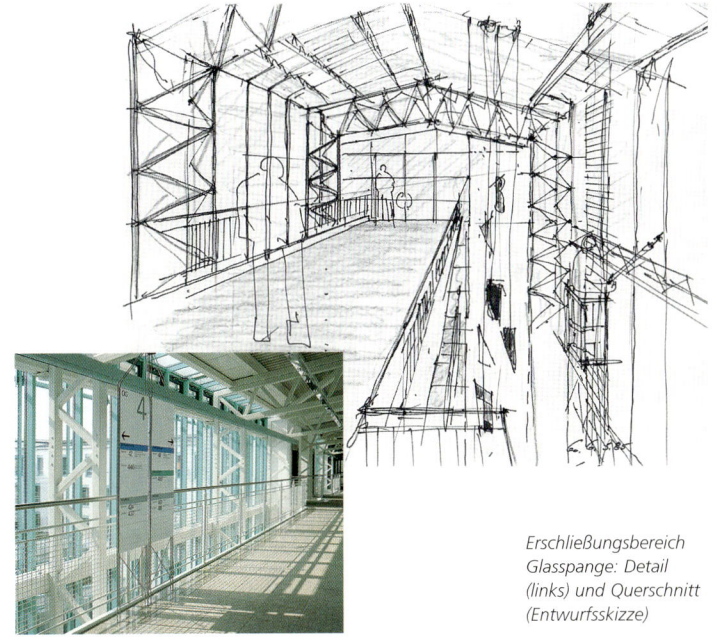

Erschließungsbereich Glasspange: Detail (links) und Querschnitt (Entwurfsskizze)

Circulation within glazed tract: detail (left) and perspective design sketch

Querschnitt der Glasspange

Cross-section through glazed tract

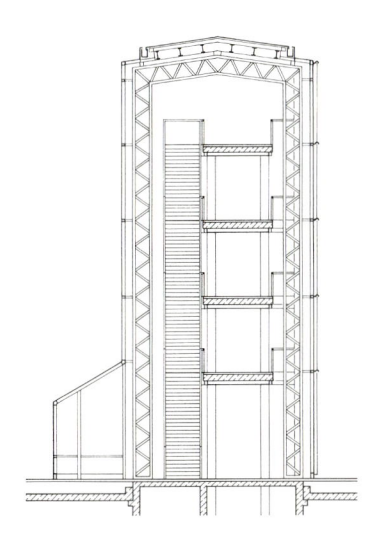

The main structure consists of solid, rendered brick walls with reinforced concrete floors and internal columns. The individual windows are in wood and aluminium. Forming a bold contrast to this, the central access tract is fully glazed and transparent from top to bottom. It divides the space within the block into two courtyards, to which there are direct visual links through the glass walls.

The building was not conceived as a bureaucratic palace in which members of the public are forced to err around in search of help and advice like underlings begging favours.

There are no barriers here. Everyone can go everywhere. The form of the building and the corresponding shape of the corridors – curving, rectilinear and straight – together with the transparency of the glazed access tract provide visitors with a clear overall view and a sense of orientation.

The building adopts the traditional architectural language of the 1920s and 50s, extrapolating it with modern means.

Arbeitsamt Augsburg

Durchgehendes Fensterband und vertikale Elemente im Raster der Hauptstützen

Continuous horizontal window strip with vertical elements; based on the dimensions of the main column grid

Die Hallen sind weitgehend von Installationen und fertigungsbedingten Nebenflächen freigehalten.

The halls are almost entirely free of mechanical services and ancillary spaces for the production process.

Das Werk der Siemens AG für Computersysteme in Augsburg, dessen ersten Bauabschnitt – eine Doppelhalle – wir 1985 planten, ist ein Beispiel für eine Industriearchitektur, die auf der Grundlage sehr konkreter Bauherrnwünsche und -vorstellungen in erster Linie technologisch-fertigungstechnisch orientiert ist. Das architektonische Erscheinungsbild ist nahezu ausschließlich determiniert durch die verbindlichen Vorgaben der Funktionen, der Kosten und der Termine.

Angesichts der geforderten Kürze der Fluchtwege waren im ersten Bauabschnitt zwei gleich große Hallen mit etwa je 8.000 m² realisierbar. Dabei sollte jede Halle für sich als selbstständige Fertigungseinheit funktionieren: durch ein Versorgungsbasement kann das Umrüsten von Fertigungslinien störungsfrei vorbereitet werden. Beide Hallen sind durch einen dazwischenliegenden dreigeschossigen Verbindungsbau mit Nebenräumen und Büros zusammengefasst. Bei einem Stützenraster von 21,60 x 10,80 m können in jeder Halle Fertigungslinien von 75 bzw. 108 m Länge eingerichtet werden. Die Hallen sind durch drei Überfahrten miteinander verbunden, so dass auch 150 m lange Fertigungslinien realisiert werden können. Sie sind so konzipiert, dass sie weitgehend von Installationen und fertigungsbedingten Nebenflächen frei sind. Installationsebene, gebäudetechnische Anlagen und fertigungsbedingte Nebenflächen sind der Halle im Untergeschoss und im Mitteltrakt direkt zugeordnet. Das Untergeschoss ist als Installationsbasement in gleicher Größe unter der Fertigungsebene angeordnet und fungiert in seiner Gesamtheit als Zuluftkanal zum Klimatisieren der Halle für die hoch anspruchsvolle, feuchtigkeits- und temperaturkonstante Computerfertigung. Die aufbereitete Luft wird durch Klimageräte direkt in das Untergeschoss eingeblasen, wo sie über Drallauslässe im Raster 90 x 90 cm in die Halle gelangt.

The first stage of this computer manufacturing works in Augsburg, a double hall structure we planned in 1985 for the Siemens company, is an example of industrial architecture designed to the specific wishes and concepts of the client. It is oriented largely to the needs of a technical production process. The architectural appearance of the building is determined almost exclusively by functional considerations as well as cost and time constraints.

In view of the short escape routes required in the brief, the design for the first phase of construction foresaw two halls of equal size, each with a floor area of roughly 8,000 m². Each hall was also to function as an independent production unit. A services basement allows any reorganization of the production lines to be prepared in advance without disrupting the working process. Between the two halls is a three-storey linking tract in which the ancillary spaces and offices are grouped together. The column grid, with axes at 21.60 x 10.80 m centres, allows the installation of production lines 75 m and 108 m long in each of the halls. The halls are linked by three transport bridges, which allow the servicing of production lines up to 150 m in length. The halls are conceived in such a way that they are largely free of mechanical services and ancillary production spaces, both of which are housed in the basement and the middle tract in direct proximity to the production lines. The basement storey with service installations occupies the same area as the production level above it. This entire subfloor space functions as an air-intake duct for the indoor climate-control system within the hall, where the highly sensitive computer production areas require constant humidity and temperature levels. The conditioned air is blown directly into the basement space, from where it enters the hall via rotary fan inlets in the floor at 90 x 90 cm centres.

Die Fassadengestaltung ermöglicht jedem Arbeitsplatz einen Ausblick ins Freie.

The façade design allows a view out of the building from every workplace.

Siemens AG Augsburg

16   **Siemens Building, Augsburg**

1985 – 1986 Werk für Systeme, Standort 2
1. Bauabschnitt · Planung und Realisierung

1985 – 1986 Computer works, location 2
1st stage of development:
planning and construction

Technologisch-fertigungstechnisch orientierte Industriearchitektur

Industrial architecture for technology and manufacturing

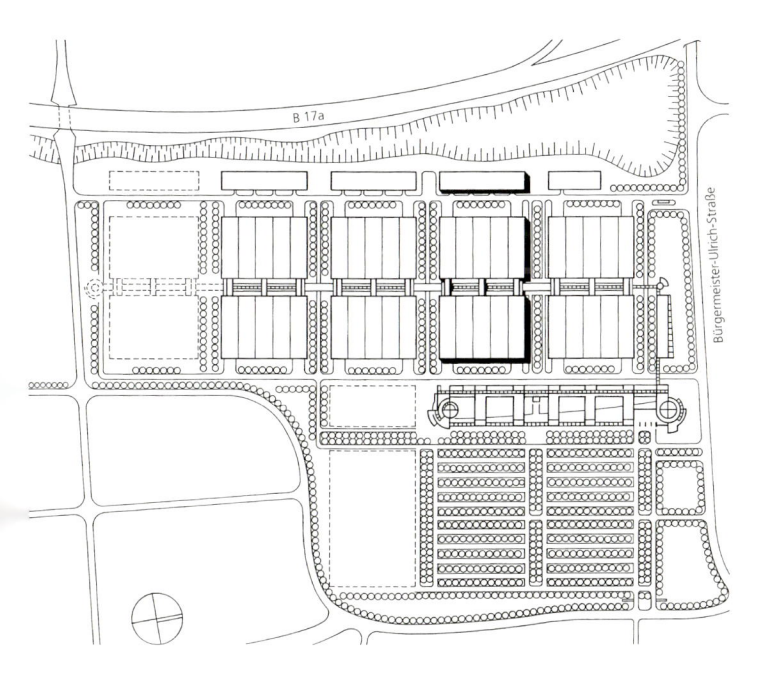

Gesamtlageplan mit erstem Bauabschnitt

Site plan, showing first stage of construction

Begonnen hat unsere Arbeit vor dreißig Jahren am Kaiserplatz in München-Schwabing mit einer Bürogemeinschaft, die über zwei Jahrzehnte lang bestanden hat. Alle Mitglieder dieser Gruppe waren selbstständig und voneinander unabhängig: Wir haben grundsätzlich nur eigene Aufträge und Wettbewerbe bearbeitet. Wenn es gelegentlich zu einer Arbeitsgemeinschaft kam, war sie immer projektbezogen. Das Ausstellen von Wettbewerbsbeiträgen, Entwürfen und Skizzen im gemeinsamen Flur sorgte auch für kollegiale Kritik. Diese Bereitschaft zur offenen Diskussion hat vermutlich die Art geprägt, wie wir heute arbeiten: eher kollegial und partnerschaftlich als autoritär und weisungsorientiert.

Unser Büro umfasst derzeit vier Partner, sechs Projektpartner und rund 100 Mitarbeiter. Die meisten sind Architekten, Innenarchitekten und Stadtplaner; hinzu kommen einige Bauingenieure. Diese Mischung garantiert eine effiziente, arbeitsteilige und noch übersichtliche Struktur unseres Büros, wobei sich die vier Partner durch ihre unterschiedlichen Temperamente und Fähigkeiten gegenseitig stützen und ergänzen. Jedes Projekt wird jedoch nach außen wie nach innen von einem Partner allein verantwortet. Auch bei Wettbewerben hat uns die Erfahrung gelehrt: letztlich darf nur ein Partner darüber entscheiden, welcher Lösungsansatz ausgearbeitet wird, und das wird vor Beginn jeder Bearbeitung festgelegt.

Fast immer ist es uns gelungen, alle Leistungsphasen einer Aufgabe bearbeiten zu können, vom Vorentwurf bis zur Bauleitung.

Für dieses Bemühen von unserer Seite gibt es zwei wesentliche Gründe. Erstens: Nur wenn der Architekt den Auftrag erhält, sein Projekt bis zum Ende zu betreuen, hat er auch die Möglichkeit, das Erscheinungsbild seines Gebäudes zu beeinflussen, das ganz entscheidend von den Materialien, den Farben, den Details und der Qualität ihrer Ausführung bestimmt wird. Der zweite Grund hat generelle Bedeutung: Die freiwillige Selbstbeschränkung des Architekten auf die vergleichsweise besser honorierten Planungsleistungen wirkt sich als Eigentor aus, weil die ausführungsorientierten Leistungen wie Ausschreibung, Vergabe und Bauleitung auch von Auftragnehmern erbracht werden können, die etwas vom Bauen verstehen, aber nicht entwerfen können. Dies kommt vielen Auftraggebern und Investoren entgegen, die Planungskosten sparen wollen und die Architekten nur noch mit den notwendigen Mindestleistungen beauftragen.

Die Arbeit in unserem Büro ist durch eine „flache Hierarchie" geprägt. Dies bedeutet, viele Mitarbeiter an möglichst vielen Entscheidungen beteiligen, ihre Selbstständigkeit auch in gestalterischen Fragen respektieren und darauf vertrauen, dass im gesamten Team sowohl fehlende Kenntnisse abgefragt als auch Erfahrungen weitergegeben werden. Unser Prinzip lautet: Kontrolle ist gut, Vertrauen ist besser.

Wie wir arbeiten

The way we work

Our work began 30 years ago in Kaiserplatz, a public square in Schwabing, Munich. The joint practice we shared existed for more than 20 years. Every member of the group had his own office and worked independently of the others. In principle, each of us had his own contracts and worked on his own competitions. On the rare occasions that we undertook something jointly, it was always limited to a specific project. The exhibition of competition entries, designs and sketches in the common entrance hall ensured an element of mutual criticism among colleagues. This readiness to participate in and expose oneself to open discussion probably had a great influence on the way our office works today. Our working relationships are distinguished by collegiality and partnership rather than authoritarian structures with directions handed down from above.

At present, our office comprises four partners, six project partners and roughly 100 assistants. Most of them are architects, interior designers or urban planners. There are also a number of building engineers. This mixture of disciplines guarantees an efficient, clear office structure based on a division of responsibilities. The four partners complement and support each other through their different temperaments and skills. Nevertheless, every project is represented by a single partner, both within the office and outside. Even in competitions, we have learned that ultimately only one partner may decide which solution should be pursued, and a decision is made in this respect before work begins on a scheme.

In almost every project, we have had the responsibility for all phases of the work, from the preliminary design to construction management.

There are two main reasons for our wishing to do this. Firstly, only when an architect is commissioned to supervise his project to the very end does he have the opportunity to control the appearance of the building, which will depend largely on the materials, colours, details and the quality of the execution. The second reason is of more general significance. Although it may be in the interests of many clients and investors who wish to save planning costs and award architects contracts only for the necessary minimum services, an architect's voluntary self-restriction to the comparatively better-paid planning work will usually backfire on him. This is because the construction-related phases of a project (preparation of specifications, tender procedure, site supervision, etc.) may be undertaken by people who have a knowledge of building, but who cannot design.

The work in our office is distinguished by a "flat hierarchy". This means that assistants are encouraged to participate in as many decision-making processes as possible. In this way, respect is shown for their independent judgement in design matters; and one trusts that, in the context of a larger team, any gaps in a person's knowledge will be closed by asking questions, and that experience will be passed on at the same time. The principle might be formulated as follows: control is good, but trust is better.

Im Jahr 1980 beschloss die BMW AG im Norden Münchens ein großes Forschungs- und Ingenieurzentrum zu errichten. Für diese riesige Baumaßnahme wurden wir und zwei weitere Büros mit einem Plangutachten zu den „Strukturellen Lösungsmöglichkeiten unter städtebaulichen und gestalterischen Gesichtspunkten" beauftragt. Hierbei sollten Lösungsvorschläge insbesondere den Gesichtspunkten unterschiedlicher und schrittweiser Realisierung Rechnung tragen.

Die Studie hatte Beurteilungsgrundlage für die Tragfähigkeit eines städtebaulichen und funktionellen Konzepts zu sein und die Möglichkeit zu prüfen, Einzelobjekte innerhalb einer Gesamtstruktur schrittweise und austauschbar zu realisieren.

In 1980, the BMW company decided to erect a large research and engineering centre in the north of Munich. Together with two other offices, we were commissioned to draw up a planning study for this huge construction programme. The study was to explore "possible structural solutions in respect of the urban planning and design" of the centre. In particular, we were asked to investigate the possibility of implementing the scheme step by step in a series of flexible phases.

The study was, therefore, to provide a basis for judging the feasibility of urban planning and functional concepts and the scope for constructing individual units of the overall complex in separate stages and in a variable, interchangeable form.

BMW Forschungs- und Ingenieurzentrum München

17 BMW Research and Engineering Centre, Munich

*1981 – 1982 Gutachten und Überarbeitung
für ein Forschungs- und Ingenieurzentrum
auf dem „Alabama-Gelände" München
Architekten: Koch · Benedek + Partner*

*1981 – 1982 Design study and revised proposals
for a research and engineering centre
on the "Alabama" site in Munich
Architects: Koch · Benedek + Partner*

Bausteine zur Realisierung eines Industriekomplexes in variablen Bauabschnitten, die auch nach Baubeginn Konzeptänderungen zulassen

Units for an industrial complex erected in a series of flexible building stages, in which conceptual changes are possible even after the commencement of construction

Modellansicht von Südosten, im Vordergrund ein Parkhaus für 3.200 Stellplätze

Model viewed from south-east; in the foreground, a parking block with space for 3,200 vehicles

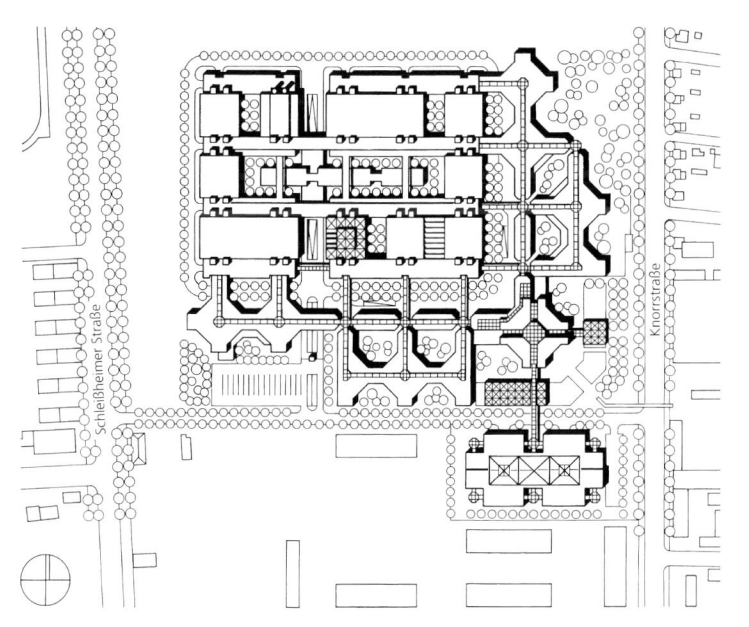

Lageplan

Site plan

In our search for an acceptable solution, various layouts were explored in which the workshops and offices were related to each other in different ways. The development plan required the location of administrative functions west of Knorrstrasse because of emissions in the area. Initially, therefore, a south-north linear development seemed appropriate; and in view of the location of the underground railway station and the Hufelandstrasse development area, the south-east corner of the site was seen as the ideal location for the main entrance.

In the light of the required ratio of office space to workshop space (with gross floor areas of 105,200 m² and 123,500 m² respectively) and the self-imposed planning constraint that high-rise structures were to be avoided, it soon became apparent that more areas than envisaged had to be assigned to office uses. Furthermore, by using a T- or L-shaped layout for the office areas, zones could be created that would facilitate more intense contacts between the offices and workshops.

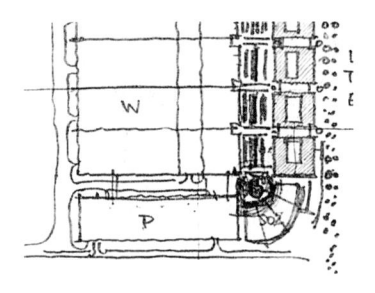

The linear south-north concept consists of office areas to the east, circulation and linking zones in an intermediate tract, and workshops and a parking block to the west.

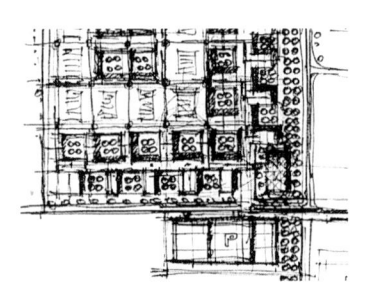

An L-shaped arrangement of the office zones allows adequate scope for the creation of links between the offices and workshops; at the same time, the lines of access are clearly comprehensible, and the layout can be extended in a number of ways.

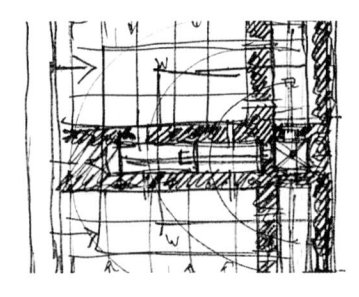

The advantage of a T-shaped layout of the office zones lies in the fact that it affords a maximum area of contact between offices and workshops. It has the disadvantage, however, that the workshop areas cannot be laid out in a continuous form.

The next stage comprised a search for forms that would permit the greatest number of combinations of pure office areas, workshop offices, and the actual workshops and testing areas. These three types of zones were to be knit together as tightly as possible, while still remaining flexible and variable in themselves.

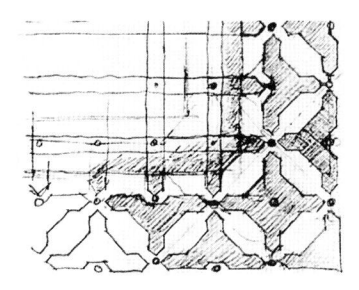

Ein einheitliches Festpunkt- und Erschließungsraster soll die Orientierung erleichtern und das Austauschen einzelner Elemente ermöglichen.

The uniform grid of reference points and access lines is designed to aid orientation and to facilitate the replacement of individual elements.

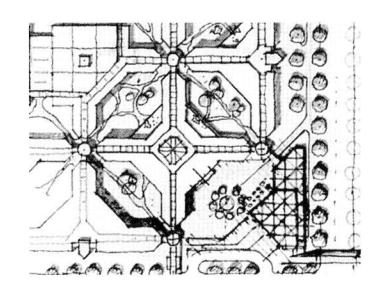

Die Ausbildung diagonal orientierter Innenhöfe im Verwaltungsbereich schafft unterschiedliche Grundrissformen, welche nach Belieben Einzelbüros, Gruppenräume oder Großraumbüros und Sondernutzungsflächen aufnehmen.

The courtyards within the administration zone are oriented to each other on the diagonal and have various layouts which can accommodate individual office spaces, group rooms or open-plan offices as well as areas for special uses.

Aus diesen Konzepten entstand der Entwurf mit folgenden Merkmalen: Anordnung zweier Bürozonen in Winkelform entlang der Knorrstraße und der südlichen Verbindungsstraße; Haupteingang für Beschäftigte und Besucher in dem Gelenk zwischen den beiden Bürozonen, auf kurzem Wege von der U-Bahn und vom Beschäftigten-Parkhaus erreichbar; innerer, beliebig oft überbaubarer Erschließungsring zwischen Büro- und Werkstattzone zur internen Versorgung und Anlieferung, Zufahrt mit Werkstor von Süden. Entwicklung von „Bausteinelementen", die eine Realisierung in vielfältig variablen Bauabschnitten zulassen und auch nach Baubeginn weitgehende Änderungen am Gesamtkonzept wie auch an Einzelheiten des Raum- und Funktionsprogramms zulassen.

Nach der Entscheidung des Vorstands für dieses Konzept wurden wir 1982 mit einer Überarbeitung beauftragt. Die weiteren Ziele waren: höhere Verdichtung, noch größere Flexibilität der Bürobereiche und stärkere städtebauliche Differenzierung der Innen- und Außenräume.

Dieses unser zweites Gutachten wurde dann Grundlage und Vorgabe für die spätere Gesamtbebauung. Das von uns gelieferte Konzept hat sich seither in hohem Maße bewährt, so dass es zu einer derzeit in Planung befindlichen Erweiterung des ganzen Komplexes auf der gleichen Basis kommen wird.

The design was developed from these concepts and was distinguished by the following features. Pairs of L-shaped office tracts were laid out along Knorrstrasse and the southern linking road. The main entrance for employees and visitors was located in the connecting tract at the angle between the two office zones and only a short distance from the underground railway station and the staff parking block. Between the office and workshop zones, an inner access and circulation route was proposed, over which linking structures could be built at any point. This route was to serve as an internal services and supply line, with access from the works gate to the south. A flexible unit system was developed that could be erected additively in a number of stages and that would be capable of accommodating major changes to the overall concept and modifications to the spatial and functional programme even after the commencement of construction.

In 1982, after the board had decided in favour of this concept, we were commissioned to revise it in order to achieve a higher building density, an even greater flexibility in the office areas and clearer distinctions between the internal and external spaces.

This second study formed the basis for the later overall development. Since then, our concept has demonstrated its validity to a very high degree – so much so, that a further extension of the complex based on the same principles is now being planned.

Das grundsätzliche Erschließungsprinzip im Gutachten und in der Überarbeitung: enge Verzahnung von Büros und Werkstätten

The basic principle of the access and services system in both the design study and the revised proposals: close links between offices and workshops

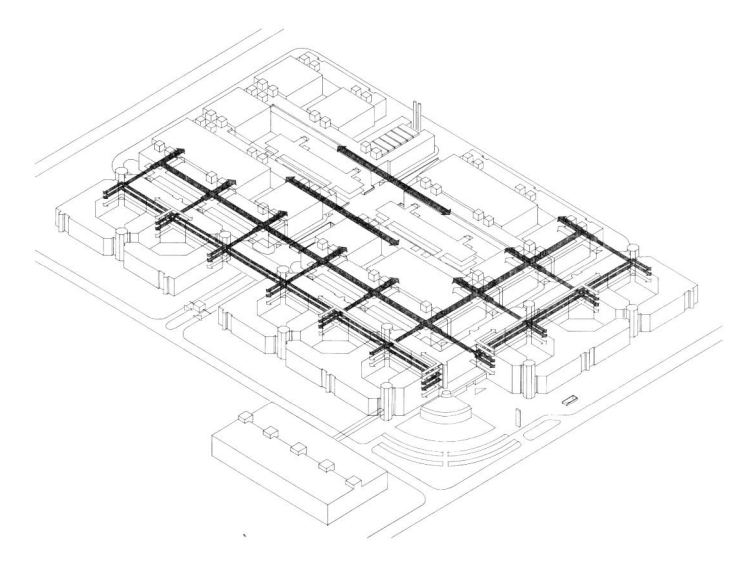

Die Salzachhalle mit Stadtmauer und Flussaue

Salzach Hall with town walls and river meadows

Salzachhalle Laufen

18   **Salzach Hall, Laufen**

*1972 – 1974 Gutachten zur Stadtentwicklung
und Altstadtsanierung*
*1979 – 1982 Neubau der Stadthalle
Planung und Realisierung*

*1972 – 1974 Study for urban development and
rehabilitation of historic town centre*
1979 – 1982 New civic hall: planning and construction

Die eigenwillige Form dieser Stadthalle antwortet auf eine besondere städtebauliche Situation und verbindet regionale Gestaltungselemente mit zeitgerechter Architektur.

The singular form of the civic hall, which combines regional design elements with modern architectural design, responds to the specific urban situation.

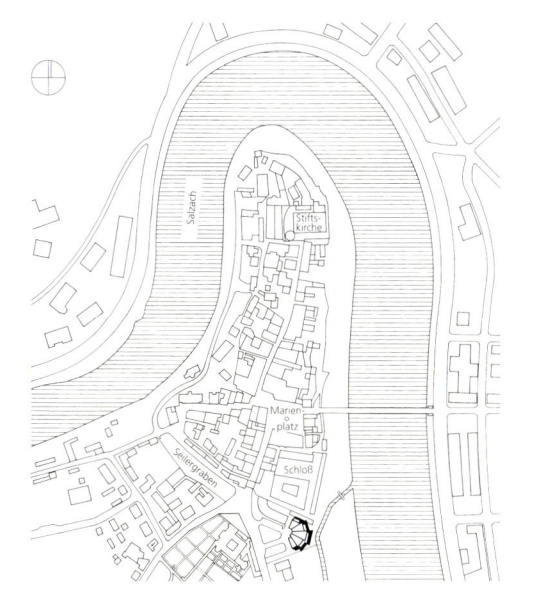

*Lageplan der Altstadt
von Laufen
(Oberbayern)*

*Plan of old town centre
of Laufen, Upper
Bavaria*

Der Baukörper sollte in Form und Größe dem benachbarten Schlossgebäude keine Konkurrenz machen, er sollte sich vielmehr diesem eindeutig unterordnen. So kam es zur realisierten Form, die den Schlossplatz baulich umschließt und abrundet, den Blick über den Platz auf das Schloss nicht verstellt, die vorgegebenen Baulichkeiten aufnimmt und in die gesamte Platzgestaltung einbezieht. Aus diesem Grund ist das Gebäude zum Schlossplatz hin in der Traufhöhe niedrig und orientiert sich mit Sicht- und Blickbeziehungen eindeutig zur Salzach. Die Salzachfront, die Aussichtsseite also, ist deshalb höher, wichtiger und markanter als die Fassade zum Schlossplatz hin. Dennoch sollte auch hier die Firsthöhe unter der Traufhöhe des Schlosses bleiben. An diesem, aus städtebaulicher Sicht idealen Standort konnte man nun ein Gebäude entwerfen, welches formal eigenständig und mit zeitgemäßem Erscheinungsbild auftritt und dennoch die Bezüge zur historischen Laufener Bauweise (der sogenannten Salzach-Bauweise) deutlich macht: Vorschussmauer, Grabendächer mit außenliegender Dachentwässerung, geputzte Wandflächen, Holzvorbauten und Erker. Ebenso verpflichtete die Nachbarschaft des Schlosses: Die Gebäudeproportionen und der Fensterrhythmus gaben den Maßstab für die Fassadengestaltung.

Auch die Funktion prägt die Gestalt. Hier war das wichtigste Entwurfskriterium die Forderung der Stadt nach einer möglichst flexiblen Nutzung des Saalbereiches. Der Besucher kommt vom Schlossplatz her; er wird durch das Foyer im Erdgeschoss geführt, erlebt während des Hinaufsteigens in die Saalebene die städtebauliche Situation durch den herrlichen Blick auf die Flusslandschaft und die Salzachbrücke und wendet sich dann, um von der Rückseite den Saal zu betreten.

Saalbereich und Vereinsbereich im Obergeschoss sind durch eine Schiebewand getrennt und können bei Bedarf zu einem großen Saal zusammengefasst werden.

Das Gebäude ist als Mauerwerksbau errichtet, wobei die nicht ausgesteiften Wände durch Stahlbeton stabilisiert sind. Die Decken und die Kellerumfassung sind in Stahlbeton ausgeführt, gleichfalls die Treppen. Soweit möglich, sind auch in den Untergeschossen die Innentragwände aus Mauerwerk. Das Dach ist mit Kupferblech gedeckt. Innenwände und Decken sind teilweise aus raumakustischen Gründen mit Naturholzpaneelen verkleidet, im Übrigen sind die Wände verputzt und mit textilem Wandbelag versehen. Die Außenwände sind ebenfalls verputzt, die Umgänge an der Ostseite mit Holz verkleidet.

Ansicht vom Schlossplatz nach Osten

View of complex looking east from Schlossplatz

Ansicht der Salzachseite mit vorgesetzten Foyerumgängen

Elevation of Salzach front with projecting foyer/circulation spaces

Detail der Eingangssituation

Detail of entrance situation

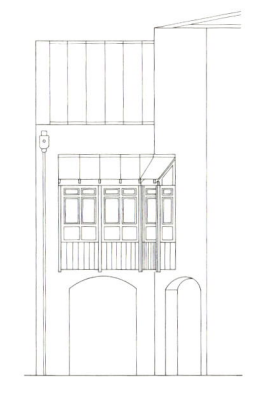

Gesamtraum mit Reihenbestuhlung – der Unterzug im Hintergrund kennzeichnet die Lage der Schiebewand.

Overall view of main hall with rows of seating. The downstand beam in the background marks the line of the sliding wall.

Die als Erker ausgebildeten Wandelgänge

Circulation space in oriel construction

In its size and configuration, the building had to subordinate itself to the nearby palace and avoid entering into competition with it. In the form in which it was finally realized, the hall closes the palace square, the Schlossplatz, without impeding the view of the older building. It accommodates itself to the existing urban structure and at the same time serves to integrate this fabric into a new overall design concept for the square. That is why the complex addresses the Schlossplatz with its lower eaves face and is clearly oriented, in terms of views and visual links, towards the River Salzach. This front – the main elevation – is taller and more striking than that overlooking the palace square. Even so, the upper eaves level is still lower than that of the palace itself. In view of the ideal urban location, a formally independent development of modern appearance was called for that would nevertheless reflect the form of construction found in many historical buildings in Laufen – the so-called "Salzach style" – with wall planes that extend up above the line of the eaves, sunken roof slopes with external drainage, rendered walls, projecting timber structures and oriels. Other buildings in the vicinity of the palace imposed a certain obligation, too. Their proportions and the rhythm of the windows, for example, set the scale for the design of the new façades.

The form also follows the function. In this respect, the most important design criterion, as defined by the civic authorities, was the need for maximum flexibility in the use of the hall. Visitors approach the building from the palace square and pass through the ground floor foyer. In ascending to hall level, they become aware of the urban surroundings, with a magnificent view to the river and the bridge across the Salzach. The route turns, and the hall is entered from the rear.

The hall and the club rooms on the upper floor are separated by a sliding wall. If necessary, they can be opened up to form a single large space.

The building is in brick construction. The non-braced walls are stabilized by the reinforced concrete elements: the floors, the outer walls of the basement, and the stairs. Wherever possible, the internal load-bearing walls in the basement were also executed in brickwork. The roof has a sheet-copper covering. For acoustic reasons, the internal walls and soffits are clad in part with natural wood panels. In other cases, the walls are plastered and finished with fabric linings. The external walls are rendered. The circulation routes along the east side are clad in wood.

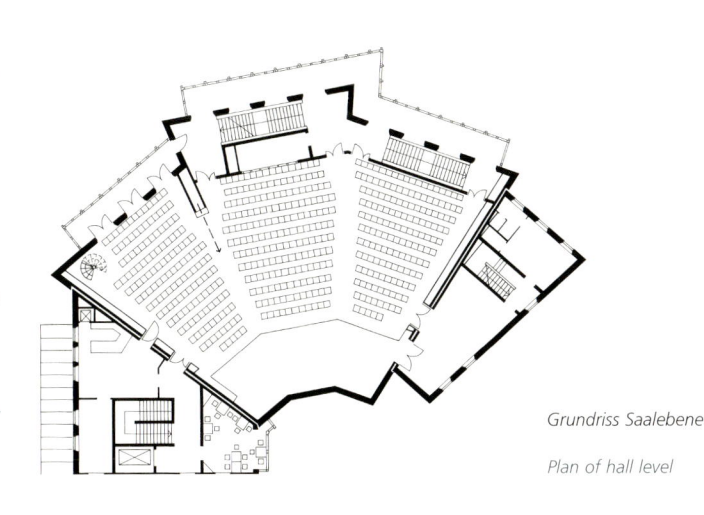

Grundriss Saalebene

Plan of hall level

Salzachhalle Laufen | 137

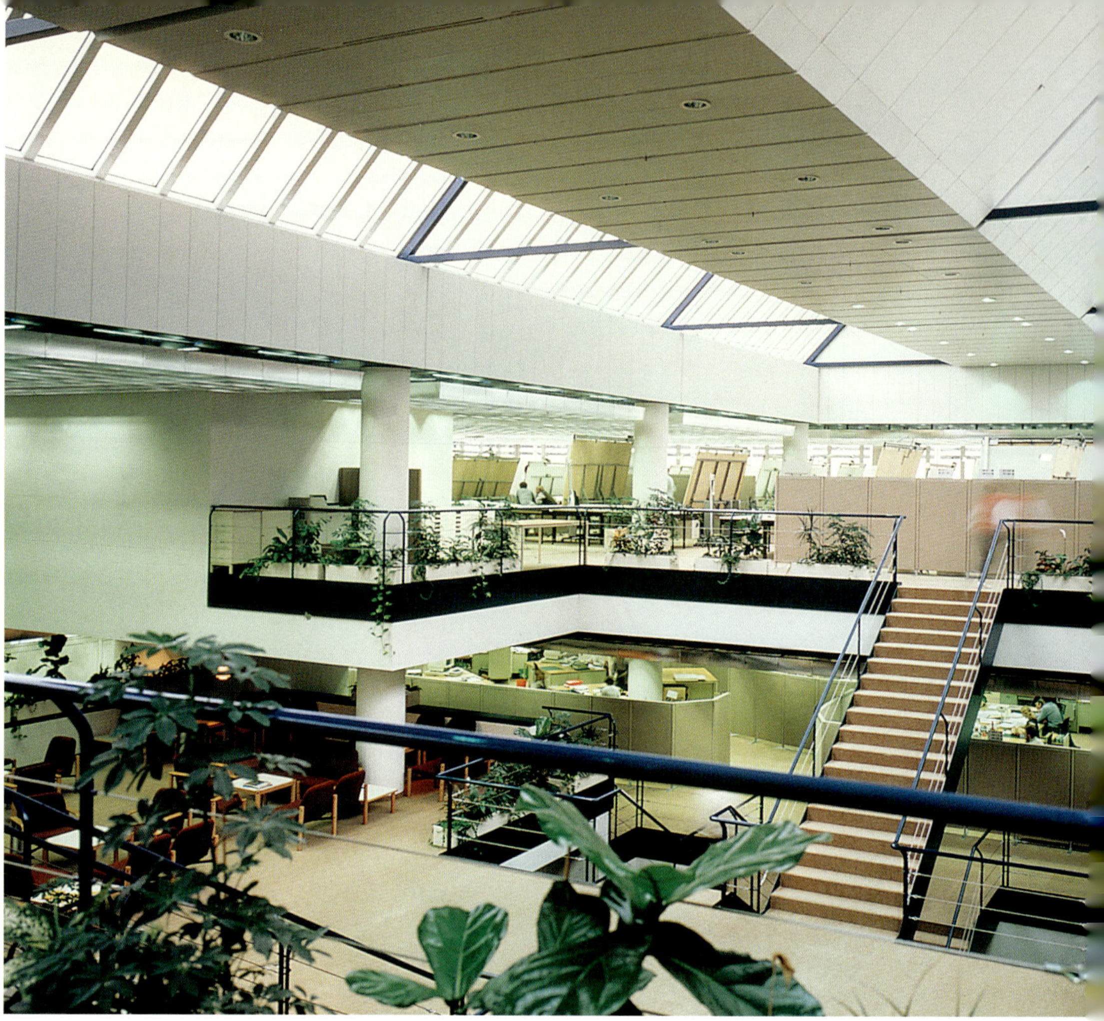

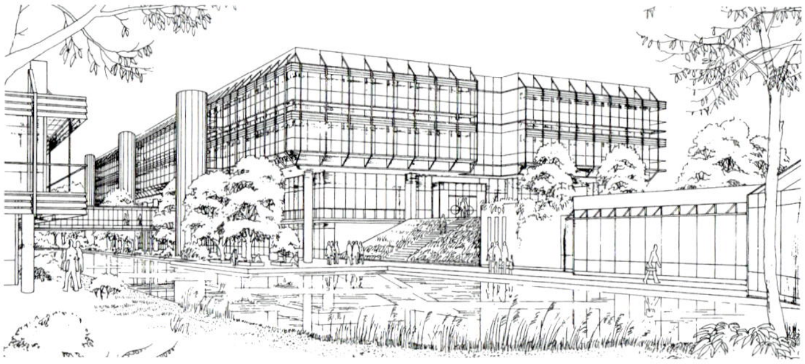

19 BMW Verwaltungsgebäude Dingolfing
BMW Administration Building, Dingolfing

Die 3 m hohen, schrägen Oberlichter und die gegenüberliegenden Spiegelflächen – gleichzeitig Verkleidung der Entrauchungsanlage – transportieren Tageslicht bis ins Untergeschoss.

The 3-metre-high sloping roof lights and the mirrored surfaces opposite them – which also serve as cladding to the smoke-extract plant – ensure that daylight penetrates to the lower ground floor.

1977 Wettbewerb · 1. Preis
1977 – 1980 Planung und Realisierung
　　　Architekten: Norbert Koch + Gabor Benedek

1977 Competition: first prize
1977 – 1980 Planning and construction
　　　Architects: Norbert Koch + Gabor Benedek

Das signifikante Verwaltungsgebäude für das Werk Dingolfing bringt außer seinem industriellen Zweck die Bedeutung des Unternehmens für die Region Niederbayern zum Ausdruck.

This important administration building for the company's Dingolfing works is an expression not only of the industrial purpose, but of the significance of the concern for the region of Lower Bavaria.

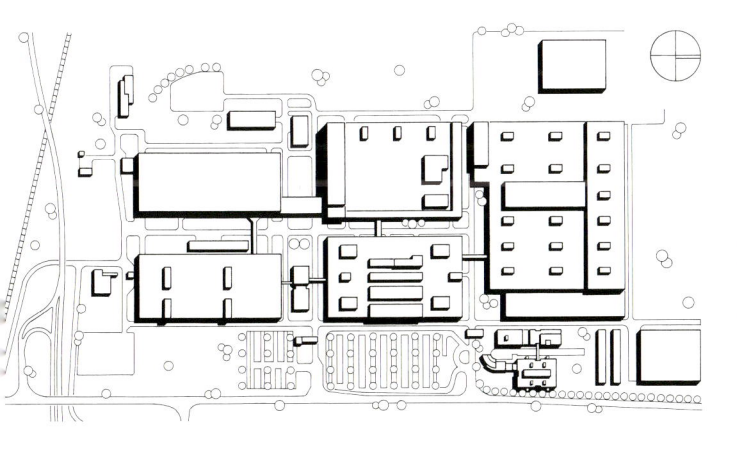

Die aus drei Einzelgebäuden bestehende Verwaltung liegt am Rande des großen Werks, gewissermaßen als „Kopf", als „Kommandobrücke" für die Produktionsanlagen.

Situated at the edge of the large works complex, the administration tract consists of three individual buildings and forms the head or "bridge" from where the production plant is controlled.

*Seite 140/141:
Der große Feuerlöschteich ist Mittelpunkt des Verwaltungsbereiches und als üppige Grünanlage gestaltet.*

*pp. 140/141:
The large fire-fighting lake forms the centre of the administration area and is extensively landscaped.*

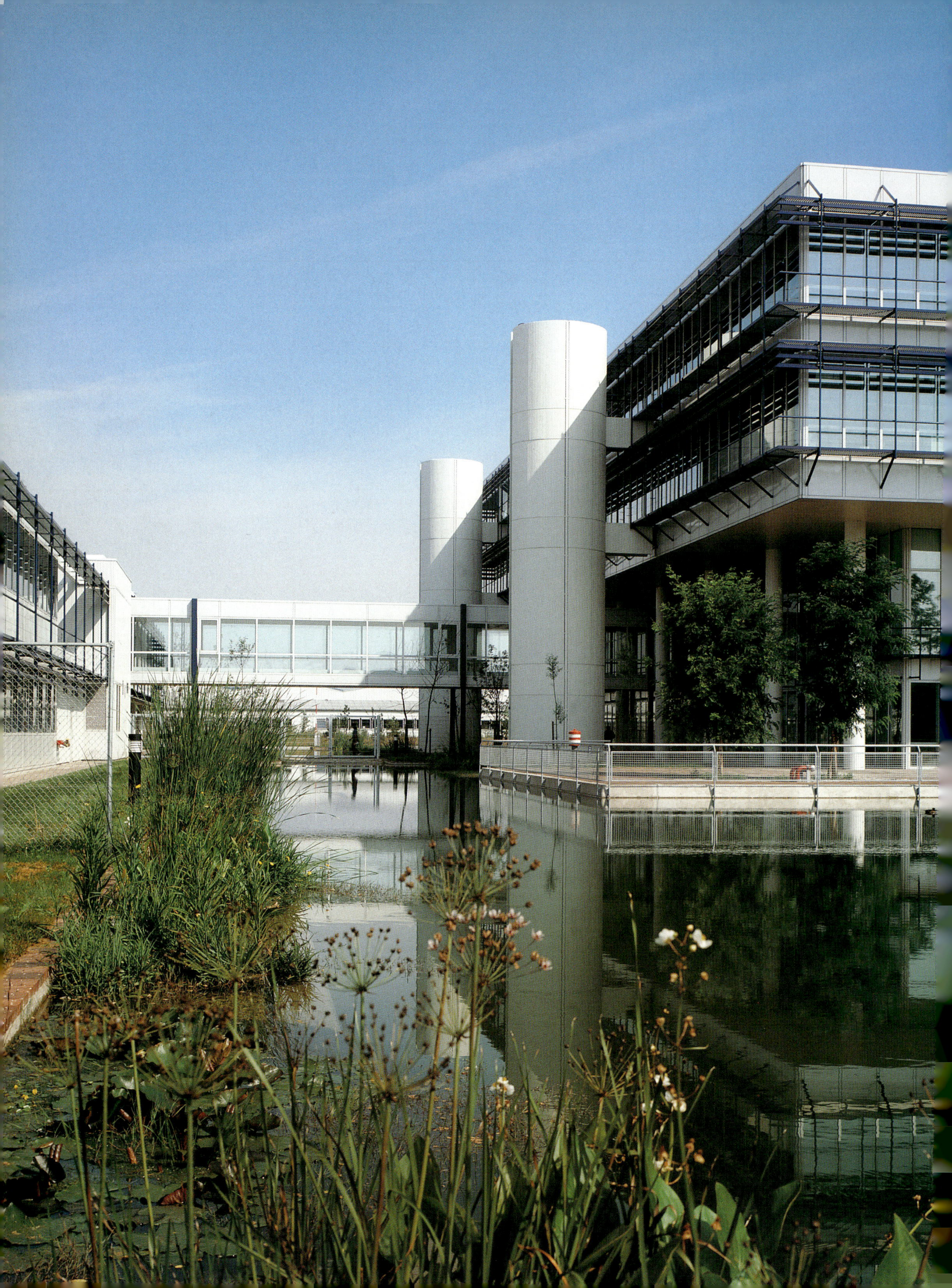

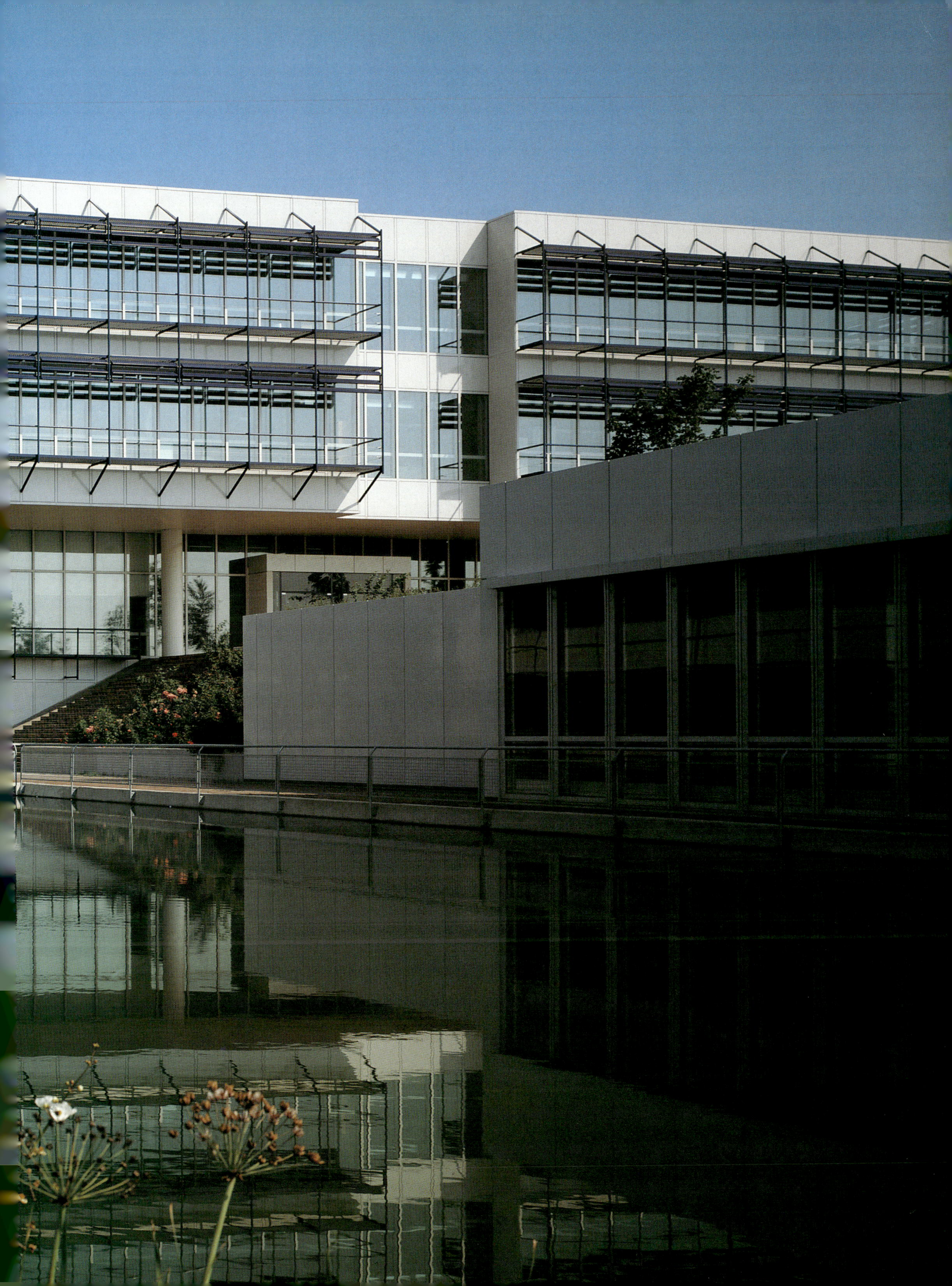

Für die gesamte Anlage ist eine konsequente Flachbebauung gewählt, die eine Anzahl funktionaler Vorzüge hat; man kann sie auch als gestalterische Alternative zum Münchner BMW-Hochhaus sehen.

Dem linearen Planungskonzept der Werksanlage mit mehrfachen, voneinander unabhängigen Erweiterungsmöglichkeiten entspricht die Anordnung dreier Zonen: an der Werksstraße angelagert und von hier erschlossen ist die Zone der „Dienste": Gesundheitsdienst, Kantine und Personalabteilung, funktionell und räumlich mehr dem Werkbereich zugeordnet. Die gesamte Anlieferung findet hier statt. Die üppig bepflanzte, nach Norden erweiterungsfähige Grünzone – als Erholungs- und Freiraum mit Wasserflächen (Feuerlöschteich) und mit Sitz- und Ruhemöglichkeiten für die Arbeitspausen – gliedert und verbindet die Gesamtanlage; sie bildet auch den grünen Rahmen und Hintergrund sowohl für die Kantine wie auch für die dritte Gebäudezone, die Büros, die ebenfalls abschnittsweise von Süden nach Norden bebaubar ist. Die durchgehende, großzügige Eingangshalle berücksichtigt bereits den nördlich anschließenden künftigen zweiten Bauabschnitt.

Den südlichen Abschluss des Ensembles bildet der viertelkreisförmig angelegte Ausstellungspavillon, der die ausgestellten Objekte in einen visuellen Zusammenhang zu den gesamten Produktionsanlagen stellt.

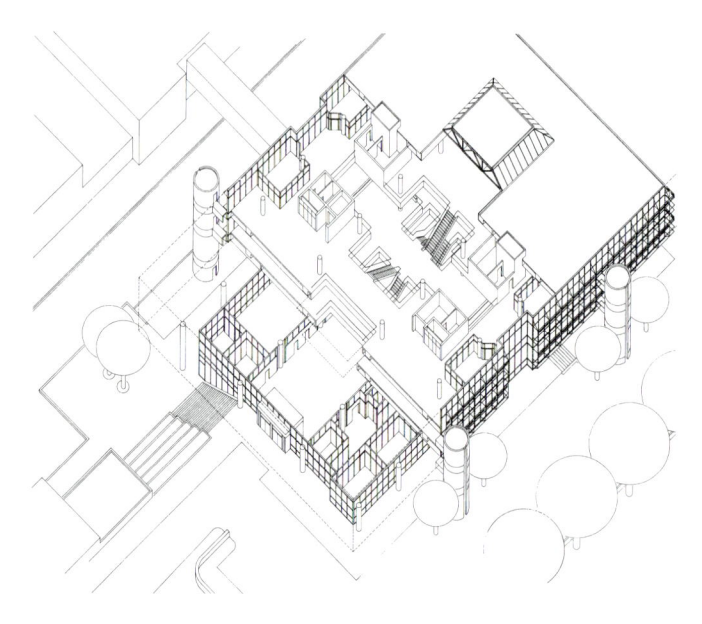

The low-rise form of development used for the entire complex offered a number of functional advantages. It may also be seen as a formal contrast to the BMW tower in Munich.

The linear planning concept on which the plant is based offers scope for a number of extensions that can be made independently of each other. The complex is divided into three zones. Adjoining the works road and with access from it is a "services zone", housing the company health service, the canteen and the staff department. Functionally and spatially, this zone is closely related to the works area; also located here is the central deliveries point. The profusely planted landscaped zone, which can be extended to the north, functions as a recreational open space with areas of water (fire-fighting lake) and with seating and other facilities for relaxation during work breaks. This zone serves to articulate the entire site and knit the various sections of the complex together. In addition, it forms a green setting for the canteen and for the third zone – the offices – which can also be developed step by step from south to north. The spacious entrance hall, extending through the building, already anticipates the future second stage of construction, which will adjoin it to the north.

To the south, the ensemble is terminated by an exhibition pavilion – a quarter circle on plan – that sets the objects on display in a visual relationship to the entire production complex.

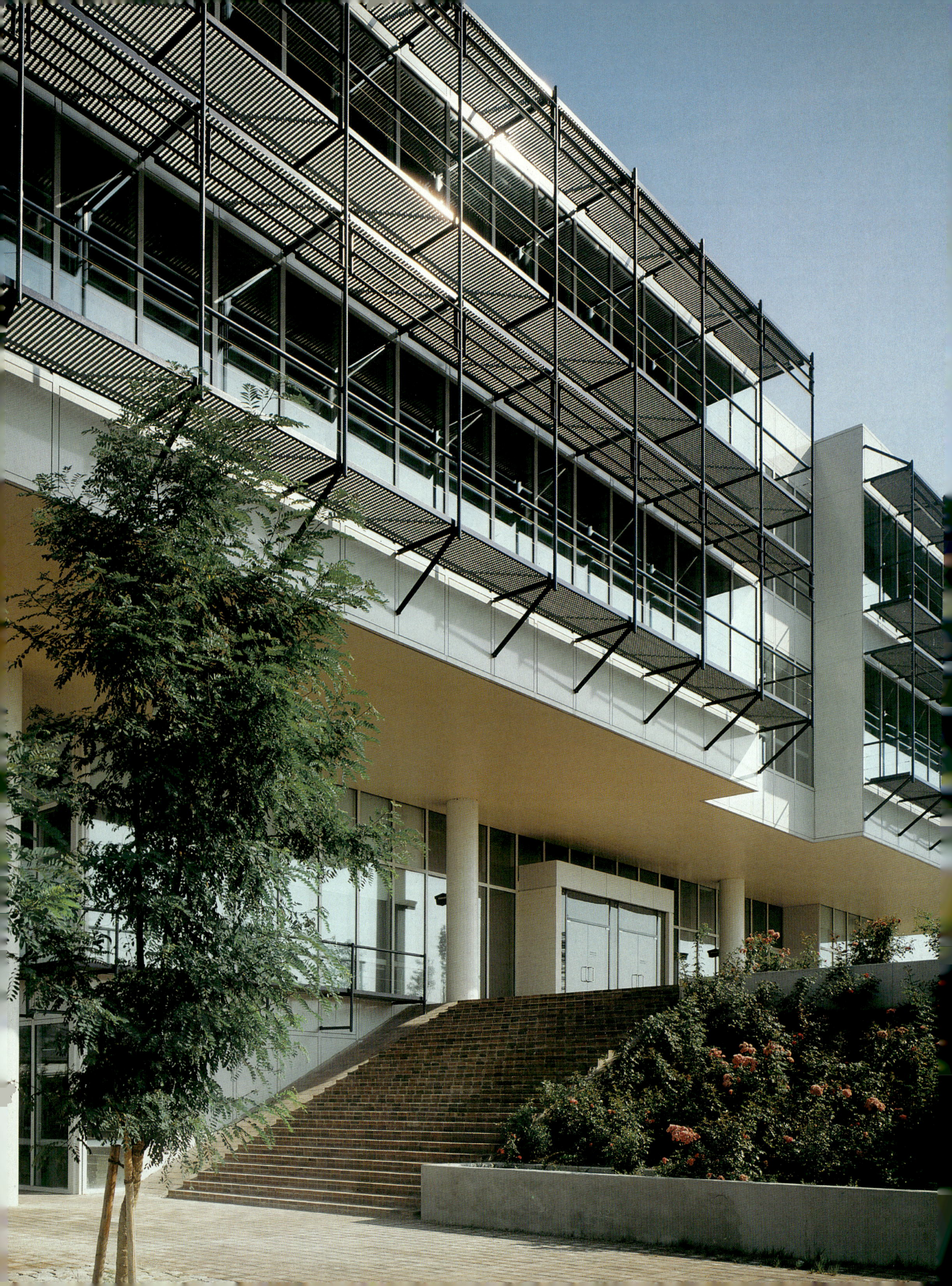

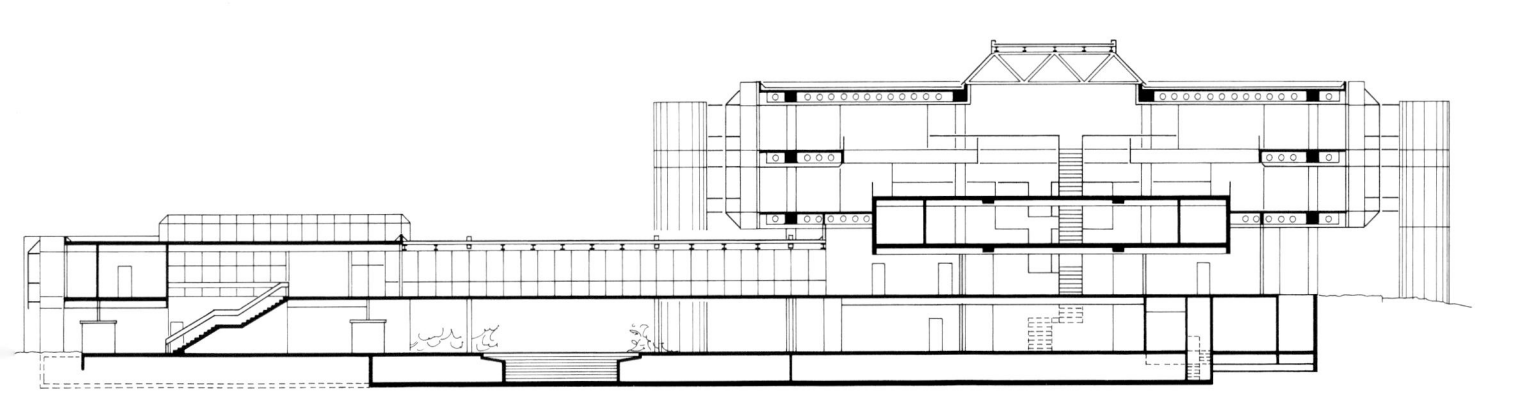

Trotz der gebotenen Wirtschaftlichkeit ist für den Verwaltungsneubau eine großzügige und freundliche Gestaltung erreicht. Dies ist in Anordnung und Größe der Eingangs- und Ausstellungsbereiche ebenso wie in der Gestaltung der Außenräume und der Fassade spürbar. Besonderer Wert ist auf die Transparenz aller Bauteile gelegt; Sichtbeziehungen von innen nach außen wie auch von außen nach innen sind möglich, um den optischen Zusammenhang mit den Werksanlagen erlebbar zu machen. Aus diesem Grund ist kein spiegelndes Sonnenschutzglas verwendet.

Für die Fassade des Hauptgebäudes ist eine zweischalige „Klimafassade" mit außenliegenden Reinigungsbalkonen entwickelt, außen raumhoch mit 3-fach Klarglas (k-Wert 1,6 kcal/m² h °C), innen Einfach-Sicherheitsverglasung, zum Reinigen zu öffnen. Die Raumabluft wird über die Leuchten abgesaugt und nach unten durch den 10-cm-Scheibenzwischenraum der Fassade geführt, die Zuluft strömt über die Spiegelrasterdecke.

Despite the need for economy, it was possible to design the new administration building in a spacious, friendly form. This is evident both in the layout and dimensions of the entrance and exhibition areas and in the design of the external spaces and the façade. Special emphasis was placed on transparency in all sections of the building. Links were created between inside and outside and vice versa in order to establish a visual relationship with the works areas. For this reason, reflective solar-control glass was not used.

The face of the main building was designed as a two-layer climate-control façade with external maintenance balconies. The outer skin consists of room-height, clear triple glazing (U = 1.6 kcal/m² h °C); the inner skin, which can be opened for cleaning purposes, comprises a single layer of toughened safety glass. Exhaust air is sucked out via outlets integrated into the design of the light fittings and drawn down through the 10 cm cavity between the layers of façade glazing. The fresh-air intake enters via a mirrored-grid soffit.

Die Fassaden sind als Klimafassaden ausgeführt. Sie senken die Betriebskosten, vermeiden Kältestrahlung und Zug und bieten bessere Schalldämmung.

The building is enclosed within climate-control façades that help to lower operating costs, avoid draughts and cold radiation, and provide a higher degree of sound insulation.

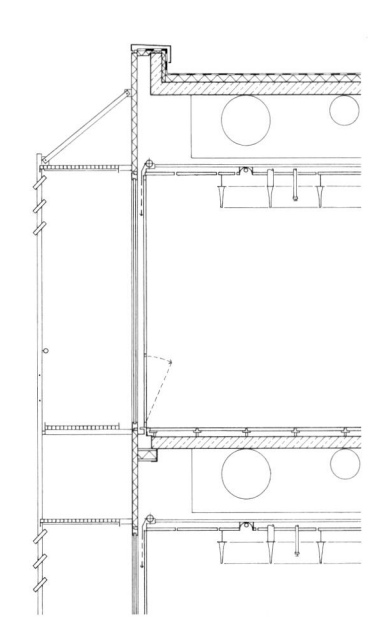

*Zwischenebenen auf
Treppenpodestniveau
für Besprechungen und
Kaffeepausen*

*Intermediate floors at
staircase landing level,
used for discussions
and coffee breaks*

Für das Verwaltungsgebäude ist eine eigenständige Konzeption der Großraumgestaltung entwickelt. Alle Büroarbeitsplätze sind in nur zwei offenen Funktionsraum-Obergeschossen um einen großen, bestimmenden Innenraum angeordnet.

Diese klare Raumkonzeption macht aufwendige Interieur-Ausstattung an den Arbeitsplätzen entbehrlich. Darüber hinaus ist hiermit eine zusätzliche, wirksame natürliche Belichtung von oben für beide Ebenen, also auch für die innenliegenden Arbeitsplätze, möglich. Dies führt besonders bei Raum-in-Raum-Lösungen mit vielen Stellwänden zu einer erheblichen Verbesserung der Arbeitsplatzqualität.

Das gesamte Gebäude kann somit zu Fuß erreicht werden; Aufzüge dienen in erster Linie für Transporte und Behinderte.

Öffnungen und Durchbrüche sowie das Einhängen von „Kommunikationsebenen" als Zwischengeschosse ermöglichen einen vielfältig erlebbaren und überschaubaren, dreidimensionalen Gesamtraum, der Sichtverbindungen zu allen Bereichen ermöglicht.

Dennoch sind die einzelnen Arbeitsbereiche individuell differenziert und gegliedert. Das Verhältnis von Nutzfläche zu Verkehrsfläche bzw. zu umbautem Raum ist damit überdurchschnittlich günstig.

Wegen des hohen Grundwasserstandes ist kein eigenes Kellergeschoss vorgesehen, sondern die Eingangsebene ist auf 2 m über Gelände gelegt. Das Untergeschoss des Verwaltungsgebäudes erhält damit eine zum Innenraum orientierte, voll belichtete Fassade und kann entsprechend gut genutzt werden.

An individual design concept was developed for the administration building. All office workplaces are on two open-plan functional upper floors laid out around a large, dominant internal space.

This clear spatial concept makes an elaboration of the interior design for the workplaces superfluous. Furthermore, it means that both levels receive additional daylight from above, to the benefit of the interior workplaces. This ensures better working conditions, especially in the context of room-within-room solutions where numerous temporary partitions may be installed.

The entire building is thus accessible on foot, and lifts are provided in the first instance for the disabled and for transporting goods. Openings, breaks and suspended "communication levels" in the form

Der innenliegende Konferenzbereich ist optisch in den Büroraum einbezogen und erhält von dort Tageslicht.

The internal conference area is visually integrated into the office space and also receives daylight from the same source.

of intermediate floors all serve to heighten the three-dimensional quality of the overall space and make it comprehensible in a variety of ways, as well as allowing visual links between the different parts of the building. The individual working areas are, nevertheless, distinctly articulated. The relation of functional floor area to circulation area and to building volume is well above average.

In view of the high groundwater level, the building has no proper basement. Instead, the entrance level was raised two metres above the ground. The lower ground floor has a fully daylighted façade, which allows light to penetrate deep into the interior and full use to be made of this storey.

Grundriss Erdgeschoss und erstes Zwischengeschoss

Plans of ground floor and first intermediate level

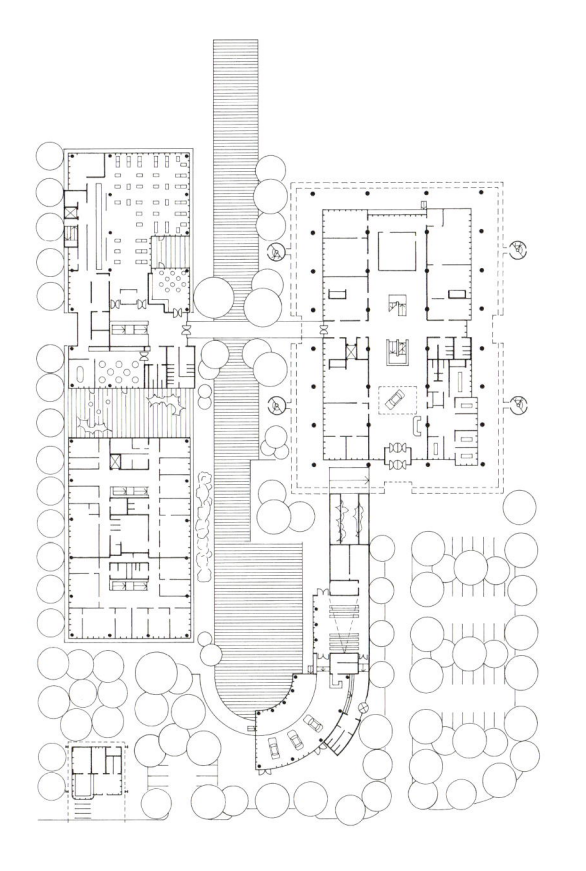

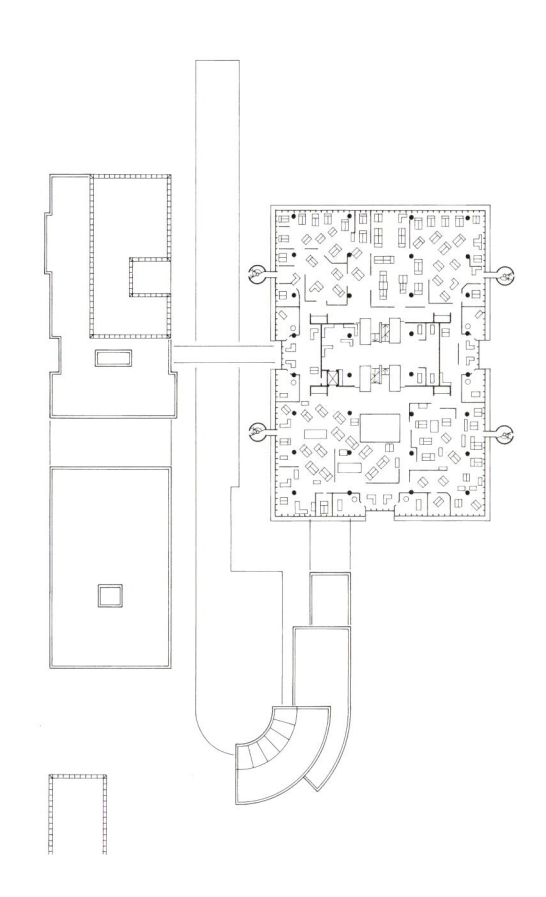

BMW Verwaltungsgebäude Dingolfing | 147

Cor-Ten-Stahl und Sichtbeton sind die dominierenden Elemente der Fassaden; sie werden ergänzt durch rote Handläufe an den Fluchtbalkonen.

Preoxidized steel and exposed concrete are the dominant materials used in the facades, complemented by red handrails to the escape balconies.

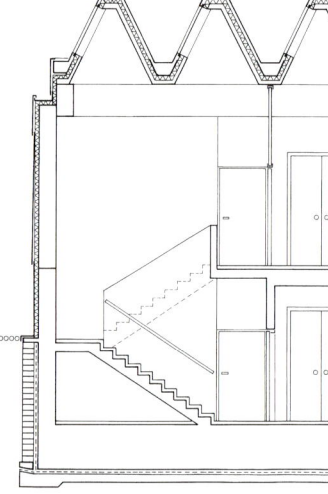

Ein Wettbewerb für eine Bundesforschungsanstalt, gewonnen im Dezember 1968, gemeinsam mit Ludwig Wagner und Wilfried Schneeberger – die erste wissenschaftliche Einrichtung für Fleischforschung in der Bundesrepublik. Sie gliedert sich in verschiedene wissenschaftliche Institute mit unterschiedlichen Arbeitsbereichen: Chemie und Physik, Bakteriologie und Histologie, Fleischerzeugung, Technologie.

Die Planung hatte dementsprechend viele unterschiedliche hochinstallierte Nutzungen und vielfältige funktionelle Zusammenhänge zu berücksichtigen, kurz die Vielfalt eines Raumprogramms wie bei einer kompletten wissenschaftlichen Hochschule.

Diese Vielfalt des Raumprogramms spiegelt sich in der Differenziertheit der Bauanlage wider: ein viergeschossiges Hauptgebäude mit den hochinstallierten Labor- und Arbeitsräumen wird durch Flachbauten mit Shed-Oberbelichtung für die technologischen Einrichtungen, Klimaställe sowie durch einen Vortragssaal und ein Personalwohngebäude ergänzt.

Gestaltungsziel war, die unterschiedlichen, in den Baukörpern und Fassaden ablesbaren Nutzungen durch ein einheitliches Fassadenmaterial zu verbinden. Hierfür bot sich wetterfester Baustahl (damalige Bezeichnung: Cor-Ten) an, der durch seine robuste Oberflächenstruktur die Vielfalt der unterschiedlichen Nutzungen, vom hochsensiblen radiologischen Labor bis zum Versuchstierstall, zum Ausdruck bringen konnte. So wurde dieses Material konsequent für sämtliche Fassadenelemente – von den Gitterrosten auf den Fluchtbalkonen über die Fensterprofile bis zu den Shed-Dachverkleidungen – unter genauester Berücksichtigung aller damals vorliegenden Erkenntnisse der Detailausbildung angewendet.

Nach Jahren hat sich heute herausgestellt, daß die von der Stahlindustrie behauptete langfristige und wartungsfreie Wetterbeständigkeit nicht zutrifft: Der Oxydationsprozeß setzte sich kontinuierlich fort und kam nie zum Abschluß. Deshalb sind alle Cor-Ten-Anwendungen im Hochbau heute sanierungsbedürftig.

In December 1968, first prize in a competition – won jointly with Ludwig Wagner and Wilfried Schneeberger – for a federal research institute: the first scientific body for meat research in the Federal Republic of Germany. This organization is divided into various scientific institutes, which are responsible for different areas: chemistry and physics, bacteriology and histology, meat production, and technology.

The planning, therefore, had to take account of many different activities with complex installations and sets of functional relationships. In other words, the diversity of the spatial programme was comparable to that of an entire science university.

The great spatial variety required by the brief is reflected in the contrasting forms of the complex. The four-storey main building, with its intensively serviced laboratories and workspaces, is complemented by low-rise structures with north-light roofs. These lower tracts accommodate spaces for technology, air-conditioned stalls for livestock, a lecture hall and a staff housing block.

One aim of the design was to unify the different functions – legible in the various volumes and façade forms – through the use of a uniform cladding material. A weatherproof preoxidized steel was chosen, known at the time as "Cor-Ten" steel. Its robust surface texture was seen as a means of articulating the different uses of the building, from the highly sensitive radiological laboratory to the stalls for test animals. The material was used for all elements of the outer skin, including the escape balcony gratings, the window frames and the shed-roof coverings. The detailing was wholly in accordance with established rules of construction at that time.

After many years, the long-term, maintenance-free, weatherproof quality claimed for this material by the steel industry has proved to be false. The oxidization process continued progessively without coming to an end. For that reason, all buildings in which this product was used require rehabilitation work today.

Bundesanstalt für Fleischforschung Kulmbach

20   Federal Institute for Meat Research, Kulmbach

1968   Wettbewerb · 1. Preis
1969 – 1976   Planung und Realisierung

1968   Competition: first prize
1969 – 1976   Planning and construction

Als Schluss des Werkberichtes das erste große Projekt – der Start in die Selbstständigkeit

At the end of this review of work: the first major project – the start of one's own practice

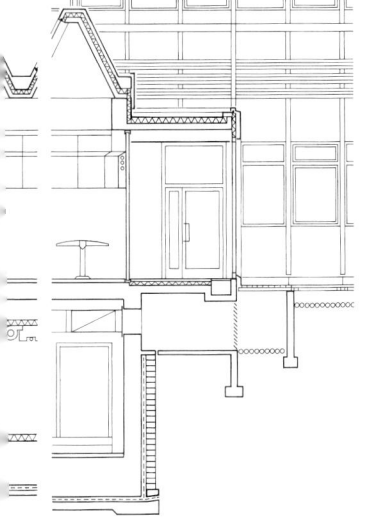

In den flachen Shed-Bauteilen sind Klimaställe zu Versuchszwecken und technologische Einrichtungen untergebracht.

The low-rise tracts with north-light roofs house spaces for technology and air-conditioned stalls for livestock used for testing purposes.

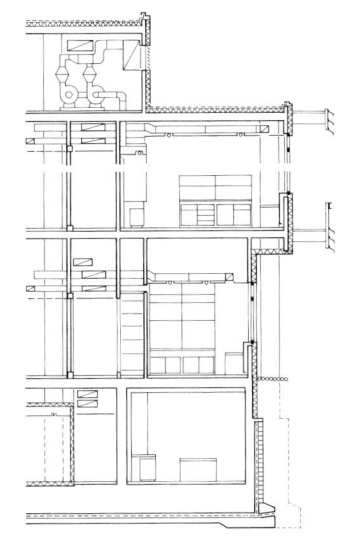

Lüftungszentralen und Rückkühlwerke in einem allseits geschlossenen Dachgeschoss

Ventilation plant and recooling units in the roof storey, which is closed on all sides

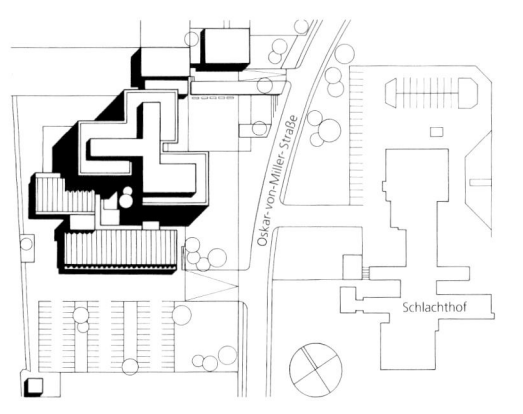

Lageplan: Das Schlacht- und Zerlegetechnikum der Forschungsanstalt befindet sich im benachbarten Schlachthof.

Site plan: the research institute's technical school for slaughtering and cutting is housed in the neighbouring slaughterhouse.

Anhang

Appendix

Zahlen und Daten der Projekte 1 – 20   152
Facts and figures to projects 1 – 20

Arbeiten und Projekte 1970 – 2000   170
Works and projects 1970 – 2000

Biografien der Partner   184
Biographies of partners

Projektpartner und Mitarbeiter 1970 – 2000   186
Project partners and assistants 1970 – 2000

1	**Flughafen München** Munich Airport	**1970**	**Plangutachten zum Masterplan** / **Planning report for master plan** Geländenutzungs- und Funktionsplan für die theoretisch mögliche Endkapazität mit Darstellung der ersten Ausbaustufe / Site Use and Functional Plan for potential ultimate capacity with representation of first extension stage

Bauherr / Client	Flughafen München GmbH
Architekt / Architects	Studiengruppe Luftfahrt – Aviation Consultants
Gesamtkoordination, Nahbereichsplanung und Bericht / Overall co-ordination, planning of surrounding areas and planning report	Norbert Koch, München
Entwurf und Bericht / Design and planning report	Hans J. Grube, Starnberg; Scott Wilson Kirkpatrick & Partners, London; Gollins Melvin Ward & Partners, London (auch Layout)
Beratung und Entwurf / Consultancy and design	Tippetts Abbett McCarthy Stratton, New York
Beratung technische Einrichtungen / Consultancy for technical installations	International Aero Limited, Southall, Middlesex
Mitarbeit / Assistants	W. A. D. Sterling, B.W. Mihlenstedt, J. Friedenberg, A. F. D. Russell, H.G. Dietz, A. Erhard, I. Schmidt
Bearbeitungszeit / Planning period	1970 – 1971
Für 1985 prognostizierte Passagiere pro Jahr / Estimated number of passengers for year 1985	ca. 12 Mio.
Prognostizierte Arbeitsplätze / Estimated number of jobs	9.000
Lage im Raum / Location	heutiges Flughafengelände MUC, Landkreis Erding

1975	**Fortschreibung Masterplan** / **Ongoing development of master plan** Fortschreibung Geländenutzungs- und Funktionsplan und Plan der baulichen Anlagen als Planfeststellungsunterlage / Preparation of Site Use and Functional Plan as basis for Building Development Plan

Bauherr / Client	Flughafen München GmbH
Architekt / Architects	Norbert Koch, München mit Hubert Schraud, München
Projektverantwortung / Overall responsibility for project	Norbert Koch
Mitarbeit / Assistants	Dieter Graf, Richard Hiemer, Michael Schneider
Landschaftsplanung / Landscape planning	Professor Günther Grzimek, Grünplan GmbH, Freising
Verkehrsplanung / Traffic planning	Dorsch Consult Ingenieursgesellschaft m.b.H., München
Bearbeitungszeit / Sequence of work	Jan. – Jul. 1975
Prognostizierte Passagiere pro Jahr / Estimated number of passengers per annum	ca. 12 Mio. – 20 Mio.
Prognostizierte Fracht pro Jahr / Estimated freight volume per annum	ca. 100.000 t – 300.000 t
Prognostizierte Arbeitsplätze / Estimated number of jobs	ca. 9.800
Lage im Raum / Location	heutiges Flughafengelände MUC, Landkreis Erding

1987 – 1991	**Allgemeine Luftfahrt** / **General Aviation** Terminal und Hangar / Terminal and hangar

Bauherr / Client	Flughafen München GmbH
Architekt / Architects	Koch + Partner
Projektverantwortung / Overall responsibility for project	Norbert Koch

Zahlen und Daten der Projekte 1 – 20

Facts and figures to projects 1 – 20

Projektleitung / Project architect	Werner Hofmaier
Bauleitung / Construction management	Werner Hofmaier, Erich Müller
Mitarbeit / Assistants	Christian Bendomir, Waltraut Eberle
Tragwerksplanung / Structural engineering	Seeberger und Friedl, München
Freiflächenplanung / Planning of external areas	Cordes und Partner, Ottobrunn
Heizung, Lüftung, Sanitär / Heating, ventilation, sanitary planning	Kühn und Bauer, München
Elektrotechnik / Electrical planning	Ing.-Büro Oskar von Miller GmbH, München
Planungsbeginn / Start of planning	1987
Baubeginn / Start of construction	1989
Gebäudefertigstellung / Completion of works	1991
Grundstücksgröße / Site area	ca. 125.700 m^2
Bebaute Fläche / Built area	Terminal: ca. 2.400 m^2, Hangar: ca. 10.800 m^2
BRI / Gross volume	Terminal: ca. 20.400 m^3, Hangar: ca. 129.600 m^3
BGF / Gross floor area	Terminal: ca. 4.000 m^2, Hangar: ca. 10.800 m^2
Bauvolumen / Construction costs	ca. 43 Mio. DM
Adresse / Address	Flughafen München, Landkreis Erding

1997 – 1998   **Terminal 2 / Terminal 2**
Realisierungswettbewerb mit zwei Überarbeitungsstufen /
Construction competition with two revision stages

Ergebnis / Result	1. Preis / 1st prize
Auslober / Competition promoter	Flughafen München GmbH
Architekt / Architects	Koch + Partner
Projektverantwortung / Overall responsibility for project	Norbert Koch, Michael Schneider
Projektleitung / Project architect	Richard Wolf
Mitarbeit / Assistants	Almut Abt, Anita Moum, Monika Pöppl, Ondrej Tomàsek
Verkehrsplanung / Traffic planning	Cordes + Partner, Ottobrunn
Landschaftsplanung / Landscape planning	Prof. Rainer Schmidt, München
Tragwerksplanung / Structural engineering	Seeberger Friedl und Partner, München
Ökologie, Energie / Environment and energy	Intep GmbH, München
Kosten / Cost planning	Ing.-Büro Schmid, Ges. für Projektsteuerung und Bauüberwachung m.b.H., München
Gesamtbearbeitungszeit / Planning period	Okt. 1997 – Jul. 1998
Erste Überarbeitung / First revision	Jul. 1998
Zweite Überarbeitung / Second revision	Jul. 1998
Wettbewerb / Competition	
BGF / Gross floor area	246.700 m^2
Programmflächen / Net main floor area	132.100 m^2
BRI / Gross volume	1.742.600 m^3
Erste Überarbeitung / First revision	
BGF / Gross floor area	214.000 m^2
Programmflächen / Net main floor area	136.100 m^2
BRI / Gross volume	1.442.000 m^3
Zweite Überarbeitung / Second revision	
BGF / Gross floor area	212.000 m^2
Programmflächen / Net main floor area	138.100 m^2
BRI / Gross volume	1.442.600 m^3
Adresse / Address	Flughafen München, Landkreis Erding

2	Stadtwerkszentrale München	1989 – 1995	**Labor / Laboratory**

Municipal Department of Works

Neubau nach Realisierungswettbewerb für die Stadtwerkszentrale 1980, 1. Preis / Construction of new centre for the Municipal Department of Works based on competition, 1980 (1st prize)

Bauherr / Client	Landeshauptstadt München
Architekt / Architects	Koch + Partner
Projektverantwortung / Overall responsibility for project	Wolf-Dieter Drohn
Projektleitung / Project architect	1. BA: Mechthild Peron, 2. BA: Gregor Tymke
Bauleitung / Construction management	1. BA: Erich Müller, 2. BA: Gregor Tymke
Mitarbeit / Assistants	Sylvia Neudecker, Elke Wolf
Tragwerksplanung / Structural engineering	CBP Cronauer, München
Heizung, Lüftung, Sanitär / Heating, ventilation, sanitary planning	HL-Technik, München
Elektrotechnik / Electrical planning	Ing.-Büro Werner, München

Planungsbeginn / Start of planning	1. BA / 1st stage:	Jun. 1989,	2. BA / 2nd stage:	Okt. 1998
Baubeginn / Start of construction	1. BA / 1st stage:	Jun. 1993,	2. BA / 2nd stage:	Apr. 1999
Fertigstellung / Completion of works	1. BA / 1st stage:	Nov. 1995,	2. BA / 2nd stage:	Nov. 1999
BRI / Gross volume	1. BA / 1st stage:	12.780 m³,	2. BA / 2nd stage:	1.180 m³
BGF / Gross floor area	1. BA / 1st stage:	3.750 m²,	2. BA / 2nd stage:	220 m²
HNF / Net main floor area	1. BA / 1st stage:	310 m²,	2. BA / 2nd stage:	20 m²

Bauvolumen / Construction costs	ca. 12 Mio. DM
Adresse / Address	Dachauer Straße, München

1992 – 1995 **24-Stunden-Trakt / 24-hour tract**

Neubau der Leitzentrale der Gas- und Wasserversorgung Münchens nach Realisierungswettbewerb für die Stadtwerkszentrale 1980, 1. Preis / New control centre for Munich's gas and water supply based on construction competition, 1980 (1st prize)

Bauherr / Client	Landeshauptstadt München
Architekt / Architects	Koch + Partner
Projektverantwortung / Overall responsibility for project	Wolf-Dieter Drohn
Projektleitung / Project architect	Mechthild Peron
Bauleitung / Construction management	Erich Müller
Mitarbeit / Assistants	Elena Buschmann, Wolfgang Dietze
Vermessung / Surveying services	Ing.-Ges. Karner, München
Bodenaustausch / Soil replacement	Dorsch Consult, München
Tragwerksplanung / Structural engineering	CBP Cronauer, München
Freiflächenplanung / Planning of external areas	Gottfried Hansjakob, München
Schallschutz / Sound insulation	Müller BBM, Planegg
Heizung, Lüftung, Sanitär / Heating, ventilation, sanitary planning	HL-Technik, München
Elektrotechnik / Electrical planning	Ing.-Büro Werner, München
Planungsbeginn / Start of planning	Aug. 1992
Baubeginn / Start of construction	Jun. 1993
Fertigstellung / Completion of works	Mai 1995
BRI / Gross volume	13.750 m³
BGF / Gross floor area	3.220 m²
HNF / Net main floor area	1.810 m²
Bauvolumen / Construction costs	ca. 17 Mio. DM
Adresse / Address	Dachauer Straße, München

1995 – 1997 **Gasdruckregler / Gas-pressure control centre**

Neubau nach Realisierungswettbewerb für die Stadtwerkszentrale 1980, 1. Preis / New municipal works centre based on construction competition, 1980 (1st prize)

Bauherr / Client	Landeshauptstadt München
Architekt / Architects	Koch + Partner
Projektverantwortung / Overall responsibility for project	Michael Schneider
Projektleitung / Project architect	Elke Wolf
Bauleitung / Construction management	Gregor Tymke
Mitarbeit / Assistant	Robert Rechenauer

Vermessung / Surveying services	Ing.-Ges. Karner, München
Bodengutachten / Soil report	Dorsch Consult, München
Tragwerksplanung / Structural engineering	Sailer Stepan und Partner, München
Freiflächenplanung / Planning of external areas	Gottfried Hansjakob, München
Fassadenplanung / Façade planning	Ing.-Büro Stephan, Dillingen
Anlagenplanung / Mechanical plant planning	GABEG Anlagenbau – Engineering GmbH, München
Elektrotechnik / Electrical planning	Stadtwerke München GmbH
Akustik / Acoustics	Akustikbüro Schwartzenberger, Pöcking
Planungsbeginn / Start of planning	Aug. 1992
Baubeginn / Start of construction	Jun. 1993
Fertigstellung / Completion of works	Mai 1995
BRI / Gross volume	2.880 m³
BGF / Gross floor area	310 m²
HNF / Net main floor area	120 m²
Bauvolumen / Construction costs	ca. 5 Mio. DM
Adresse / Address	Dachauer Straße, München

1994 – 2001 Büro- und Betriebszentrum / Administration and Works Centre

Neubau nach Realisierungswettbewerb für die Stadtwerkszentrale 1980, 1. Preis /
New development based on construction competition for municipal works, 1980 (1st prize)

Bauherr / Client	Stadtwerke München GmbH
Generalplaner und Architekt / Overall planners and architects	Koch+Partner
Projektverantwortung / Overall responsibility for project	Wolf-Dieter Drohn, Michael Schneider
Projektleitung / Project architects	Christian Bendomir, Jürgen Zschornack
Bauleitung / Construction management	Bernhard Hörnig, Martin Markl, Josef Meier, Markus Walter
Planung / Planning	Thomas Braun, Heinz Szuggar
Ausschreibung / BQs and tender documents	Gerald Bader, Wolfgang Dietze, Franz Felsner, Gregor Tymke
Kosten und Termine / Cost planning and scheduling	Volker Hagen, Christian Prechtl, Peter Rosenbauer, Uli Zehfuß
Mitarbeit / Assistants	Thomas Abt, Sigrid Apel, Jeannette Bachmeier, Anja Goehler, Endre Molnar, Claudia Mühlbauer, Sylvia Neudecker, Monika Pöppl, Robert Rechenauer, Stephan Repges, Stefan Roßner, Katja Schäper, Karen Schlömer, Katharina Schott
Vermessung / Surveying services	Ing.-Ges. Karner, München
Bodengutachten / Soil report	Dorsch Consult, München
Tragwerksplanung / Structural engineering	Bürozentrum: Sailer Stepan und Partner, München Betriebszentrum: CBP Cronauer, München
Ökologie / Environmental	Prof. Steiger, Zürich; Intep GmbH, München
Technische Gebäudeausrüstung / Technical installations	CBP Cronauer, München
Thermische Bauphysik / Thermal construction physics	Waubke & Klessinger, Neubiberg
Industrieplanung / Industrial planning	Industrieplanung Backes, München
Schalltechnik / Acoustic engineering	Akustikbüro Schwartzenberger, Pöcking
Freiflächenplanung, Verkehrsanlagen / Planning of external and traffic areas	Gottfried Hansjakob, München
Fassadenplanung / Façade planning	Ing.-Büro Hans Stephan, Lauingen
Elektro- und Fördertechnik / Electrical planning and conveyance systems	Ing.-Büro Oskar von Miller GmbH, München
Lichtplanung Sonderbereiche / Lighting planning for special areas	a.g. Licht, Köln
Küchentechnik / Kitchen technology	Mühletaler Consult, Sauerlach
Orientierungs- und Leitsysteme / Directional and communication systems	Designgruppe Flath & Frank, München
Planungsbeginn / Start of planning	Sep. 1994
Grundsteinlegung / Laying of foundation stone	Okt. 1998
Fertigstellung / Completion of works	Dez. 2001
Grundstücksfläche mit Werkstraße / Site area including works road	137.120 m²
BRI / Gross volume	593.780 m³
BGF / Gross floor area	146.080 m²
HNF + NNF / Net main and ancillary floor areas	84.750 m²
Bauvolumen / Construction costs	ca. 350 Mio. DM
Adresse / Address	Dachauer Straße, München

3	**Universität Erfurt**	**1997 – 1999**	**Entwicklungsgutachten Universität Erfurt /**
			Development report University of Erfurt
	University of Erfurt		Städtebauliches Gutachten nach städtebaulichem Ideen- und Realisierungswettbewerb 1995, 1. Preis /
			Urban development study based on urban planning ideas and construction competition, 1995 (1st prize)

Auftraggeber / Client	Finanzministerium des Freistaates Thüringen
Architekt / Architects	Koch+Partner
Projektverantwortung / Overall responsibility for project	Norbert Koch
Projektleitung / Project planner	Astrid Eggensberger
Mitarbeit / Assistants	Ioana Cisek, Anita Moum
Freiflächenplanung / Planning of external areas	Peter Kluska, Landschaftsarchitekt BDLA, München
Bearbeitungszeit / Planning period	Mrz. 1997 – Jun. 1999
Entwicklungsgebiet / Development area	ca. 874.000 m²
Bruttobauland / Gross development area	ca. 310.000 m²
Nettobauland / Net development area	ca. 230.000 m²
GRZ / Site-use factor	0,22
GFZ / Floor-area factor	0,63
Lage im Raum / Location	Nordhäuser Straße, Erfurt

1996 – 1999 **Dienstgebäude / Administration building**

Umbau eines Studentenwohnheimes nach Städtebaulichem Ideen- und Realisierungswettbewerb 1995, 1. Preis /
Conversion of students' hostel based on urban planning ideas and construction competition, 1995 (1st prize)

Bauherr / Client	Finanzministerium und Ministerium für Wissenschaft, Forschung und Kultur des Freistaates Thüringen
Generalplaner und Architekt / Overall planners and architects	Koch+Partner
Projektverantwortung / Overall responsibility for project	Norbert Koch
Projektleitung / Project architect	Susanne Moog
Bauleitung / Construction management	Burkhard Möckel
Mitarbeit / Assistants	Markus Rehn, Elke Wolf
Tragwerksplanung / Structural engineering	Sailer, Stepan und Partner, München
Freiflächenplanung / Planning of external areas	Peter Kluska, Landschaftsarchitekt BDLA, München
Heizung, Lüftung, Sanitär / Heating, ventilation, sanitary planning	Scholze Ing.-Gesellschaft, Frankfurt/Main
Planungsbeginn / Start of planning	Feb. 1997
Fertigstellung / Completion of works	Dez. 1999
HNF / Net main floor area	2.210 m²
Bauvolumen / Construction costs	ca. 8 Mio. DM
Adresse / Address	Nordhäuser Straße, Erfurt

1995 – 2000 **Universitätsbibliothek / University library**

Neubau nach Städtebaulichem Ideen- und Realisierungswettbewerb 1995, 1. Preis /
Development based on urban ideas and construction competition (1st prize)

Bauherr / Client	Finanzministerium und Ministerium für Wissenschaft, Forschung und Kultur des Freistaates Thüringen
Architekt / Architects	Koch+Partner
Projektverantwortung / Overall responsibility for project	Norbert Koch
Projektleitung / Project architect	Stefan Maisch
Bauleitung / Construction management	Burkhard Möckel, Johannes Lehmann-Dronke
Mitarbeit / Assistants	Anita Moum, Sylvia Neudecker, Monika Pöppl, Robert Rechenauer, Birgit Schimmel
Tragwerksplanung / Structural engineering	Sailer, Stepan und Partner, München
Freiflächenplanung / Planning of external areas	Peter Kluska, Landschaftsarchitekt BDLA, München
Heizung, Lüftung, Sanitär / Heating, ventilation, sanitary planning	Himmen Partner, Erfurt
Elektroplanung / Electrical planning	Ing.-Büro Oskar von Miller GmbH, München

Planungsbeginn 1. BA / Start of planning (first stage)	Jul. 1996
Baubeginn / Start of construction	Jul. 1998
Fertigstellung / Completion of works	Mrz. 2000
BRI / Gross volume	78.440 m²
BGF / Gross floor area	16.960 m²
HNF / Net main floor area	9.700 m²
Bauvolumen / Construction costs	ca. 56 Mio. DM
Adresse / Address	Nordhäuser Straße, Erfurt

4 Messestadt Riem, München / Messestadt Riem, Munich

1987 — Künftige Nutzung des Flughafengeländes München-Riem / Future use of former airport site in Riem, Munich
Kooperatives Verfahren (Entwurfsseminar) / Collaborative working process (design seminar)

Auftraggeber / Client	Landeshauptstadt München
Architekt / Architects	Koch+Partner
Projektverantwortung / Overall responsibility for project	Norbert Koch, Michael Schneider
Mitarbeit / Assistant	Waltraut Eberle
Freiflächenplanung / Planning of external areas	Eberhard Krauss, Grünplan GmbH, Freising
Bearbeitungszeit / Planning period	17. – 26. Okt. 1987
Planungsgebiet / Planning area	ca. 11,9 km²
Flughafengelände / Airport site area	ca. 3,7 km²
Lage im Raum / Location	München-Riem

1991 – 1992 Künftige Nutzung des Flughafengeländes München-Riem / Future use of former airport site in Riem, Munich
Internationaler Städtebaulicher Ideenwettbewerb / International urban planning ideas competition

Ergebnis / Result	Ankauf / purchase of scheme
Auslober / Competition promoter	Landeshauptstadt München, Münchener Messegesellschaft
Architekt / Architects	Koch+Partner
Projektverantwortung / Overall responsibility for project	Norbert Koch, Wolfgang Voigt
Projektleitung / Project architect	Mechthild Peron
Mitarbeit / Assistants	Ruth Baumeister, Silvia Topp, Richard Wolf
Freiflächenplanung / Planning of external areas	Peter Kluska, Landschaftsarchitekt BDLA, München
Messeplanung / Trade-fair planning	Herrmann Te Wildt, Düsseldorf
Ökologisches Bauen / Ecological construction	Dirk Stender, München
Verkehrsplanung / Traffic planning	Dr. Gerhard Krasser, München
Tragwerksplanung / Structural engineering	Dieter Herrschmann, München
Bearbeitungszeit / Planning period	Jan. 1991 – Mai 1991
Preisgericht / Jury decision	25. Jul. 1991
Wettbewerbsgebiet / Competition area	ca. 5,62 km²
davon / of which	
Wohnen / Housing	1,10 km²
Messegelände / Trade-fair area	0,65 km²
Sondernutzung / Special uses	0,21 km²
Infrastruktur / Infrastructure	1,15 km²
Lage im Raum / Location	München-Riem

1991 – 1992 Neue Messe München / New Trade Fair, Munich
Realisierungswettbewerb / Construction competition

Ergebnis / Result	4. Preis / 4th price
Auslober / Competition promoter	Landeshauptstadt München, Münchener Messegesellschaft und Maßnahmeträger München-Riem GmbH
Architekt / Architects	Koch+Partner
Projektverantwortung / Overall responsibility for project	Norbert Koch
Projektleitung / Project architect	Wolfgang Voigt
Mitarbeit / Assistants	Bill Block, Claudia Habelt, Alexander Krizik, Stefan Maisch, Mechthild Peron, Dirk Stender, Birgit Wild-Dicke, Richard Wolf

Freiflächenplanung / Planning of external areas	Peter Kluska, Landschaftsarchitekt BDLA, München
Messeplanung / Trade-fair planning	Herrmann Te Wildt, Düsseldorf
Verkehrsplanung / Traffic planning	Dr. Gerhard Krasser, München
Tragwerksplanung / Structural engineering	Dieter Herrschmann, München
Kunstwerk / Art	Manfred Mayerle, München
CAD	Waltraut Eberle, München
Bearbeitungszeit / Planning period	Nov. 1991 – Jan. 1992
Preisgericht / Jury decision	27. Okt. 1992
Wettbewerbsgebiet / Competition area	ca. 830.000 m²
Bebaute Fläche / Built area	284.000 m²
BGF / Gross floor area	450.000 m²
Freiflächen / External areas	366.000 m²
Lage im Raum / Location	München-Riem

1993 Neuriem Mitte / Neuriem Mitte
Realisierungswettbewerb Stufe 1 und Stufe 2 / Construction competition: stages 1 and 2

Ergebnis / Result	3. Preis für Stufe 1 / 3rd prize in stage 1
Auslober / Competition promoter	Landeshauptstadt München, Referat für Stadtplanung und Bauordnung
Architekt / Architects	Koch+Partner
Projektverantwortung / Overall responsibility for project	Norbert Koch
Projektleitung / Project architect	Jürgen Zschornack
Mitarbeit / Assistants	Astrid Eggensberger, Sylvia Neudecker, Robert Rechenauer, Richard Wolf
Freiflächenplanung / Planning of external areas	Peter Kluska, Landschaftsarchitekt BDLA, München
Verkehrsplanung / Traffic planning	Dr. Gerhard Krasser, München
Bearbeitungszeit Stufe 1 / Planning period, stage 1	Mrz. 1993 – Mai 1993
Preisgericht / Jury decision	23. Mai 1993
Bearbeitungszeit Stufe 2 / Planning period, stage 2	Mai 1993 – Okt. 1993
Preisgericht / Jury decision	6. Nov. 1993
Wettbewerbsgebiet / Competition area	ca. 730.000 m²
Lage im Raum / Location	München-Riem

1994 – 1998 Messestadt Riem – Gewerbegebiet Nordwest / Messestadt Riem – north-west commercial area
Städtebaulicher Entwurf und Bebauungsplan / Urban design plan and development plan

Auftraggeber / Client	Maßnahmeträger München-Riem GmbH
Architekt / Architects	Koch+Partner
Projektverantwortung / Overall responsibility for project	Norbert Koch, Michael Schneider
Projektleitung / Project planner	Astrid Eggensberger
Mitarbeit / Assistants	Ioana Cisek, Ondrej Tomasek
Freiflächenplanung / Planning of external areas	Gottfried Hansjakob, München
Verkehrsplanung / Traffic planning	Prof. Dr.-Ing. Hansjörg Lang, Lang+Burkhardt, München
Bearbeitungszeit / Planning period	Dez. 1994 – Sep. 1998
Städtebaulicher Entwurf / Urban design plan	ca. 210.000 m²
Bebauungsplan / Development plan	ca. 130.000 m²
Lage im Raum / Location	München-Riem

1997 – 1998 Park+Ride-Anlage Messestadt Riem / Park-and-ride facilities, Messestadt Riem
Realisierungswettbewerb / Construction competition

Ergebnis / Result	2. Preis / 2nd prize
Auslober / Competition promoter	Maßnahmeträger München-Riem GmbH
Architekt / Architects	Koch+Partner
Projektverantwortung / Overall responsibility for project	Michael Schneider
Mitarbeit / Assistants	Stefan Maisch, Elke Wolf
Tragwerksplanung / Structural engineering	Sailer, Stepan und Partner, München
Freiflächenplanung / Planning of external areas	Prof. Donata Valentien, Wessling

Bearbeitungszeit / Planning period		Dez. 1997 – Apr. 1998
Preisgericht / Jury decision		23. Apr.1998
Grundstücksfläche / Site area approx.		ca. 20.700 m²
Bebaute Fläche / Built area		ca. 6.050 m²
BRI / Gross volume		ca. 51.500 m³
Parkhaus-Stellplätze / Parking block (no. of vehicles)		ca. 1.000
mit Bike+Ride Plätzen / with bike+ride stands		50 B+R
HNF / Net main floor area		ca. 13.300 m²
Adresse / Address		München-Riem, Messeeingang Ost

---

5 Innere Neustadt Dresden – Regierungsviertel

Innere Neustadt, Dresden – Government District

1992 – 1993 Innere Neustadt Dresden – Regierungsviertel / Innere Neustadt, Dresden - Government District
Städtebaulicher Ideenwettbewerb / Urban planning ideas competition

Ergebnis / Result	1. Preis / 1st prize
Auslober / Competition promoter	Freistaat Sachsen und Landeshauptstadt Dresden
Architekt / Architects	Koch+Partner
Projektverantwortung / Overall responsibility for project	Norbert Koch
Projektleitung / Project architect	Stefan Maisch, Richard Wolf
Mitarbeit / Assistants	Claudia Habelt, Walter Riedhammer
Landschaftsplanung / Landscape planning	Peter Kluska, Landschaftsarchitekt BDLA, München
Bearbeitungszeit / Planning period	Aug. 1992 – Nov. 1992
Preisgericht / Jury decision	17. Feb. 1993
weiteres Planungsgebiet / extended planning area	ca. 580.000 m²
engeres Planungsgebiet / limited planning area	ca. 170.000 m²
Lage im Raum / Location	Innenstadt Dresden / Central city of Dresden

seit 1993 / from 1993 Innere Neustadt / Innere Neustadt, Dresden
Städtebaulicher Rahmenplan / Outline urban planning

Auftraggeber / Client	Landeshauptstadt Dresden, Stadtplanungsamt
Architekt / Architects	Koch+Partner
Projektverantwortung / Overall responsibility for project	Norbert Koch
Projektleitung / Project planner	Astrid Eggensberger
Mitarbeit / Assistants	Ioana Cisek, Stefan Maisch, Silvia Pahl-Leclerque, Sylvia Neudecker, Robert Rechenauer
Freiflächenplanung / Planning of external areas	Peter Kluska, Landschaftsarchitekt BDLA, München
Bearbeitungsbeginn / Start of planning	Jun. 1993
weiteres Planungsgebiet / extended planning area	ca. 580.000 m²
engeres Planungsgebiet / limited planning area	ca. 170.000 m²
Lage im Raum / Location	Innenstadt Dresden / Central city of Dresden

1994 – 1995 Sanierung Teilgebiet Albertstraße / Rehabilitation of Albertstrasse area
Sanierungsgutachten, Machbarkeitsstudie / Rehabilitation report and feasibility study

Auftraggeber / Client	Projektgruppe Stadtentwicklung Dresden
Architekt / Architects	Koch+Partner
Projektverantwortung / Overall responsibility for project	Norbert Koch
Projektleitung / Project planner	Astrid Eggensberger
Mitarbeit / Assistants	Sylvia Neudecker, Robert Rechenauer
Freiflächenplanung / Planning of external areas	Peter Kluska, Landschaftsarchitekt BDLA, München
Bearbeitungszeit / Planning period	Jun. 1994 – Mai 1995
Teilgebiet / Project area	ca. 70.000 m²
Lage im Raum / Location	Albertstraße, Dresden

	1995 – 1998	**Innere Neustadt – Regierungsviertel /**
		Innere Neustadt – Government District
		Bebauungsplan / Development plan
Auftraggeber / Client		Landeshauptstadt Dresden, Stadtplanungsamt
Architekt / Architects		Koch + Partner
Projektverantwortung / Overall responsibility for project		Norbert Koch
Projektleitung / Project planner		Astrid Eggensberger
Mitarbeit / Assistant		Ioana Cisek
Freiflächenplanung / Planning of external areas		Peter Kluska, Landschaftsarchitekt BDLA, München
Bearbeitungsbeginn / Start of planning		Nov. 1995
Satzungsbeschluss / Statutory regulation of planning		Jan. 1999
Planungsgebiet / Planning area		75.000 m²
Lage im Raum / Location		Carolaplatz / Wigardstraße / Archivplatz, Dresden

	1995	**Ministerialgebäude / Ministerial building**
		Beschränkter Realisierungswettbewerb / Construction competition with limited entry
Ergebnis / Result		2. Preis / 2nd prize
Auslober / Competition promoter		Freistaat Sachsen
Architekt / Architects		Koch + Partner
Projektverantwortung / Overall responsibility for project		Norbert Koch
Projektleitung / Project architect		Stefan Maisch
Mitarbeit / Assistants		Thomas Braun, Robert Rechenauer
Tragwerksplanung / Structural engineering		Sailer, Stepan und Partner, München
Freiflächenplanung / Planning of external areas		Peter Kluska, Landschaftsarchitekt BDLA, München
Kantinenplanung / Planning of canteen		Hans-Peter Mühlethaler, Baldham
Bearbeitungszeit / Planning period		Feb. 1995 – Apr. 1995
Preisgericht / Jury decision		26. Apr. 1995
Grundstücksfläche / Site area (approx.)		ca. 8.500 m²
Bebaute Fläche / Built area		ca. 7.920 m²
BRI / Gross volume		ca. 122.770 m³
BGF / Gross floor area		ca. 33.030 m²
Adresse / Address		Wigardstraße, Dresden

6	**Universität Leipzig – Chemische Institute**	1995 – 1999	**Chemische Institute / Institutes for Chemistry**
			Neubau nach Realisierungswettbewerb 1994, 1. Preis; Sächsischer Staatspreis für Architektur und Bauwesen 2000, engste Wahl / Development based on construction competition, 1994 (1st prize); State Prize of Saxony for Architecture and Building 2000 (shortlist)
	University of Leipzig – Institutes for Chemistry		
	Bauherr / Client		Freistaat Sachsen
	Architekt / Architects		Koch + Partner
	Projektverantwortung / Overall responsibility for project		Wolfgang Voigt
	Projektleitung / Project architect		Mechthild Peron
	Bauleitung / Construction management		Klaus Gericke, Anja Göhler, Stefan Kunze
	Mitarbeit / Assistants		Friedrich Bröker, Wolfgang Dietze, Susanne Moog, Sylvia Neudecker, Angelika Rogler, Katja Schäper, Karen Schlömer, Heinz Szuggar
	Projektsteuerung / Project management		CBP Cronauer Beratung Planung Ber.-Ing. GmbH, Leipzig
	Tragwerksplanung / Structural engineering		Ing.-Büro Herrschmann, Leipzig
	Freiflächenplanung / Planning of external areas		Peter Kluska, Landschaftsarchitekt BDLA, München
	Heizung, Lüftung, Sanitär, Kälte, Medien / Heating, cooling, ventilation, sanitary and media planning		Ing.-Büro Scholze, Leipzig
	Elektro- und Fördertechnik / Electrical planning and conveyance systems		Ing.-Büro Oskar von Miller GmbH, Leipzig
	Labortechnik / Laboratory technology		PK Peuker-Kiefl, Dresden
	Planungsbeginn / Start of planning		Apr. 1995
	Baubeginn / Start of construction		Apr. 1997
	Fertigstellung / Completion of works		Sep. 1999

Grundstücksfläche / Site area	15.400 m²
Bebaute Fläche / Built area	3.500 m²
BRI / Gross volume	52.600 m³
BGF / Gross floor area	12.150 m²
HNF / Net main floor area	6.120 m²
Bauvolumen / Construction costs	ca. 76 Mio. DM
Adresse / Address	Philipp-Rosenthal-Straße, Leipzig

1996 – 1999 Studentenwohnheim / Students' hostel
Sanierung und Umnutzung / Rehabilitation and conversion

Bauherr / Client	Studentenwerk Leipzig
Architekt / Architects	Koch+Partner
Projektverantwortung / Overall responsibility for project	Wolfgang Voigt
Projektleitung / Project architect	Susanne Moog
Bauleitung / Construction management	Klaus Gericke, Anja Göhler, Stefan Kunze
Mitarbeit / Assistants	Sylvia Neudecker, Markus Rehn, Karen Schlömer
Projektsteuerung / Project management	CBP Cronauer Beratung Planung Ber.-Ing. GmbH, Leipzig
Tragwerksplanung / Structural engineering	Ing.-Büro Herrschmann, Leipzig
Freiflächenplanung / Planning of external areas	Peter Kluska, Landschaftsarchitekt BDLA, München
Heizung, Lüftung, Sanitär, Kälte, Medien / Heating, cooling, ventilation, sanitary and media planning	Ing.-Büro Scholze, Leipzig
Elektro- und Fördertechnik / Electrical planning and conveyance systems	Ing.-Büro Oskar von Miller GmbH, Leipzig
Planungsbeginn / Start of planning	Feb. 1996
Baubeginn / Start of construction	Jun. 1997
Fertigstellung / Completion of works	Sep. 1999
Grundstücksfläche / Site area	15.400 m²
Bebaute Fläche / Built area	1.800 m²
BRI / Gross volume	42.550 m³
BGF / Gross floor area	15.020 m²
HNF / Net main floor area	8.130 m²
Bauvolumen / Construction costs	ca. 18 Mio. DM
Adresse / Address	Philipp-Rosenthal-Straße, Leipzig

---

7 Frankona Rückversicherungs AG München

Frankona Reinsurance Building, Munich

1982 – 1985 Erster Erweiterungsbau / First extension
Neubau nach Realisierungswettbewerb, 1. Preis /
Development based on construction competition (1st prize)

Bauherr / Client	Frankona Rückversicherungs AG München
Architekt / Architects	Koch+Partner
Projektverantwortung / Overall responsibility for project	Norbert Koch
Projektleitung / Project architect	Wolfgang Voigt
Bauleitung / Construction management	Horst Rosen
Mitarbeit / Assistants	Christoph Damm, Werner Hofmaier
Tragwerksplanung / Structural engineering	Seeberger + Friedl, München
Freiflächenplanung / Planning of external areas	Holm Becher, Germering
Treppenhausbegrünung / Staircase planting	Prof. Peter Latz, Kassel
Heizung, Lüftung, Sanitär / Heating, ventilation, sanitary planning	Hänsel + Köstner, München
Elektro- und Fördertechnik / Electrical planning, conveyance systems	Karl Lackerbauer, München
Lichtplanung / Lighting planning	Christian Bartenbach, München
Küchenplanung / Kitchen planning	Interhoga, München
Planungszeit / Planning period	Okt. 1982 – Apr. 1983
Bauzeit / Construction period	Apr. 1983 – Dez. 1984
Gebäudebezug / Building taken into use	Feb. 1985
Grundstücksfläche / Site area	6.170 m²
Bebaute Fläche / Built area	1.710 m²
BRI / Gross volume	19.170 m³
BGF / Gross floor area	4.700 m²
HNF / Net main floor area	1.860 m²
Bauvolumen / Construction costs	ca. 14 Mio. DM
Adresse / Address	Törringstraße, München

		1996 – 1998	Zweiter Erweiterungsbau / Second extension
	Bauherr / Client		ERC-Frankona Rückversicherungs AG München
	Architekt / Architects		Koch+Partner
	Projektverantwortung / Overall responsibility for project		Wolfgang Voigt
	Projektleitung / Project architect		Claudia Mühlbauer
	Bauleitung / Construction management		Werner Wiehl, ERC-Francona
	Tragwerksplanung / Structural engineering		Ing.-Büro Dieter Herrschmann, München
	Freiflächenplanung / Planning of external areas		Wolfgang Barth, München
	Heizung / Heating		Fritz Hummel, München
	Lüftung / Ventilation		Mayerthaler GmbH, Freising
	Sanitär / Sanitary installation		Urban & Zwanziger, München
	Elektroplanung / Electrical planning		Ing.-Büro Hans Berlic, München
	Schall-/Wärmeschutz / Acoustic and thermal insulation		Akustikbüro Schwartzenberger, Pöcking
	Vermessung / Surveying services		Karner GmbH, München
	Planungszeit / Planning period		Dez. 1996 – Okt. 1997
	Bauzeit / Construction period		Okt. 1997 – Okt. 1998
	Gebäudebezug / Building taken into use		Nov. 1998
	Grundstücksfläche / Site area		mit erstem Erweiterungsbau 6.670 m²
	Bebaute Fläche / Built area		460 m²
	BRI / Gross volume		7.300 m³
	BGF / Gross floor area		2.200 m²
	HNF / Net main floor area		970 m²
	Bauvolumen / Construction costs		ca. 5 Mio. DM
	Adresse / Address		Törringstraße, München

8	Neue Terrasse – Ostra-Allee, Dresden	1997	Neue Terrasse – Ostra-Allee / New Terrace – Ostra-Allee
			Städtebaulicher Rahmenplan nach Städtebaulichem Ideenwettbewerb 1997, 1. Preis / Outline urban planning based on urban planning ideas competition, 1997 (1st prize)
	New Terrace – Ostra-Allee, Dresden		
	Auftraggeber / Client		Landeshauptstadt Dresden, Stadtplanungsamt
	Architekt / Architects		Koch+Partner
	Projektverantwortung / Overall responsibility for project		Norbert Koch
	Projektleitung / Project planner		Astrid Eggensberger
	Mitarbeit / Assistant		Anita Moum
	Freiflächenplanung / Planning of external area		Prof. Rainer Schmidt, München/Berlin
	Bearbeitungszeit / Planning period		Mrz. – Jul. 1997
	Planungsgebiet / Planning area		ca. 145.000 m²
	Lage im Raum / Location		ehemaliges Packhofgelände an der Elbe / former "Packhof" (dockland area) on the Elbe, Dresden
		1997	Städtebauliche Leitlinien Kongresszentrum Dresden / Urban planning guidelines for Congress Centre, Dresden
			Stellungnahme zur Ausschreibung eines Wettbewerbs / Response to competition brief
	Auftraggeber / Client		Landeshauptstadt Dresden, Stadtplanungsamt
	Architekt / Architects		Koch+Partner
	Projektverantwortung / Overall responsibility for project		Norbert Koch
	Projektleitung / Project planner		Astrid Eggensberger
	Mitautoren / Co-authors		weitere Preisträger des Städtebaulichen Ideenwettbewerbs / other competition prizewinners: von Einsiedel & Prof. Michelis, Köln Prof. Bernhard Winking, Hamburg
	Bearbeitungszeit / Planning period		Jun. 1997 – Aug. 1997
	Baugrundstück / Site area		ca. 40.000 m²
	Lage im Raum / Location		ehemaliges Packhofgelände an der Elbe / former "Packhof" (dockland area) on the Elbe, Dresden

		1998 – 1999	**Kongresszentrum Dresden / Congress Centre, Dresden**
			Realisierungswettbewerb / Construction competition
	Auslober / Competition promoter		HOCHTIEF Projektentwicklung GmbH, Niederlassung Sachsen-Thüringen, Dresden
	Architekt / Architects		Koch+Partner
	Projektverantwortung / Overall responsibility for project		Wolfgang Voigt
	Projektleitung / Project architect		Stefan Maisch
	Mitarbeit / Assistants		Fenn-Yvonne Hartmann, Sabine Hagenmiller, Karen Schlömer, Sigrid Schönenberger
	Tragwerksplanung / Structural engineering		Sailer, Stepan und Partner, München
	Ökologie / Environmental planning		Intep GmbH, München
	Kosten / Cost planning		Ing.-Büro Schmid, Ges. f. Projektsteuerung u. Bauüberwachung m.b.H., München
	Küchenplanung / Kitchen planning		Hans-Peter Mühlethaler Consult, Sauerlach
	Bearbeitungszeit / Planning period		Dez. 1998 – Apr. 1999
	Preisgericht / Jury decision		22. Apr. 1999
	Grundstücksfläche / Site area		ca. 40.000 m²
	Bebaute Fläche / Built area		ca. 9.320 m²
	BRI / Gross volume		ca. 215.000 m³
	BGF / Gross floor area		ca. 36.400 m²
	HNF+NNF / Net main + ancillary floor areas		ca. 18.800 m²
	Adresse / Address		Devrientstraße, Dresden

9	**Klärwerk München I**	**1986 – 1993**	**Maschinenhaus 2 / Hall 2 for mechanical plant**
	Gut Großlappen		
		Bauherr / Client	Landeshauptstadt München, Baureferat Hochbau 2
	Sewage Treatment Plant	Architekt / Architects	Koch+Partner
	Munich I, Grosslappen Estate	Projektverantwortung / Overall responsibility for project	Michael Schneider
		Projektleitung / Project architect	Christian Bendomir
		Bauleitung / Construction management	Klaus Gericke, Erich Müller
		Mitarbeit / Assistants	Waltraut Eberle, Werner Hofmeier, Alexander Krizik, Endre Molnar, Bernhard Roll, Peter Rosenbauer, Ariane Wöckel
		Tragwerksplanung / Structural engineering	Sailer, Stepan, Bloos, München
		Freiflächenplanung / Planning of external areas	Dieter Ruoff, Landschaftsarchitekt BDLA, Ottobrunn
		Termin- und Kostenplanung / Scheduling and cost planning	Drees & Sommer Ing.-Ges. f. Projektmanagement, München
		Haustechnik / Mechanical services	Sailer, Stepan, Bloos, München
		Planungsbeginn / Start of planning	Jun. 1986
		Baubeginn / Start of construction	Apr. 1990
		Gebäudebezug / Building taken into use	Apr. 1993
		Bebaute Fläche / Built area	2.590 m²
		BRI / Gross volume	31.500 m³
		BGF / Gross floor area	5.800 m²
		HNF / Net main floor area	1.290 m²
		Bauvolumen / Construction costs	ca. 63 Mio. DM
		Adresse / Address	Klärwerk München I, Gut Großlappen
		1987 – 1988	**Zweite Biologische Reinigungsstufe / Second stage biological purification**
			Konzept und Gestaltung / Concept and design
		Bauherr / Client	Landeshauptstadt München
		Architekt / Architects	Koch+Partner
		Projektverantwortung / Overall responsibility for project	Michael Schneider
		Projektleitung / Project architect	Christian Bendomir
		Übergreifendes Erscheinungsbild / Overall design appearance	Prof. Eberhard Stauß, München
		Bearbeitungszeit / Planning period	Jan. 1987 – Feb. 1989
		1991 – 1996	**Verwaltungs- und Laborgebäude / Administration and laboratory tracts**
		Bauherr / Client	Landeshauptstadt München
		Architekt / Architects	Koch+Partner
		Projektverantwortung / Overall responsibility for project	Michael Schneider
		Projektleitung / Project architects	Wolfgang Dietze, Jürgen Zschornack
		Bauleitung / Construction management	Erich Müller

	Mitarbeit / Assistants	Monika Düchting, Susanne Moog, Sylvia Neudecker, Mechthild Peron, Katja Schäper	
	Tragwerksplanung / Structural engineering	Sailer, Stepan und Partner GmbH, München	
	Termin- und Kostenplanung / Scheduling and cost planning	Ing.-Büro EDR GmbH, München	
	Haustechnik / Mechanical services	Ing.-Büro Anton Kaiser, München	
	Elektrotechnik / Electrical planning	IBE, Ing.-Büro Elektrotechnik, Oberhaching	
	Lichtplanung Turm und Foyer / Lighting planning for tower and foyer	Ing.-Büro Lampl, Dießen am Ammersee	
	Freiflächenplanung / Planning of external areas	Dieter Ruoff, Landschaftsarchitekt BDLA, Ottobrunn	
	Planung / Planning period	Okt. 1991 – Okt. 1993	
	Baubeginn / Start of construction	Jul. 1994	
	Gebäudebezug / Building taken into use	Jun. 1996	
	BRI / Gross volume	ca. 17.470 m³	
	BGF / Gross floor area	3.680 m²	
	HNF / Net main floor area	ca. 3.060 m²	
	Bauvolumen / Construction costs	ca. 21 Mio. DM	
	Adresse / Address	Klärwerk München I, Gut Großlappen	

---

10 Büro- und Wohnhaus Wittstockstraße Leipzig

1992 – 1995

Büro- und Wohnhaus Wittstockstraße Leipzig / Office and Housing Block in Wittstockstrasse, Leipzig

Office and Housing Block in Wittstockstrasse, Leipzig

Bauherr / Client	Norbert Koch
Architekt / Architects	Koch + Partner
Projektverantwortung / Overall responsibility for project	Norbert Koch
Projektleitung / Project architect	Susanne Moog
Bauleitung / Construction management	Peter Ernst
Mitarbeit / Assistants	Christian Bendomir, Claudia Habelt, Sylvia Neudecker, Jürgen Reimann, Katja Schäper, Stephan von Schickfuß, Richard Wolf
Ausschreibung / BQs and tender documents	Monika Odoj, München
Tragwerksplanung / Structural engineering	Ing.-Büro Herrschmann, München
Prüfstatik / Testing engineers (structure)	Prof. Dr.-Ing. habil. L. Schubert, Prüfing. f. Baustatik VPI, Leipzig
Freiflächenplanung / Planning of external areas	Peter Kluska, Landschaftsarchitekt BDLA, München
Haustechnik / Mechanical services	CBP Cronauer, München
Planungsbeginn / Start of planning	Nov. 1992
Bauzeit / Construction period	Okt. 1993 – Mai 1995
Gebäudebezug / Building taken into use	Okt. 1995
Grundstücksfläche / Site area	400 m²
Bebaute Fläche / Built area	250 m²
BRI (inkl. Halle) / Gross volume (inc. hall)	4.900 m³
BGF / Gross floor area	1.400 m²
HNF / Net main floor area	960 m²
Bauvolumen / Construction costs	ca. 2 Mio. DM
Adresse / Address	Wittstockstraße, Leipzig

---

11 Postbank Leipzig

1991 – 1995

Postbank Niederlassung Leipzig / Branch Post Office Bank, Leipzig

Post Office Bank, Leipzig

Bauherr / Client	Postbank-Immobilien und Baumanagement GmbH & Co, Bonn / Objekt Leipzig KG
Architekt / Architects	Koch + Partner
Projektverantwortung / Overall responsibility for project	Wolf-Dieter Drohn, Wolfgang Voigt
Projektleitung / Project architect	Andreas Schneider
Bauleitung / Construction management	Bernhard Hörnig, Gilbert Bullok, Klaus Gericke, Rolf Seliger, Gregor Tymke
Mitarbeit / Assistants	Friedrich Bröker, Elena Buschmann, Monika Düchting-Loose, Peter Ernst, Godwin Idehen, Endre Molnar, Mechthild Peron, Angelika Rogler, Peter Rosenbauer, Katja Schäper, Helena Sedlacek, Heinz Szuggar, Martin Sonnenberg, Christel Tampé, Birgit Wild-Dicke
Projektsteuerung / Project management	CBP Cronauer, Beratende Ingenieure GmbH, München
Tragwerksplanung / Structural engineering	Ingenieurbüro Herrschmann, München
Prüfstatik / Testing engineers (structure)	Ing.-Büro Dr.-Ing. Max Mühlhaus, München/Leipzig
Freiflächenplanung / Planning of external areas	Peter Kluska, Landschaftsarchitekt BDLA, München
Haustechnik / Mechanical services	HL-Technik AG, München
Küchentechnik / Kitchen technology	Ing.-Büro Welskopp, München
Grundbau / Foundation engineering	Erd- und Grundbauinstitut Dr. Christoph Batereau, Dresden
Brunnen / Fountain	Herbert Peters, München

Planungsbeginn / Start of planning		Mrz. 1991
Bauzeit / Construction period		Okt. 1992 – Dez. 1994
Gebäudebezug / Building taken into use		Feb. 1995
Grundstücksfläche / Site area		16.110 m²
Bebaute Fläche / Built area		10.740 m²
BRI (inkl. Halle) / Gross volume (inc. hall)		320.000 m³
BGF / Gross floor area		68.320 m²
HNF / Net main floor area		30.240 m²
Bauvolumen / Construction costs		ca. 170 Mio. DM
Adresse / Address		Rohrteichstraße, Leipzig

---

12 Großes Ostragehege – IGA Dresden 2003

Grosses Ostragehege – International Horticultural Show (IGA), Dresden, 2003

1995

Großes Ostragehege – IGA Dresden 2003 / Grosses Ostragehege – International Horticultural Show, Dresden, 2003
Städtebaulich-landschaftsplanerischer Ideenwettbewerb / Urban and landscape planning ideas competition

Ergebnis / Result	3. Preis / 3rd prize
Auslober / Competition promoter	Landeshauptstadt Dresden, Projektgruppe IGA Dresden 2003
Architekt / Architects	Koch+Partner in Arbeitsgemeinschaft mit / in collaboration with Prof. Rainer Schmidt, München/Berlin
Projektverantwortung / Overall responsibility for project	Norbert Koch und Prof. Rainer Schmidt
Projektleitung / Project architect	Stefan Maisch
Mitarbeit / Assistants	Thomas Braun, Robert Rechenauer, Petra Becker, Jeannette Hönge, Christina Löw, Stefan Müller, Herman Salm, Peter Wich
Bearbeitungszeit / Planning period	Mrz. – Mai 1995
Preisgericht / Jury decision	14./15. Jun. 1995
Weiteres Planungsgebiet / Extended planning area	ca. 4,3 km²
Engeres Planungsgebiet / Limited planning area	ca. 2,9 km²
Davon IGA-Gelände / Of which, IGA site	ca. 2 km²
Lage im Raum / Location	Großes Ostragehege (ehemaliges Schlachthofgelände an der Elbe) / Former abattoir area on the Elbe, Dresden

---

13 Deutscher Bundestag Berlin, Alsenblock

German Bundestag, Berlin: Alsen Block

1994

Deutscher Bundestag Berlin, Alsenblock / German Bundestag, Berlin: Alsen Block
heute: Paul-Löbe-Haus, Realisierungswettbewerb / now, Paul Löbe Building; construction competition

Ergebnis / Result	2. Preis / 2nd prize
Auslober / Competition promoter	Bundesrepublik Deutschland
Architekt / Architects	Koch+Partner
Projektverantwortung / Overall responsibility for project	Norbert Koch, Michael Schneider
Projektleitung / Project architect	Stefan Maisch
Mitarbeit / Assistant	Robert Rechenauer
Tragwerksplanung / Structural engineering	Sailer, Stepan, Bloos, München
Bearbeitungszeit / Planning period	Apr. 1994 – Sep. 1994
Preisgericht / Jury decision	27./28. Okt. 1994
Grundstücksfläche / Site area	ca. 17.240 m²
Bebaute Fläche / Built area	ca. 11.640 m²
BRI / Gross volume	373.380 m³
BGF / Gross floor area	104.110 m²
HNF / Net main floor area	ca. 45.000 m²
Adresse / Address	Am Spreebogen, Berlin

14	Postsparkassenamt München	1986 – 1993	**Postsparkassenamt München / Post Office Savings Bank, Munich**

Post Office Savings Bank, Munich

Neubau nach Realisierungswettbewerb 1983, 1. Preis / New development based on construction competition, 1983 (1st prize)

Bauherr / Client	Deutsche Bundespost Postbank, Oberpostdirektion München
Architekt / Architects	Koch, Benedek + Partner
Projektverantwortung / Overall responsibility for project	Wolf-Dieter Drohn, Michael Schneider
Projektleitung / Project architect	Jürgen Zschornack
Bauleitung / Construction management	Thomas Barra, Gilbert Bullok, Bernhard Hörnig, Gregor Tymke
Mitarbeit / Assistants	Birgit Ackermann, Franz Josef Amstorfer, Volker Hagen, Alexander Krizik, Peter Rosenbauer, Richard Pentlehner, Peter Übelacker, Josef Zaunseder
Projektsteuerung / Project management	Ing.-Büro CBP Cronauer, München
Tragwerksplanung / Structural engineering	Ing.-Büro Herrschmann, München
Prüfstatik / Testing engineers (structure)	Ing.-Büro Dr. Mühlhaus, München
Freiflächenplanung / Planning of external areas	Peter Kluska, Landschaftsarchitekt BDLA, München
Haustechnik / Mechanical services	Kuehn + Bauer, Beratende Ing. München
Elektrotechnik / Electrical planning	Ing.-Büro ptz, München
Küchentechnik / Kitchen technology	Ing.-Büro Herrmann, München
Grundbau / Foundation engineering	Dorsch Consult, München
Vermesung / Surveying services	Ing.-Büro Bott, München
Fassadenberatung / Facade consultants	Ing.-Büro Stephan, Lauingen
Schutzraumplanung / Air-raid shelter planning	Ing.-Büro Lindau, München
Haustechnische Bauleitung / Construction management (mechanical services)	Ing.-Büro Schmitt, München
Planungsbeginn / Start of planning	Jul. 1986
Bauzeit / Construction period	Mai 1989 – Okt. 1992
Gebäudebezug / Building taken into use	Jun. 1993
Grundstücksfläche / Site area	15.320 m²
Bebaute Fläche / Built area	11.070 m²
BRI / Gross volume	270.460 m³
BGF / Gross floor area	69.630 m²
HNF / Net main floor area	37.000 m²
Bauvolumen / Construction costs	ca. 160 Mio. DM
Adresse / Address	Bayerstraße, München

15	Arbeitsamt Augsburg	1984 – 1989	**Arbeitsamt Augsburg / Jobcentre, Augsburg**

Jobcentre, Augsburg

Neubau nach Realisierungswettbewerb 1981, 1. Preis / New development based on construction competition, 1981 (1st prize)

Bauherr / Client	Bundesanstalt für Arbeit
Architekt / Architects	Koch + Partner
Projektverantwortung / Overall responsibility for project	Wolfgang Voigt
Projektleitung / Project architect	Wolfgang Voigt
Bauleitung / Construction management	Hans-Jörg Kramer
Mitarbeit / Assistants	Birgit Ackermann, Franz Josef Amstorfer, Michael Bergmann, Waltaut Eberle, Alexander Krizik, Monika Odoj, Joachim Wahlich
Tragwerksplanung / Structural engineering	Ing.-Büro Steinherr/Duval, Ing.-Büro Hillenbrand, Augsburg
Freiflächenplanung / Planning of external areas	Gottfried Hansjakob, München
Haustechnik / Mechanical services	HL-Technik GmbH, München
Elektrotechnik / Electrical planning	BMS Ing.-Gesellschaft, München
Künstler. Gestaltung Innenhöfe, Lichtstelen / Artistic design of courtyards; lighting stelae	Manfred Mayerle, München, und Florian Lechner, Nußdorf
Planungsbeginn / Start of planning	Mrz. 1984
Bauzeit / Construction period	Jul. 1986 – Okt. 1989
Gebäudebezug / Building taken into use	Okt. 1989
Grundstücksfläche / Site area	18.330 m²
Bebaute Fläche / Built area	3.780 m²
BRI / Gross volume	77.240 m³
BGF / Gross floor area	22.150 m²
HNF / Net main floor area	14.160 m²
Bauvolumen / Construction costs	ca. 41 Mio. DM
Adresse / Address	Wertachstraße, Augsburg

16	Siemens AG Augsburg	1985 – 1987	**Werk für Systeme, Standort 2** / Siemens computer works, location 2
			Erster Bauabschnitt / First stage of construction
	Siemens Building, Augsburg		
		Bauherr / Client	Siemens AG, Zentrale Abt. für Bauten und Anlagen, München
		Architekt / Architects	Koch+Partner
		Projektverantwortung / Overall responsibility for project	Norbert Koch, Michael Schneider
		Projektleitung / Project architects	Roland Woltmann, Richard Pentlehner
		Bauleitung / Construction management	Bernhard Hörnig, Wolfgang Thumann
		Mitarbeit / Assistants	Birgit Ackermann, Michael Bergmann, Stefan Burger, Waltraut Eberle, Klaus Freudenfeld, Jürgen Zschornack
		Projektsteuerung / Project management	Ing.-Büro Stössl, München
		Tragwerksplanung / Structural engineering	Sailer, Stepan und Partner, München
		Freiflächenplanung / Planning of external areas	Gottfried Hansjakob, München
		Haustechnik / Mechanical services	Ing.-Büro Korner
		Planungsbeginn / Start of planning	Okt. 1985
		Bauzeit / Construction period	Apr. 1986 – Jan. 1987
		Grundstücksfläche / Site area	321.500 m²
		Bebaute Fläche / Built area	20.000 m²
		BRI / Gross volume	222.450 m³
		BGF / Gross floor area	23.150 m²
		HNF / Net main floor area	20.840 m²
		Bauvolumen / Construction costs	ca. 36 Mio. DM
		Adresse / Address	Augsburg Haunstetten

17	BMW Forschungs- und Ingenieurzentrum München	1981 – 1982	**Strukturuntersuchung für ein Forschungs- und Ingenieurzentrum** / Structural investigation for a research and engineering centre
			Gutachten und Überarbeitung / Design study and revised proposals
	BMW Research and Engineering Centre, Munich		
		Auftraggeber / Client	Bayerische Motorenwerke AG, München
		Architekt / Architects	Koch, Benedek+Partner
		Projektverantwortung / Overall responsibility for project	Gabor Benedek, Norbert Koch
		Projektleitung / Project architect	Michael Schneider
		Mitarbeit / Assistant	Klaus Bachmann
		Verkehrsplanung / Traffic planning	Prof. Dipl.-Ing. K. Schaechterle, Dr.-Ing. Harald Kurzak, Lehrstuhl für Verkehrs- und Stadtplanung TU München
		Freiflächenplanung / Planning of external areas	Gottfried Hansjakob, München
		Bearbeitung Gutachten / Design study	1981
		Bearbeitung Überarbeitung / Revisions	1982
		Untersuchungsgebiet / Area under investigation	ca. 190.000 m²
		BRI / Gross volume	1.309.170 m³
		BGF / Gross floor area	321.200 m²
		davon Büroflächen / of which offices	105.200 m²
		Werkstätten / workshops	123.500 m²
		Lage im Raum / Location	Alabama Gelände, Knorrstraße, München

18	Salzachhalle Laufen	1972 – 1974	**Gutachten zur Stadtentwicklung und Altstadtsanierung** / Study for urban development and rehabilitation of historic town centre
	Salzach Hall in Laufen		
		Auftraggeber / Client	Stadt Laufen
		Architekt / Architect	Norbert Koch
		Projektleitung / Project architect	Fritz Hubert
		Mitarbeit / Assistants	Udo Bünnagel, Erhard Engel
		Soziale Grundlagen und Fremdenverkehr / Social context and tourism	Felizitas Lenz-Romeiss, München
		Bearbeitungszeit / Planning period	Mrz. 1973 – Jul. 1974
		Untersuchungsgebiet Stadtentwicklung / Area investigated: urban development	ca. 2,23 km²
		Untersuchungsgebiet Altstadt / Area investigated: historic town centre	ca. 0,14 km²
		Lage im Raum / Location	Laufen an der Salzach

		1979 – 1982	**Salzachhalle / Salzach Hall**
	Bauherr / Client		Stadt Laufen
	Architekt / Architects		Koch + Partner
	Projektverantwortung / Overall responsibility for project		Norbert Koch, Michael Schneider
	Projektleitung / Project architect		Wolfgang Voigt
	Bauleitung / Construction management		Horst Rosen
	Statik, HLT, Sanitär / Structural engineering and mechanical services		Sailer, Stepan, Bloos, München
	Bauphysik / Constructional physics		H. Sorge, AIV, Zirndorf
	Elektrotechnik / Electrical planning		BMS – Ingenieur-GmbH, München
	Bühnentechnik / Stage technology		G. Zimmermann, Laufen
	Planungsbeginn / Start of planning		1979
	Bauzeit / Construction period		Okt. 1980 – Okt. 1982
	Eröffnung / Opening		Jan. 1983
	Bebaute Fläche / Built area		ca. 3.000 m²
	BRI / Gross volume		13.110 m³
	HNF / Net main floor area		1.810 m²
	Bauvolumen / Construction costs		ca. 6 Mio. DM
	Adresse / Address		Schloßplatz, Laufen

19	**BMW Verwaltungsgebäude Dingolfing** **BMW Administration Building, Dingolfing**	1977 – 1980	**BMW Verwaltungsgebäude Werk 2, Dingolfing /** **BMW administration building, Works 2, Dingolfing** Neubau nach Realisierungswettbewerb 1977, 1. Preis / New development based on construction competition, 1977 (1st prize) Deutscher Architektenpreis – lobende Erwähnung / German Architecture Prize: honourable mention BDA Preis Bayern 1981 / BDA Prize for Bavaria, 1981
	Bauherr / Client		Bayerische Motorenwerke AG, München
	Architekt / Architects		Arge Norbert Koch + Gabor Benedek, München
	Projektverantwortung / Overall responsibility for project		Gabor Benedek, Norbert Koch
	Projektleitung / Project architect		Gabor Benedek
	Bauleitung / Construction management		Horst-Dieter Rosen
	Mitarbeit / Assistants		Günther Burkhardt, Christa Giesecke, Dieter Graf, Peter Ottoway, Peter Rosenbauer, Michael Schneider
	Projektsteuerung / Project management		Dieter Graf, Arge Norbert Koch + Gabor Benedek, München
	Tragwerksplanung / Structural engineering		Obermeyer Projektmanagement, München
	Bauphysik / Constructional physics		Hans Sorge Ingenieure AIV, Zirndorf
	Freiflächenplanung / Planning of external areas		Gottfried Hansjakob, München
	Haustechnik / Mechanical services		Obermeyer Projektmanagement, München
	Planungszeit / Planning period		Dez. 1977 – Apr. 1978
	Bauzeit / Construction period		Jul. 1978 – Mai 1980
	Gebäudebezug / Building taken into use		Jun. 1980
	Grundstücksfläche / Site area		18.420 m²
	Bebaute Fläche / Built area		6.820 m²
	BRI / Gross volume		71.270 m³
	BGF / Gross floor area		15.160 m²
	HNF / Net main floor area		Fläche für 420 Beschäftigte / Area for 420 employees
	Bauvolumen / Construction costs		ca. 30 Mio. DM
	Adresse / Address		BMW Werksgelände, Dingolfing

20	**Bundesanstalt für Fleisch- forschung Kulmbach** **Federal Institute for Meat Research, Kulmbach**	1969 – 1976

**Bundesanstalt für Fleischforschung Kulmbach /
Federal Institute for Meat Research, Kulmbach**
Neubau nach Realisierungswettbewerb 1968, 1. Preis /
New development based on construction competition, 1968 (1st prize)

Bauherr / Client	Bundesrepublik Deutschland, BM für Ernährung, Landwirtschaft und Forsten, BM für Wirtschaft und Finanzen, Freistaat Bayern
Architekt / Architects	Planungsgruppe BAF: Norbert Koch, München mit Wilfried Schneeberger und Ludwig Wagner, Weiden
Projektverantwortung / Overall responsibility for project	Norbert Koch
Projektleitung / Project architect	Poul Leckband
Bauleitung / Construction management	Peter Leitholf, Kulmbach
Mitarbeit / Assistant	Udo Bünagel
Tragwerksplanung / Structural engineering	Sailer und Stepan, München
Heizungs-, Klima-, Lüftungsplanung / HVA planning	Ing.-Büro Hübner, München
Elektrische Anlagen / Electrical planning	Brown, Boveri + Cie, Nürnberg
Planungszeit / Planning period	1969 – 1972
Bauzeit / Construction period	1972 – 1976
Gebäudebezug / Building taken into use	Sep. 1976
BRI / Gross volume	63.000 m^3
BGF / Gross floor area	11.000 m^2
HNF + NNF/ Net main and ancillary floor areas	7.500 m^2
Bauvolumen / Construction costs	ca. 40 Mio. DM
Adresse / Address	Oskar-von-Miller-Straße, Kulmbach

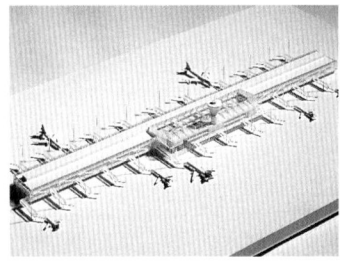

1998 – 2003 Flughafen München, Terminal 2	1998 – 2003 Munich Airport: Terminal 2
2000 – 2003 Flughafen München, 1. Satellit	2000 – 2003 Munich Airport: first satellite
1997 – 2002 Allianz Ludwigstraße München, Generalsanierung HPP – Koch+Partner	1997 – 2002 Allianz Insurance, Ludwigstrasse, Munich: general refurbishment HPP – Koch+Partner
1994 – 2001 Stadtwerke München, Stadtwerkszentrale	1994 – 2001 Municipal Department of Works centre, Munich
1997 – 2000 Stadt Geretsried, Bebauungsplan Karl-Lederer-Platz	1997 – 2000 Municipality of Geretsried: development plan for Karl-Lederer-Platz
1995 – 2000 Universität Erfurt, Universitätsbibliothek	1995 – 2000 University of Erfurt: university library
1993 – 2000 Innere Neustadt Dresden, Städtebaulicher Rahmenplan	1993 – 2000 Innere Neustadt, Dresden: outline urban planning
1999 Flughafen München, Konzeptstudie 1. Satellit Dorsch Consult – Koch+Partner u.a.	1999 Munich Airport: conceptual study for first satellite; Dorsch Consult – Koch+Partner and others
1999 Herzogingarten Dresden, Gutachten	1999 Herzogingarten, Dresden: planning report
1999 Flughafen Wien, Wettbewerb	1999 Vienna Airport; competition
1999 Kongresszentrum Dresden, Wettbewerb	1999 Congress Centre, Dresden; competition
1998 – 1999 Messestadt Riem, Gestaltungsleitlinien	1998 – 1999 Messestadt Riem, Munich: design guidelines

Arbeiten und Projekte 1970 – 2000

Works and projects 1970 – 2000

1998 – 1999 Stadtwerke München, Gesamtlabor 2. BA	1998 – 1999 Municipal Department of Works, Munich: laboratory; 2nd stage of construction
1998 – 1999 Allianz Versicherung München, Umbau Theresienstraße 1 – 7	1998 – 1999 Allianz Insurance company, Munich: conversion of Theresienstrasse 1 – 7
1997 – 1999 Universität Erfurt, Entwicklungsgutachten	1997 – 1999 University of Erfurt: development study
1995 – 1999 Universität Erfurt, Umbau Wohnheim in ein Dienstgebäude	1995 – 1999 University of Erfurt: conversion of students' hostel into administration building
1995 – 1999 Regierungsviertel Dresden, Bebauungsplan	1995 – 1999 Government district, Dresden: development plan
1994 – 1999 Universität Leipzig, Chemische Institute	1994 – 1999 University of Leipzig: Institutes for Chemistry
1994 – 1999 Universität Leipzig, Studentenwohn- heim, Sanierung und Umnutzung	1994 – 1999 University of Leipzig: rehabilitation and conversion of students' hostel
1994 – 1999 Postbankareal Sonnenstraße München	1994 – 1999 Post Office Bank site, Sonnenstrasse, Munich
1998 Flughafen München 2, Terminal 2, Wettbewerb 1. Preis	1998 Munich Airport 2, Terminal 2; competition: 1st prize
1998 P+R-Anlage, Messestadt Riem, München, Wettbewerb 2. Preis	1998 Messestadt Riem, Munich: park-and-ride facilities; competition: 2nd prize
1998 Universität Brixen, Wettbewerb	1998 University of Bressanone; competition
1998 Universität Bozen, Wettbewerb	1998 University of Bolzano; competition
1997 – 1998 Frankona Rückversicherungs AG München, Verwaltungsgebäude	1997 – 1998 Frankona Reinsurance company, Munich: administration building

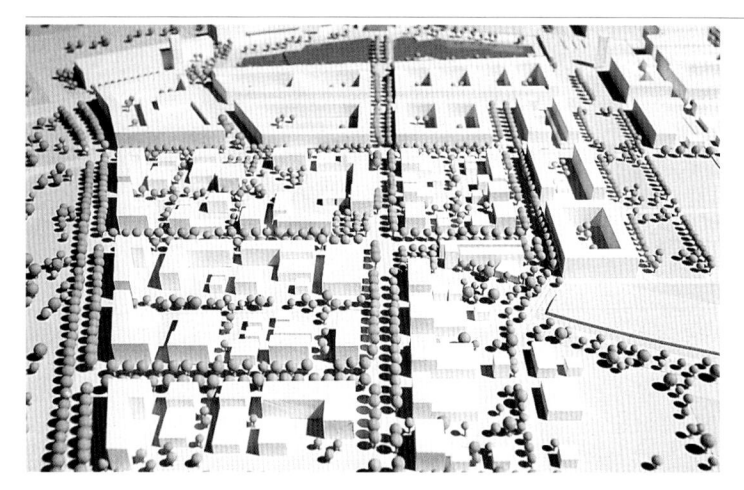

1994 – 1998 Messestadt Riem, Gewerbegebiet Nord/West, Struktur- und Bebauungsplan	1994 – 1998 Messestadt Riem, Munich: structural and development plan for north-west commercial area
1994 – 1998 Klärwerk München I, Gut Großlappen, Fassadensanierung	1994 – 1998 Sewage Treatment Plant Munich I: facade refurbishment
1994 – 1998 Klärwerk München I, Gut Großlappen, Geräte- und Elektrowerkstatt	1994 – 1998 Sewage Treatment Plant Munich I: hall for equipment and electrical supply
1994 – 1998 Klärwerk München I, Gut Großlappen, Betriebshof Nord	1994 – 1998 Sewage Treatment Plant Munich I: northern works yard
1993 – 1998 Postbankfiliale Sonnenstraße München	1993 – 1998 Post Office Bank branch, Sonnen- strasse, Munich
1992 – 1998 Gemeinde Rottach-Egern, Flächen- nutzungsplan und Bebauungspläne	1992 – 1998 Municipality of Rottach-Egern: land-use and development plans
1997 Kongresszentrum Dresden, Städtebauliche Leitlinien	1997 Congress Centre, Dresden: urban planning guidelines
1997 Neue Terrasse – Ostra-Allee Dresden, Städtebaulicher Rahmenplan	1997 New Terrace – Ostra-Allee, Dresden: outline urban planning
1997 Neue Terrasse – Ostra-Allee Dresden, Wettbewerb 1. Preis	1997 New Terrace – Ostra-Allee, Dresden; competition: 1st prize
1997 Bayerische Rückversicherung Unterföhring, Wettbewerb	1997 Bavarian Reinsurance company, Unterföhring; competition
1997 Flughafen Stuttgart, Wettbewerb	1997 Stuttgart Airport; competition
1997 IGA 2003 Rostock, Wettbewerb	1997 International Horticultural Show 2003, Rostock; competition
1996 – 1997 Karl-Liebknecht-Straße Leipzig, Grundrissstudien für Bebauungsplan	1996 – 1997 Karl-Liebknecht-Strasse, Leipzig: layout studies for development plan
1996 – 1997 Gemeinde Ismaning, Bebauungsplan Bildungszentrum	1996 – 1997 District of Ismaning: development plan for educational centre
1996 – 1997 Schützenplatz Dresden, Bebauungsstudie	1996 – 1997 Schützenplatz, Dresden: development study
1995 – 1997 Stadtwerke München, Gasdruckregler	1995 – 1997 Municipal Department of Works, Munich: gas-pressure control centre

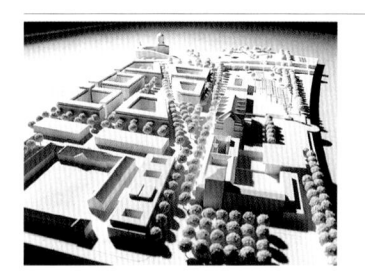

1994 – 1997 Klärwerk München I, Gut Großlappen, Wärmezentrale	1994 – 1997 Sewage Treatment Plant Munich I: heating plant
1996 Stadtwerke München, Gaswerksgelände Nordteil	1996 Municipal Department of Works, Munich: gasworks site, northern area
1996 Universität Jena, Bibliothek, Wettbewerb Ankauf	1996 University of Jena: library; competition: purchase of scheme
1996 Fraunhofer Gesellschaft München, Zentralverwaltung und Institut für Festkörpertechnologie, Wettbewerb	1996 Fraunhofer Society, Munich: central administration and institute for solid-state technology; competition
1996 Umgestaltung ehemalige Flintkaserne Bad Tölz, Wettbewerb Ankauf	1996 Former Flint Barracks, Bad Tölz: conversion and redesign; competition: purchase of scheme
1996 Universitätsklinikum 2000 Jena, Wettbewerb 1. Stufe, Preisgruppe	1996 University Clinic 2000, Jena; competition first stage: shortlist
1996 Thüringer Landtag Erfurt, Wettbewerb	1996 Thuringian State Parliament, Erfurt; competition
1996 Landesfunkhaus Thüringen Erfurt, Wettbewerb	1996 Thuringian State Broadcasting building, Erfurt; competition
1994 – 1996 Foto Sauter München, Ladenumbau	1994 – 1996 Foto Sauter, Munich: shop conversion
1992 – 1996 IGL Halle, Bürogebäude	1992 – 1996 IGL office building, Halle
1991 – 1996 Klärwerk München I, Gut Großlappen, Verwaltung	1991 – 1996 Sewage Treatment Plant Munich I: administration building
1991 – 1996 Klärwerk München I, Gut Großlappen, Labor	1991 – 1996 Sewage Treatment Plant Munich I: laboratories
1995 Jahn-Baum-Klenzestraße München Bebauungsstudie	1995 Jahn-, Baum- and Klenzestrasse area, Munich: development study
1995 IGA Dresden 2003, Großes Ostragehege, Wettbewerb 3. Preis	1995 International Horticultural Show, Dresden, 2003; competition: 3rd prize
1995 Ministerialgebäude Dresden, Wettbewerb 2. Preis	1995 Ministerial building, Dresden; competition: 2nd prize
1995 Wohnen im Moabiter Werder Berlin, Wettbewerb	1995 Housing in Moabiter Werder, Berlin; competition

1995 Humboldt Universität, Berlin, Adlershof, Chemische Institute, Wettbewerb	1995 Humboldt University, Adlershof, Berlin: Institutes for Chemistry; competition
1995 Universität und Bibliothek Erfurt, Wettbewerb 1. Preis	1995 University and library, Erfurt; competition: 1st prize
1995 Fachhochschule Magdeburg, Wettbewerb 4. Preis	1995 University of Applied Science, Magdeburg; competition: 4th prize
1993 – 1995 Stadt Geretsried, Bebauungsplan Jeschkenstraße	1993 – 1995 Municipality of Geretsried: development plan for Jeschkenstrasse
1992 – 1995 Wittstockstraße Leipzig, Büro- und Wohnhaus	1992 – 1995 Wittstockstrasse, Leipzig: office and housing block
1992 – 1995 Stadtwerke München, 24-Stunden-Trakt	1992 – 1995 Municipal Department of Works, Munich: 24-hour tract
1991 – 1995 Postbank Leipzig	1991 – 1995 Post Office Bank, Leipzig
1989 – 1995 Stadtwerke München, Stadtwerkszentrale, Gesamtlabor (1. BA)	1989 – 1995 Municipal Department of Works, Munich: laboratory
1994 Bebauungsstudien Leipzig	1994 Development studies for Leipzig
1994 Deutscher Bundestag Berlin, Alsenblock, Wettbewerb 2. Preis	1994 German Bundestag, Berlin: Alsen Block; competition: 2nd prize
1994 Theater Frankfurt/Oder, Wettbewerb Ankauf	1994 Theatre in Frankfurt/Oder; competition: purchase of scheme
1994 Hauptbahnhof Leipzig, Wettbewerb Ankauf	1994 Leipzig Main Station; competition: purchase of scheme
1994 Universität Leipzig, Chemische Institute, Wettbewerb 1. Preis	1994 University of Leipzig, Institutes for Chemistry; competition: 1st prize
1994 Mitteldeutscher Rundfunk Leipzig, Wettbewerb	1994 Mitteldeutscher Rundfunk (Central German Broadcasting), Leipzig; competition
1993 – 1994 Innere Neustadt Dresden, Teilgebiet Albertstraße Sanierung, Gutachten	1993 – 1994 Innere Neustadt, Dresden: planning study for rehabilitation of Albertstrasse area
1993 – 1994 Körnerstraße Leipzig, Büro- und Wohngebäude	1993 – 1994 Körnerstrasse, Leipzig: office and housing block

1992 – 1994 Stadtwerkszentrale München, Entwurfsanpassung	1992 – 1994 Municipal Department of Works, Munich: planning modifications
1990 – 1994 Klärwerk München I, Gut Großlappen, Energiezentrale	1990 – 1994 Sewage Treatment Plant Munich I: energy-generating plant
1993 Terreno Bürogebäude München, Wettbewerb 3. Preis	1993 Terreno office building, Munich; competition: 3rd prize
1993 Wigardstraße Dresden, Bebauungsstudie	1993 Wigardstrasse, Dresden: development study
1993 Max-Planck-Gesellschaft Jena, Wettbewerb Ankauf	1993 Max Planck Society, Jena; competition: purchase of scheme
1993 Neuriem Mitte Stufe 1, Wettbewerb 3. Preis	1993 Neuriem Mitte, stage 1; competition: 3rd prize
1993 Max-Planck-Gesellschaft, Generalverwaltung München, Wettbewerb	1993 Max Planck Society: general administration building, Munich; competition
1993 Haus der Bayerischen Wirtschaft München, Wettbewerb	1993 Haus der Bayerischen Wirtschaft, Munich; competition
1993 Regierungsviertel Dresden, Wettbewerb 1. Preis	1993 Government district, Dresden; competition: 1st prize
1989 – 1993 Telekom Ismaning, Berufsbildungszentrum und Fernmeldeschule	1989 – 1993 Telekom Ismaning, Munich: training centre and telecommunications school
1987 – 1993 Klärwerk München I, Gut Großlappen, 2. Biologie, Gestaltung	1987 – 1993 Sewage Treatment Plant Munich I, second-stage biological purification plant: concept and design
1986 – 1993 Klärwerk München I, Gut Großlappen, Maschinenhaus	1986 – 1993 Sewage Treatment Plant Munich I: hall 2 for mechanical plant
1986 – 1993 Gemeinde Gmund, Flächennutzungsplan, Bebauungspläne	1986 – 1993 Municipality of Gmund: land-use plan and development plans
1979 – 1993 Gemeinde Bad Wiessee, Flächennutzungsplan, Bebauungspläne	1979 – 1993 Municipality of Bad Wiessee: land-use plan and development plans
1978 – 1993 Gemeinde Bad Wiessee, Bebauungsplan Spielbank	1978 – 1993 Municipality of Bad Wiessee: development plan for casino

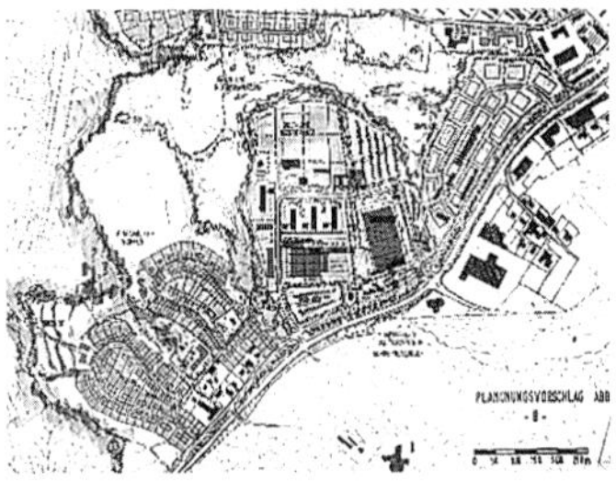

1992 Stadt Passau, Gutachten Kasernengelände Deutsche Akademie für Städtebau und Landesplanung – Koch+Partner	1992 Municipality of Passau: report on barracks site; German Academy for Urban and Regional Planning – Koch+Partner
1992 Bayerische Vereinsbank Leipzig, Wettbewerb	1992 Bayerische Vereinsbank, Leipzig; competition
1992 Juliusspital Würzburg, Wettbewerb	1992 Juliusspital, Würzburg; competition
1991 – 1992 Klärwerk München I, Gut Großlappen, Werkstätten	1991 – 1992 Sewage Treatment Plant Munich I: workshops
1990 – 1992 Stadt Plauen, Altstadtsanierung	1990 – 1992 Municipality of Plauen: rehabilitation of old city centre
1988 – 1992 Flughafen München 2, Allgemeine Luftfahrt, Städtebaulicher Entwicklungsplan, Terminal und Hangar, Planfeststellungsänderung	1988 – 1992 Munich Airport 2, general aviation, urban development plan, terminal and hangar: revisions to statutory planning (Building Development Plan)
1986 – 1992 Krankenhaus Weilheim Koch+Partner Brökelmann	1986 – 1992 Weilheim Hospital Koch+Partner Brökelmann
1983 – 1992 Postsparkassenamt München Koch, Benedek+Partner	1983 – 1992 Post Office Savings Bank, Munich Koch, Benedek+Partner
1991 Vereinte Versicherungen München, Wettbewerb	1991 Vereinte Versicherungen, Munich; competition
1991 Arbeitsamt Memmingen, Plangutachten	1991 Jobcentre, Memmingen: planning report
1991 Neue Messe München, Wettbewerb 4. Preis	1991 New Trade Fair, Munich; competition: 4th prize
1991 Arbeitsamt Augsburg, SIS + BIS Gebäude	1991 Jobcentre, Augsburg: job and career information building
1991 Künftige Nutzung des Flughafengeländes München Riem, Wettbewerb Ankauf	1991 Future use of former airport site in Riem, Munich; competition: purchase of scheme
1987 – 1991 Münchner Yachtclub, Starnberg, Clubhausumbau	1987 – 1991 Munich Yacht Club, Starnberg: redesign of clubhouse
1990 Stadt Saalfeld, Vorbereitende Untersuchung Arge Computergestützte Bauaufnahme ACB	1990 Municipality of Saalfeld; preliminary investigations; working group for computer-aided building surveys (ACB)

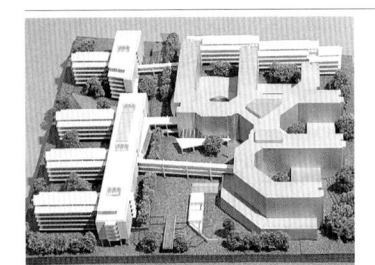

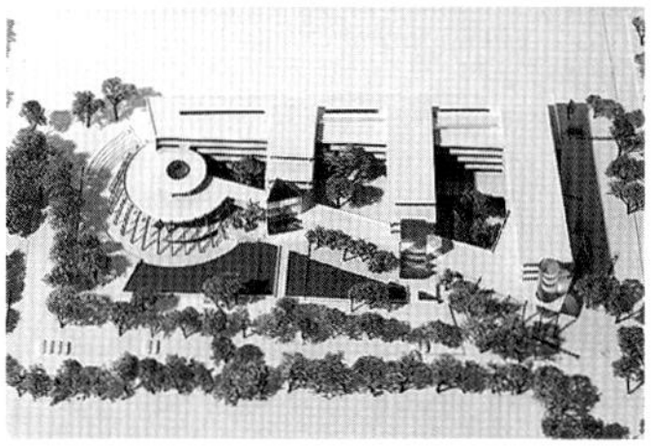

1990 Sparkasse Regensburg, Wettbewerb	1990 Savings Bank in Regensburg; competition
1989 – 1990 Kammerspiele München, Bestandsdokumentation Arge Computergestützte Bauaufnahme ACB	1989 – 1990 Kammerspiele theatre in Munich: survey and report of existing structure; working group for computer-aided building surveys (ACB)
1989 Max-Planck-Institut München, Laborgebäude, Wettbewerb	1989 Max Planck Institute, Munich: laboratory building; competition
1989 Europäisches Patentamt Den Haag, Wettbewerb	1989 European Patent Office, The Hague; competition
1989 Arbeitsamt Meschede, Wettbewerb	1989 Jobcentre, Meschede; competition
1988 – 1989 Bad Feilnbach, Gutachten Blumenhofklinik	1988 – 1989 Bad Feilnbach: report on Blumenhof Clinic
1988 – 1989 Arbeitsamt Augsburg, Hausmeisterhaus	1988 – 1989 Jobcentre, Augsburg: caretaker's house
1988 – 1989 Gut Schwibich, Scheunenausbau	1988 – 1989 Schwibich Estate: conversion of barn
1987 – 1989 Flemingstraße 36, München, Umbau	1987 – 1989 Flemingstrasse 36, Munich: conversion
1984 – 1989 Arbeitsamt Augsburg	1984 – 1989 Jobcentre, Augsburg
1988 Stadthalle Schongau, Wettbewerb	1988 Civic hall in Schongau; competition
1987 – 1988 Klärwerk München I, Gut Großlappen, Faulbehälter, Gestaltung	1987 – 1988 Sewage Treatment Plant Munich I: design of sapropel chambers
1974 – 1988 Gemeinde Burgkirchen, Studie Ortszentrum	1974 – 1988 Municipality of Burgkirchen: study for town centre
1987 BMW Kundenzentrum München, Plangutachten Koch, Benedek + Partner	1987 BMW Customer Centre, Munich: planning report Koch, Benedek + Partner
1987 Künftige Nutzung des Flughafengeländes München Riem, Gutachterliches Verfahren	1987 Future use of Munich Airport site in Riem: advisory report

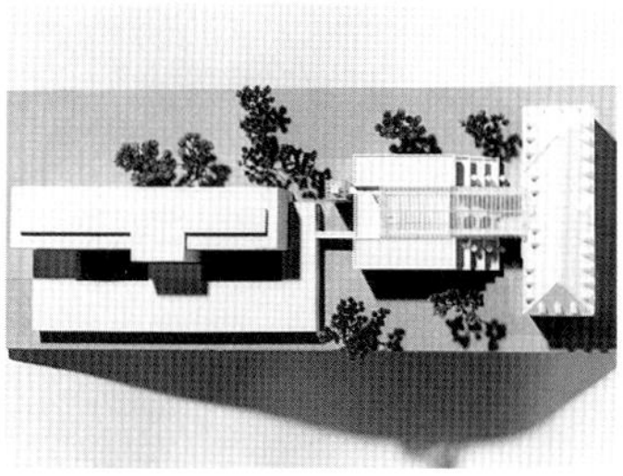

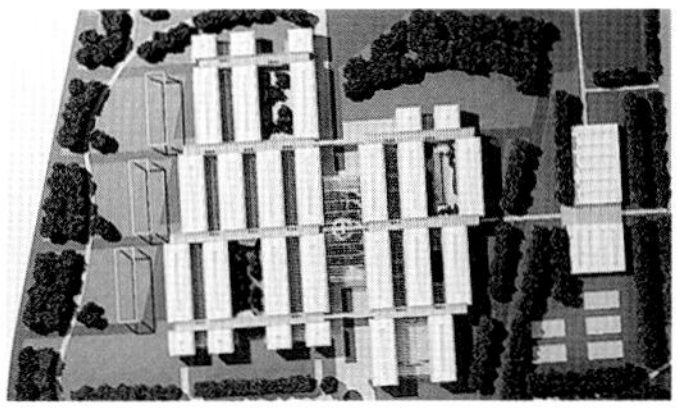

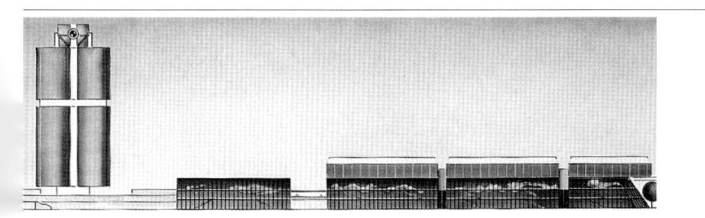

Arbeiten und Projekte 1970 – 2000

1986 – 1987 Rechenzentrum Fernmeldeamt, Perlach Koch, Benedek + Partner	1986 – 1987 Computer centre for telephone office in Perlach, Munich Koch, Benedek + Partner
1985 – 1987 Vereinte Krankenversicherungs AG, Mozartstraße München, Umbau	1985 – 1987 Vereinte Krankenversicherungs AG (health insurance company), Mozartstrasse, Munich: redesign and conversion
1975 – 1987 Stadt Friedberg, Flächennutzungsplan	1975 – 1987 Municipality of Friedberg: land-use plan
1986 Theater Hof, Wettbewerb	1986 Theatre in Hof; competition
1986 Marienhof München, Wettbewerb	1986 Marienhof public square, Munich; competition
1985 – 1986 Siemens AG Augsburg, WS 2 Standort 2	1985 – 1986 Siemens company, Augsburg: computer works, location 2
1973 – 1986 Gemeinde Burgkirchen, Entwicklungsplan	1973 – 1986 Municipality of Burgkirchen: development plan
1985 Stadt Laufen, Friedhof	1985 Municipality of Laufen: cemetery
1985 Herzzentrum München, Wettbewerb 2. Preis	1985 Heart Centre, Munich; competition: 2nd prize
1985 Bayerische Backwaren München, Studie Fabrikneubau	1985 Bayerische Backwaren, Munich: study for new bakery factory
1985 BMW Kurfürstendamm Berlin, Wettbewerb	1985 BMW, Kurfürstendamm, Berlin; competition
1985 Deutsche Botschaft Helsinki, Wettbewerb	1985 German Embassy in Helsinki; competition
1982 – 1985 Wildhaus Ambach, Personalwohngebäude	1982 – 1985 Wildhaus, Ambach: staff housing
1984 Zahnradfabrik Friedrichshafen, Ent- wicklungs- und Konzernzentrum, Plangutachten Koch, Benedek + Partner	1984 Cog factory in Friedrichshafen: development centre and company centre; planning report Koch, Benedek + Partner
1983 – 1984 Haus Fingerhut München, Umbau	1983 – 1984 Fingerhut House, Munich: redesign and conversion

1983 – 1984 BMW München, Werkschutzgebäude Süd Koch, Benedek+Partner	1983 – 1984 BMW, Munich: works security building south Koch, Benedek+Partner
1982 – 1984 Frankona Rückversicherungs AG München, Verwaltungsgebäude	1982 – 1984 Frankona Reinsurance company, Munich: administration building
1975 – 1984 Zentralgebäude Universität Augsburg Benedek, Hagen, Koch, Uhlmann	1975 – 1984 University of Augsburg: central building; Benedek, Hagen, Koch, Uhlmann
1983 Bayerische Vereinsbank Nürnberg, Wettbewerb Ankauf	1983 Bayerische Vereinsbank, Nuremberg; competition: purchase of scheme
1983 Postsparkassenamt München, Wettbewerb 1. Preis Koch, Benedek+Partner	1983 Post Office Savings Bank, Munich; competition: 1st prize; Koch, Benedek+Partner
1983 Goetheinstitut München, Wettbewerb	1983 Goethe Instutute, Munich; competition
1983 Altenheim Percha, Wettbewerb	1983 Old People's Home, Percha; competition
1982 Daimler Benz AG Stuttgart, Wettbewerb 1. Stufe qual.	1982 Daimler Benz company, Stuttgart; competition: 1st stage
1982 Baasel Lasertechnik Starnberg, Studie Bürogebäude	1982 Baasel Lasertechnik, Starnberg: study for office building
1982 Frankona Rückversicherung München, Verwaltungsgebäude, Wettbewerb 1. Rang	1982 Frankona Reinsurance company, Munich; competition for administration building: 1st prize
1981 – 1982 Haus Martens, München	1981 – 1982 Martens House, Munich
1981 – 1982 BMW München, Forschungs- und Ingenieurzentrum, Gutachten	1981 – 1982 BMW, Munich: planning report for research and engineering centre
1979 – 1982 Stadt Laufen, Neubau der Stadthalle	1979 – 1982 Municipality of Laufen: new civic hall
1981 Bundespostministerium Bonn, Wettbewerb Ankauf	1981 Federal Ministry of Post and Telecommunications, Bonn; competition: purchase of scheme
1981 Haus Scholz, Starnberg	1981 Scholz House, Starnberg

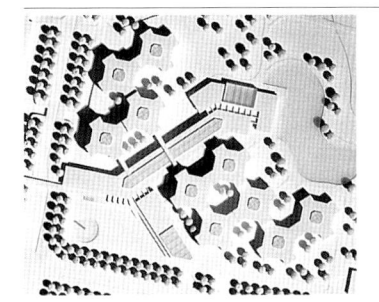

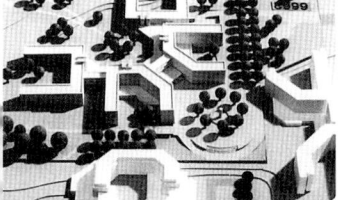

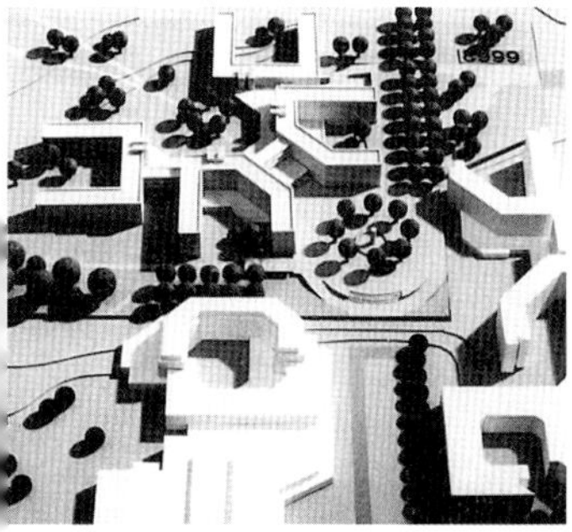

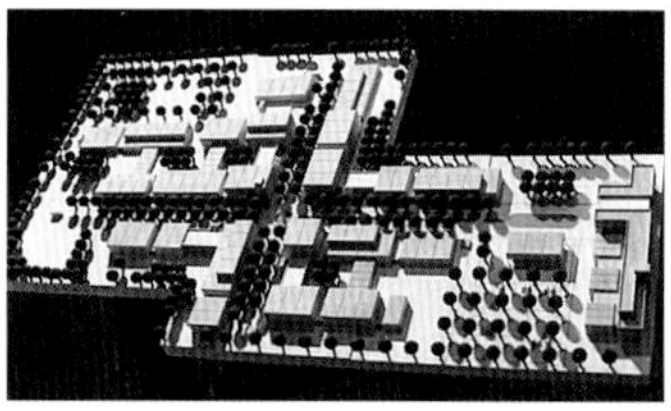

	1981 Landesgewerbeanstalt Nürnberg, Wettbewerb	1981 State Institute for Trade and Industry, Nuremberg; competition
	1981 Krankenhaus St. Josef Regensburg, Wettbewerb	1981 St Joseph's Hospital, Regensburg; competition
	1981 Bebauungsplan Orleansplatz München, Wettbewerb 4. Preis	1981 Orleansplatz development plan, Munich; competition: 4th prize
	1981 Haus Oehl, München	1981 Oehl House, Munich
	1981 Arbeitsamt Augsburg, Wettbewerb 1. Preis	1981 Jobcentre, Augsburg; competition: 1st prize
	1980 – 1981 Stadt Friedberg, Studie Subzentrum Friedberg	1980 – 1981 Municipality of Friedberg: study for Friedberg subcentre
	1977 – 1981 Stadt Neutraubling, Flächennutzungsplan	1977 – 1981 Municipality of Neutraubling: land-use plan
	1980 Stadtwerkszentrale München, Wettbewerb 1. Preis	1980 Municipal Department of Works, Munich; competition: 1st prize
	1979 – 1980 Flemingstraße 36, München, Wohnhaus	1979 – 1980 Flemingstrasse 36, Munich: house
	1977 – 1980 BMW Dingolfing, Verwaltungsgebäude	1977 – 1980 BMW administration building, Dingolfing
	1979 Stadt Neutraubling, Bebauungspläne	1979 Municipality of Neutraubling: development plans
	1974 – 1979 Stadt Kronach, Flächennutzungsplan	1974 – 1979 Municipality of Kronach: land-use plan
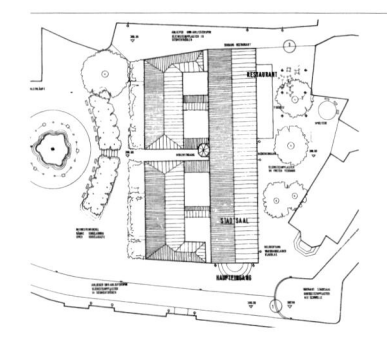	1978 Eichstätt Residenzplatz und Stadthalle, Wettbewerb 2. Preis und Ankauf	1978 Residenzplatz and civic hall, Eichstätt; competition: 2nd prize and purchase of scheme
	1978 ADAC-Hauptverwaltung München, Wettbewerb 2. Rang	1978 ADAC administrative headquarters, Munich; competition: 2nd place
	1978 AUDI-NSU Ingolstadt, Plangutachten	1978 AUDI-NSU, Ingolstadt: planning report

1976 – 1978 Stadt Neutraubling, Ortsplanung	1976 – 1978 Municipality of Neutraubling: town planning
1977 Stadt Laufen, Marienplatzgestaltung	1977 Municipality of Laufen: urban planning of Marienplatz
1977 Altstadtsanierung Ansbach, Plangutachten 2. Preis	1977 Rehabilitation of historic centre of Ansbach; planning report: 2nd prize
1977 Modell Campingplatz Wemding, Wettbewerb 3. Preis	1977 Model campsite, Wemding; competition: 3rd prize
1970 – 1977 Bundesanstalt für Fleischforschung, Kulmbach	1970 – 1977 Federal Institute for Meat Research, Kulmbach
1976 Stadt Laufen, Standortuntersuchung Stadthalle	1976 Municipality of Laufen, site investigation for civic hall
1976 Verwaltungsgebäude BMW Dingolfing, Wettbewerb 2. Preis	1976 BMW administration building, Dingolfing; competition: 2nd prize
1976 Bayerisches Arbeitsministerium München, Wettbewerb	1976 Bavarian State Ministry of Labour, Munich; competition
1976 Landratsamt Dachau, Wettbewerb Ankauf	1976 District administrative office, Dachau; competition: purchase of scheme
1976 Vermessungsamt Traunstein Wettbewerb 3. Preis	1976 Land surveying office, Traunstein; competition: 3rd prize
1976 Flughafen München 2, Betriebs- gelände Nord, Wettbewerb Ankauf	1976 Munich Airport 2: Technical Opera- tions Area North; competition: purchase of scheme
1973 – 1976 Gemeinde Neufahrn, Gemeindeentwicklung	1973 – 1976 Municipality of Neufahrn municipal development
1975 Studie Wochenendhaussiedlungen	1975 Study for weekend-house developments
1975 Flughafen München, Geländenut- zungs- und Funktionsplan mit Hubert Schraud	1975 Munich Airport 2: site use and functional plan, in collaboration with Hubert Schraud
1974 – 1975 Ortszentrum Burgkirchen, Entwurfsstudie	1974 – 1975 Burgkirchen town centre: design study
1974 – 1975 Strukturuntersuchung Münchner Nordosten	1974 – 1975 Structural investigation of north- eastern area of Munich

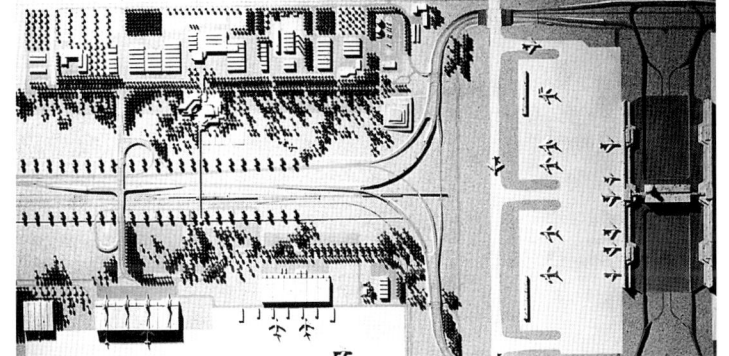

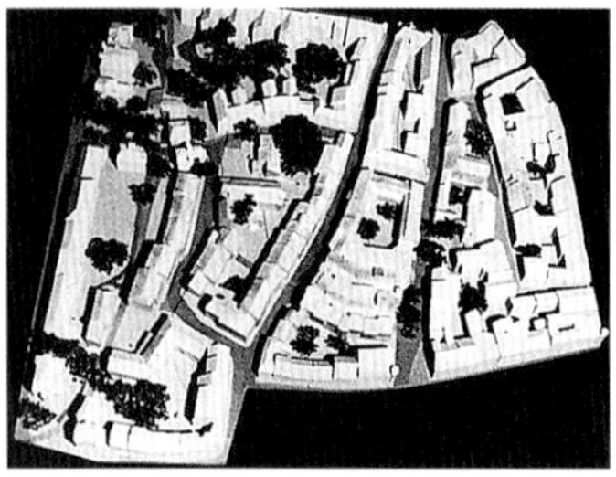

1973 – 1975 Stadt Coburg, Sanierungsgutachten Altstadt	1973 – 1975 Municipality of Coburg: report on rehabilitation of historic city centre
1973 – 1975 Fernwasserversorgung Ortwang, Betriebsgebäude	1973 – 1975 Long-distance water supply, Ortwang: works building
1974 Universität Augsburg, Bebauungsplan Zentrale Bereiche Benedek, Hagen, Koch, Uhlmann	1974 University of Augsburg: development plan for central area; Benedek, Hagen, Koch, Uhlmann
1974 Stadt Kronach, Bebauungsplan Adolf-Kolping-Straße	1974 Municipality of Kronach: development plan for Adolf-Kolping-Strasse
1974 Stadt Tittmoning, Feriendorf	1974 Municipality of Tittmoning: holiday village
1973 – 1974 Stadt Laufen, Gutachten zur Stadtentwicklung und Altstadtsanierung	1973 – 1974 Municipality of Laufen: report on urban development and rehabilitation of historic town centre
1973 – 1974 Stadt Kempten, Sanierungsgutachten	1973 – 1974 Municipality of Kempten: rehabilitation report
1973 – 1974 Poing, Städtebauliches Gutachten	1973 – 1974 Poing: urban planning report
1973 Schottenhamel, München Vorprüfung Wettbewerb	1973 Schottenhamel, Munich: preliminary investigation; competition
1973 Zentrum Universität Bayreuth, Wettbewerb Ankauf	1973 University of Bayreuth, central area; competition: purchase of scheme
1973 Siebenhausen, Vorbereitung Gutachten	1973 Siebenhausen: preliminary studies for report
1973 Zentrum Universität Augsburg, Wettbewerb 2. Preis	1973 University of Augsburg: central area; competition: 2nd prize
1973 Plangutachten Mohren-Schützen, Kempten 1. Rang	1973 Mohren-Schützen, Kempten: planning report; 1st place

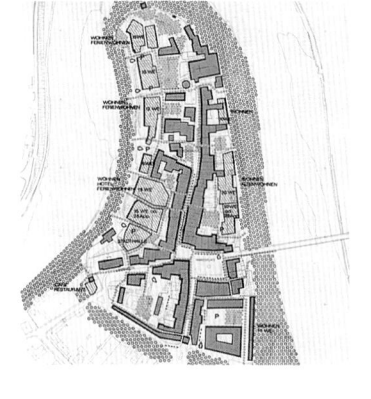

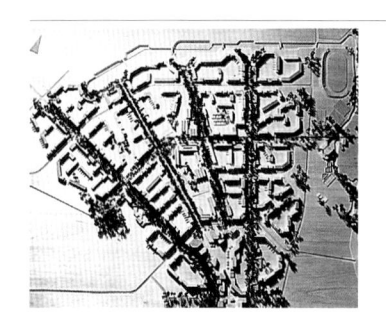

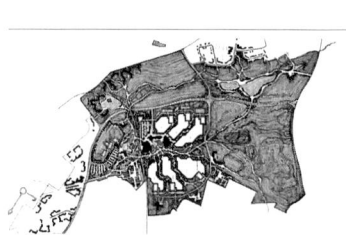

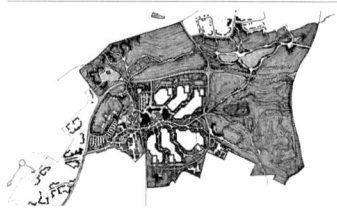

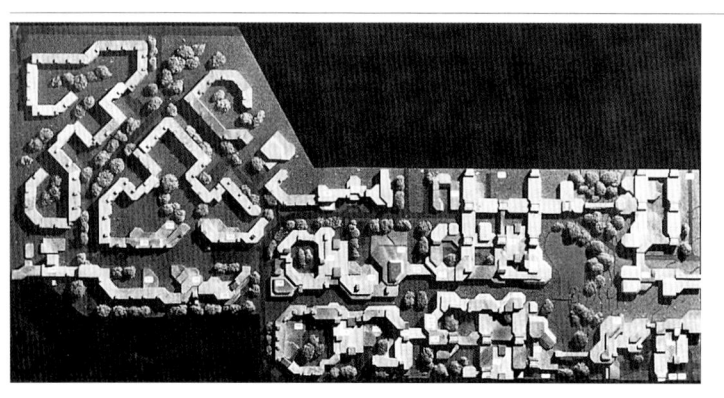

	1973 Ferienzentrum Attenkirchen	1973 Holiday centre in Attenkirchen
	1973 Rathaus Dachau, Wettbewerb	1973 Dachau town hall; competition
	1973 Stadt Ingolstadt, Sanierung, Wettbewerb	1973 Municipality of Ingolstadt: rehabilitation; competition
	1972 – 1973 Altenheim Sparrenlech, Augsburg Koch+Benedek	1972 – 1973 Sparrenlech old people's home, Augsburg; Koch+Benedek
	1972 Standortuntersuchung Oberhaching	1972 Site investigation, Oberhaching
	1972 Gemeinde Eching, Ortsentwicklungsplan	1972 Municipality of Eching: town development plan
	1972 Einfamilienhaus Houdayer	1972 Single-family house (Houdayer House)
	1972 Stadt Memmingen, Vorbereitung städtebaulicher Wettbewerb	1972 Municipality of Memmingen: preliminary work for urban planning competition
	1970 – 1971 Flughafen München 2, Plangutachten zur Gesamtstruktur, mit Studiengruppe Luftfahrt/Aviation Consultants	1970 – 1971 Munich Airport 2: planning report on overall structure as part of Aviation Study Group
	1970 – 1971 Gemeinde Vaterstetten, Struktur- und Bebauungsplan Parsdorf	1970 – 1971 Municipality of Vaterstetten: structural and development plan for Parsdorf
	1970 – 1971 Stadt Augsburg, Bebauungsplan Sparrenlech	1970 – 1971 Municipality of Augsburg: development plan for Sparrenlech
	1970 Ortszentrum Taufkirchen, Wettbewerb Ankauf	1970 Taufkirchen town centre; competition: purchase of scheme
	1970 Rathaus Taufkirchen, Wettbewerb 1. Preis	1970 Taufkirchen town hall; competition: 1st prize
	1970 Bundesanstalt für Fleischforschung, Kulmbach, Wettbewerb 1. Preis	1970 Federal Institute for Meat Research, Kulmbach; competition: 1st prize

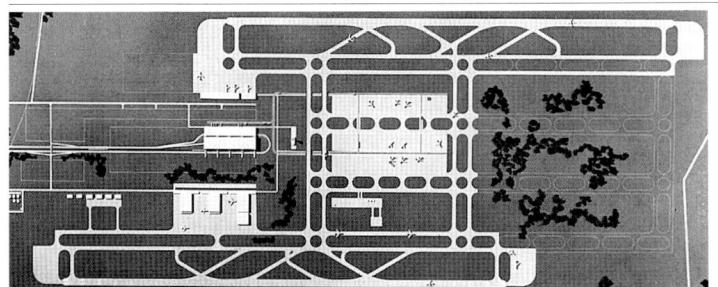

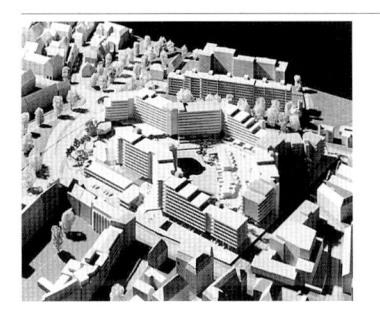

Norbert Koch

Regierungsbaumeister,
Architekt BDA
Government architect, BDA

1939	geboren in Würzburg
1959 – 1965	Architekturstudium an der Technischen Universität München
1965	Diplom an der Technischen Universität München
1965 – 1967	Mitarbeit im Büro Prof. Kurt Ackermann, München
1967 – 1968	Referendarausbildung im Vertiefungsgebiet Städtebau
1968	2. Staatsexamen
1969 – 1972	Leiter des Instituts für Städtebau, Landesplanung und Raumordnung an der Technischen Universität München
seit 1970	eigenes Architektur- und Stadtplanungsbüro
seit 1981	Partnerschaft mit Wolf-Dieter Drohn und Michael Schneider
seit 1988	Partnerschaft mit Wolfgang Voigt
1939	Born in Würzburg
1959 – 1965	Studies architecture at University of Technology, Munich
1965	Diploma at University of Technology, Munich
1965 – 1967	Assistant in office of Prof. Kurt Ackermann, Munich
1967 – 1968	Civil service training: extension studies in urban planning
1968	Second state examinations
1969 – 1972	Head of Institute for Urban, Regional and Environmental Planning at University of Technology, Munich
since 1970	Own architectural and urban planning practice
since 1981	Partnership with Wolf-Dieter Drohn and Michael Schneider
since 1988	Partnership with Wolfgang Voigt

Wolf-Dieter Drohn

Dipl.-Ing. Architekt
Dipl.-Ing., Architect

1940	geboren in Königsberg/Ostpreußen
1959 – 1965	Architekturstudium an der Technischen Universität München mit einjährigem Praktikum bei Prof. Kraemer, Braunschweig
1965	Diplom an der Technischen Universität München
1965	Freie Mitarbeit am Lehrstuhl Prof. Hassenpflug, München
1966 – 1969	Mitarbeit in Architekturbüros in Caracas, Venezuela
1969 – 1970	Organisatorische Bauplanung im Quickborner Team, Quickborn
1970 – 1981	Partner der Congena, Gesellschaft für Planung und Organisation, München, Organisatorische Bauplanung vorwiegend für große Verwaltungsbauten
seit 1981	Partnerschaft mit Norbert Koch und Michael Schneider
seit 1988	Partnerschaft mit Wolfgang Voigt
1940	Born in Königsberg, East Prussia (today, Kaliningrad)
1959 – 1965	Studies architecture at University of Technology, Munich, with one-year practical training in the office of Prof. Kraemer, Brunswick
1965	Diploma at University of Technology, Munich
1965	Freelance work in university department of Prof. Hassenpflug, Munich
1966 – 1969	Assistant in architectural offices in Caracas, Venezuela
1969 – 1970	Organizational construction planning in Quickborner Team, Quickborn
1970 – 1981	Partner in Congena, company for planning and organization, Munich: organizational construction planning mainly for large administration buildings
since 1981	Partnership with Norbert Koch and Michael Schneider
since 1988	Partnership with Wolfgang Voigt

Biografien der Partner
Biographies of partners

Michael Schneider

Dipl.-Ing. Architekt
Dipl.-Ing., Architect

1944	geboren in München
1967 – 1973	Architekturstudium an der Technischen Universität München
1973	Diplom an der Technischen Universität München
1973 – 1974	Freie Mitarbeit bei Prof. Helmut Gebhard, Technische Universität München
1974 – 1981	Mitarbeiter bei Norbert Koch, München
seit 1981	Partnerschaft mit Norbert Koch und Wolf-Dieter Drohn
seit 1988	Partnerschaft mit Wolfgang Voigt
1944	Born in Munich
1967 – 1973	Studies architecture at University of Technology, Munich
1973	Diploma at University of Technology, Munich
1973 – 1974	Freelance work with Prof. Helmut Gebhard, University of Technology, Munich
1974 – 1981	Assistant in office of Norbert Koch, Munich
since 1981	Partnership with Norbert Koch and Wolf-Dieter Drohn
since 1988	Partnership with Wolfgang Voigt

Wolfgang Voigt

Dipl.-Ing. Architekt BDA
Dipl.-Ing., Architect, BDA

1952	geboren in Bayreuth
1972 – 1977	Architekturstudium an der Technischen Universität München
1977	Diplom an der Technischen Universität München
1977 – 1987	Mitarbeiter bei Norbert Koch, München
seit 1988	Partnerschaft mit Norbert Koch, Wolf-Dieter Drohn und Michael Schneider
1952	Born in Bayreuth
1972 – 1977	Studies architecture at University of Technology, Munich
1977	Diploma at University of Technology, Munich
1977 – 1987	Assistant in office of Norbert Koch, Munich
since 1988	Partnership with Norbert Koch, Wolf-Dieter Drohn and Michael Schneider

Projektpartner

Project partners

Christian Bendomir
Dipl.-Ing. Architekt
Dipl.-Ing., Architect

Susanne Moog
Dipl.-Ing. (FH) Innenarchitektin
Dipl.-Ing., Interior Designer

Astrid Eggensberger
Dipl.-Ing. Stadtplanerin
Dipl.-Ing., Urban Planner

Richard Wolf
Dipl.-Ing. Architekt
Dipl.-Ing., Architect

Stefan Maisch
Dipl.-Ing. (FH) Architekt
Dipl.-Ing., Architect

Jürgen Zschornack
Dipl.-Ing. Architekt
Dipl.-Ing., Architect

Mitarbeiter 1970 – 2000

Assistants 1970 – 2000

Abels Udo
Abt Almut
Abt Thomas
Amuser Christa
Apel Sigrid
Armstorfer Franz Josef

Bachmeier Jeanette
Bader Gerald
Bendomir Christian
Bendomir Michaela
Bergmann Beate
Bergmann Michael
Braun Thomas
Bröker Friedrich
Bünnagel Udo
Büscher Andreas
Bullok Gilbert
Bungert-Stüttgen Angelika
Burkhard Caroline
Buschmann de Bautista Elena

Chrisam Antoinette
Christ Ursula
Cisek Ioana
Clemente Alexandra
Cremers Jan

Damm Christoph
Demal Stephanie
Dieker Andrea
Dietrich Annett
Dietze Wolfgang
Dubyk Kai
Düchting-Loose Monika

Eberle Waltraut
Eggensberger Astrid
Ehling Annemarie
Engel Erhard
Enzmann Christian
Ernst Peter

Feldmann Sebastian
Felsner Franz
Flach Margot
Freudenfeld Klaus
Fritzberg Florian
von Fuchs-Nordhoff Britta

Geist Thomas
Gericke Klaus

Giesecke Christa
Göhler Anja
Graf Dieter
Grygar Klaus

Habelt Claudia
Hagen Volker
Hein Britta
Hartmann Fenn-Yvonne
Hermann Ulrich
Hiemer Richard
Hösl Ursula
Hörnig Bernhard
Hofmaier Werner
Horneff Christl
Hubert Fritz
Hutter Monika

Idehen Godwin

Keidel Michael
Keller Kilian
Knab Jürgen
Kögl Peter
Kotte Carsten
Kronenbitter Benedikt
Krizik Alexander
Kunze Stefan
Kupka Audrey

Langer-Fuchs Hermina
Leckband Poul
Lehmann-Dronke Johannes
Leitgeb Christoph
Lindström Jan
Linke Jürgen

Maisch Stefan
Markert Hans
Markl Martin
Meier Josef
Möckel Burkhardt
Molnar Endre
Moog Susanne
Moum Anita
Mühlbauer Claudia
Müller Erich
Müller Peter-Andreas
Musierowicz Magdalena

Nery-Veit Alessandra
Neudecker Sylvia

Noll Anton
Novotny Rudolf

Odoj Monika

Pahl-Leclerque Silvia
Penthlehner Richard
Peron Mechthild
Plöckl Jutta
Pöppl Monika
Posch Barbara
Prechtl Christian

Rathjens Helga
Rechenauer Robert
Rehn Markus
Reimann Jürgen
Rembold Irene
Repges Stephan
Riedhammer Walter
Rogler Angelika
Roll Bernhard
Rose Nadine
Rosen Horst
Rosenbauer Peter
Roßner Stefan-Jörg

Sames Henning
Schabel Barbara
Schäper Katja
Schaugg Elmar
von Schickfus Stephan
Schiffer-Wortmann Cornelia
Schilling Daniela
Schilling Thomas
Schimmel Birgit
Schlömer Karen
Schmidt Ingrid
Schmidt Jutta
Schmidt Katja
Schneider Andreas
Schneider Michael
Schönenberger Sigrid
Schott Katharina
Schraud Hubert
Schulz Thomas
Schwedler Katrin
Sedlacek Helena
Seliger Rolf
Sjaaf Adjie
Späth Christoph
Spenner Elisabeth

Stangl Regine
Steinberger Christina
Stepper Rita
Stöckle Gabriele
Szuggar Heinz

Tampé Christel
Tesche Tasja
Tomásek Ondrej
Tränkner Bernd
Tymke Gregor

Voigt Wolfgang

Wahlich Joachim
Walter Markus
Weber Günther
Weinlich Cornelia
Wild-Dicke Birgit
Wöckel Ariane Alice
Wolf Elke
Wolf Richard
Woltmann Roland

Zehfuß Ulrich
Zinglersen Peer
Zipfel Karen
Zschornack Jürgen

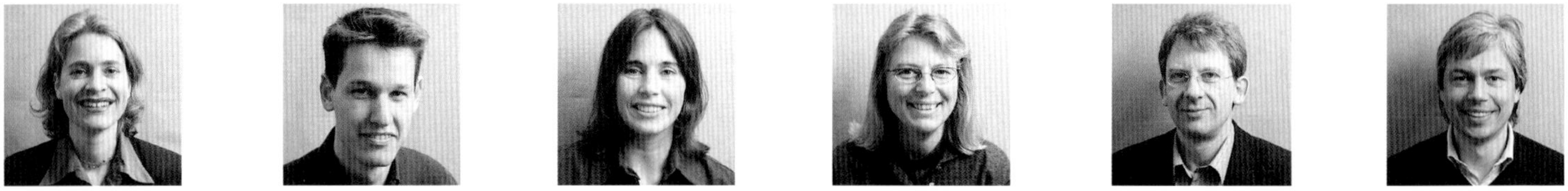
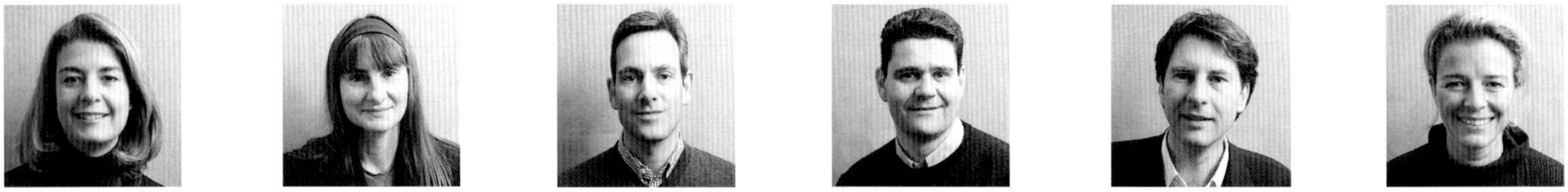
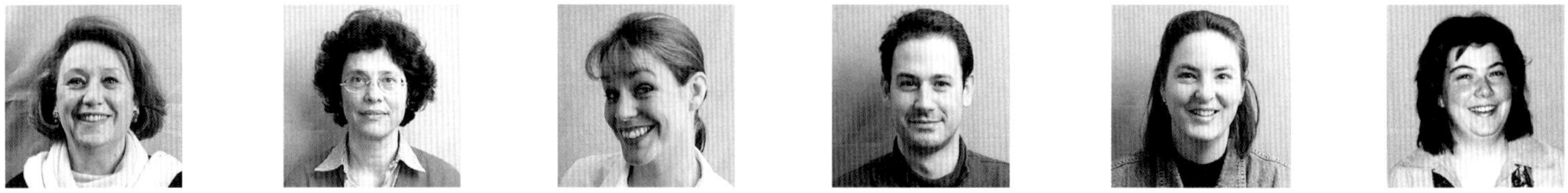
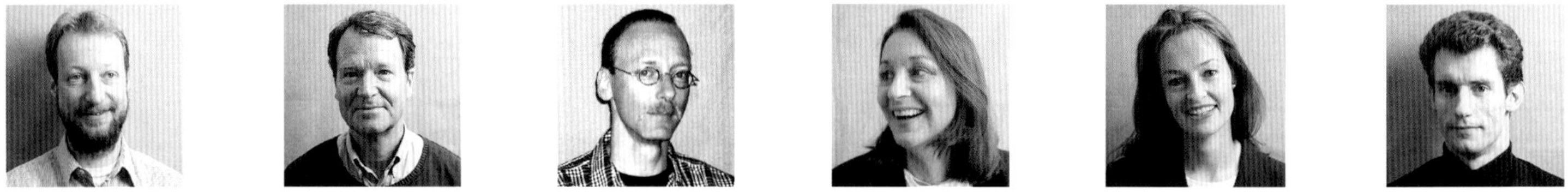
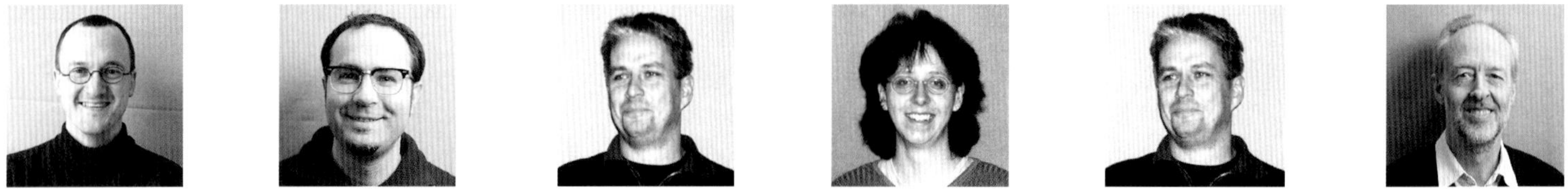
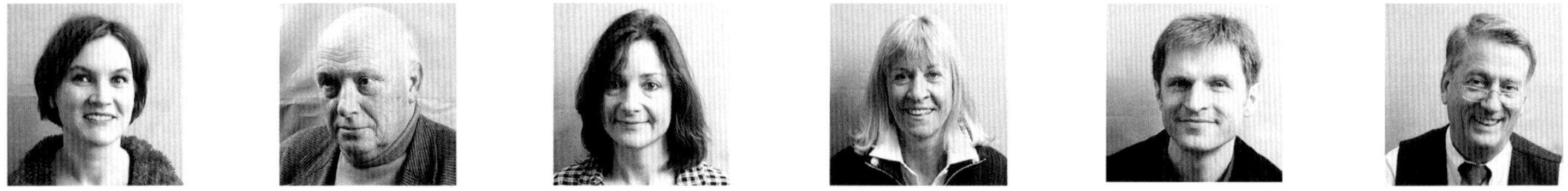
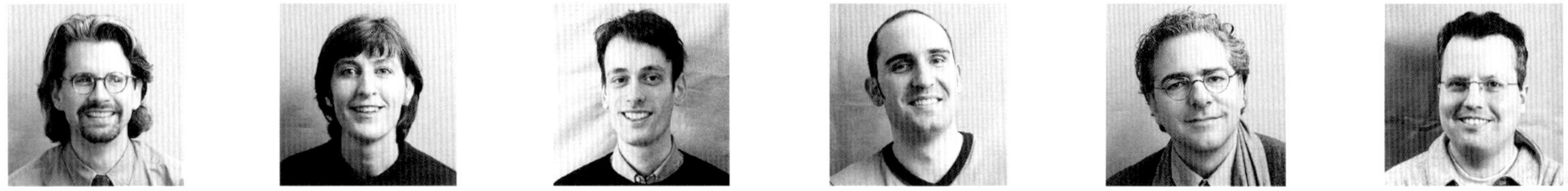

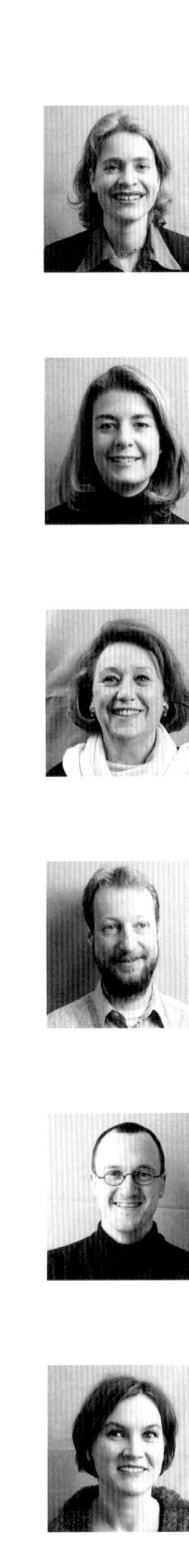

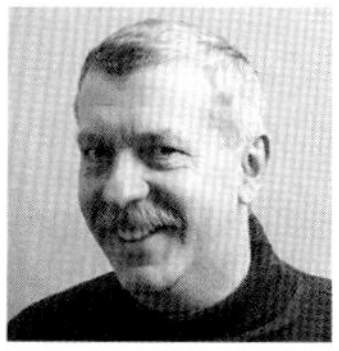
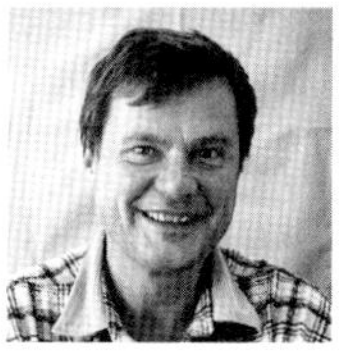
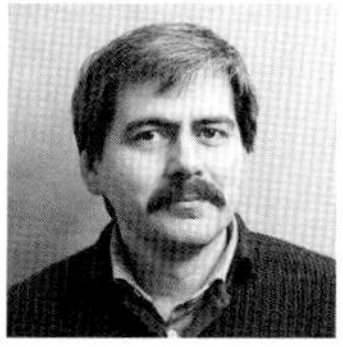
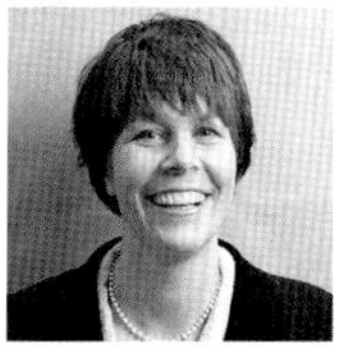
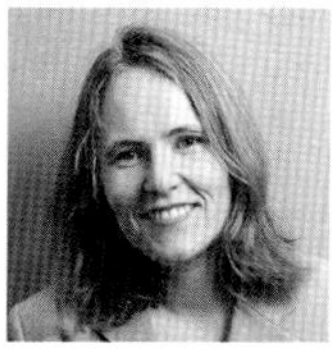
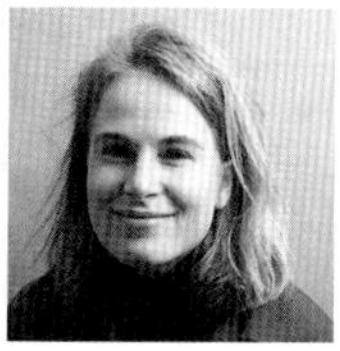
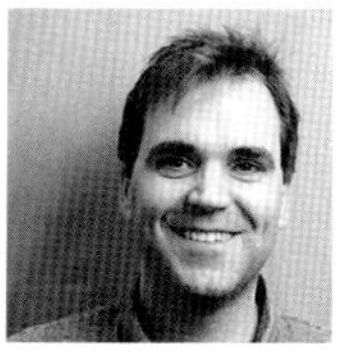
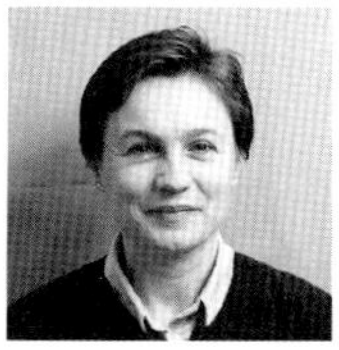
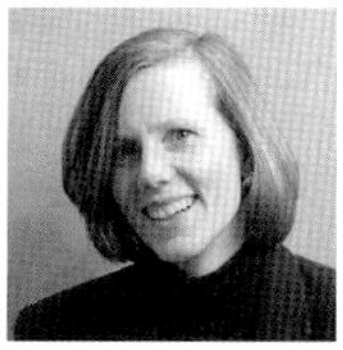
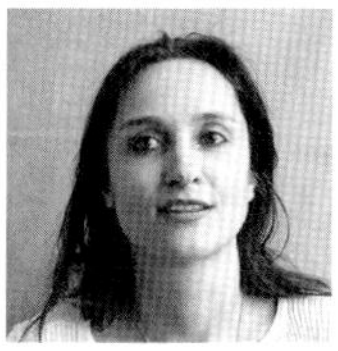
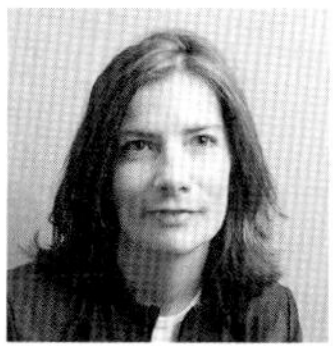
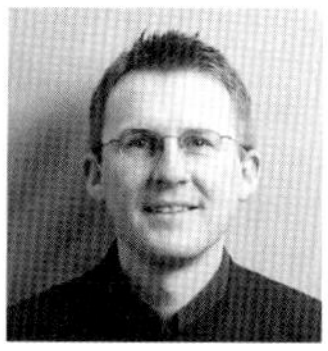
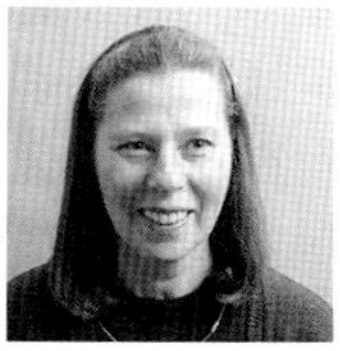
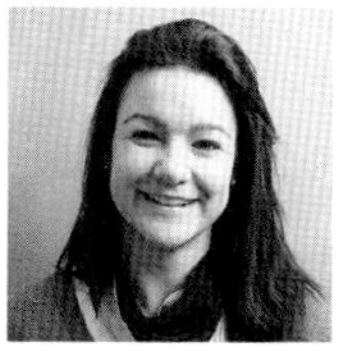
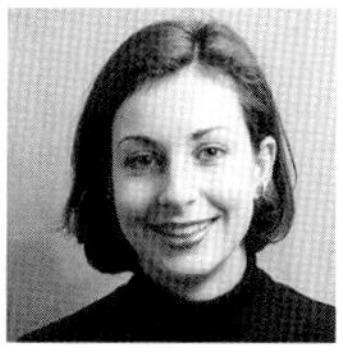
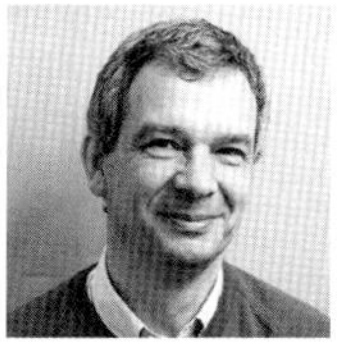
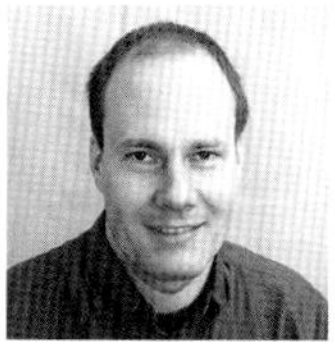
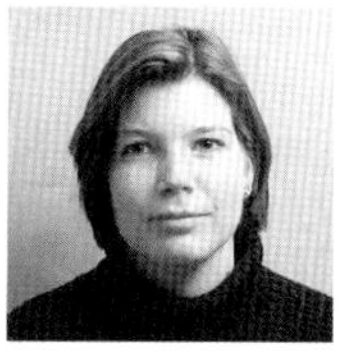
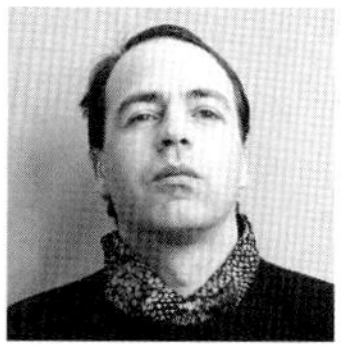
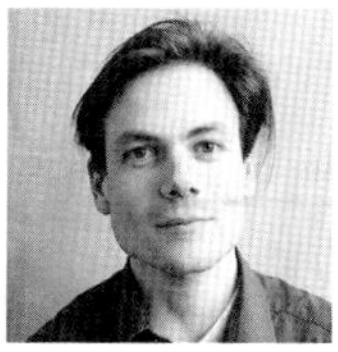
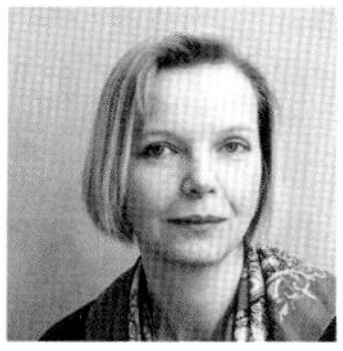
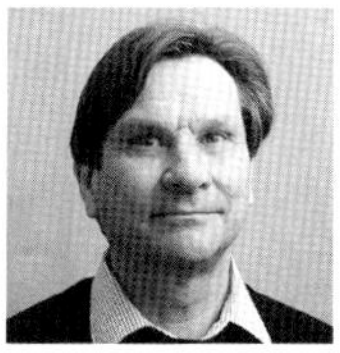
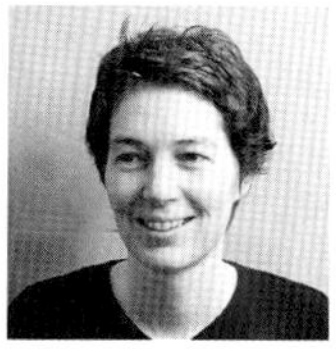
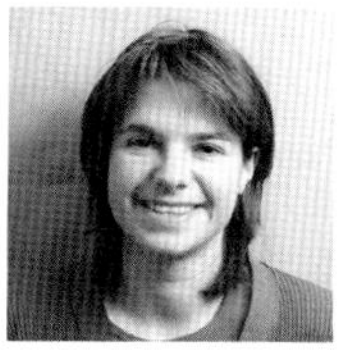
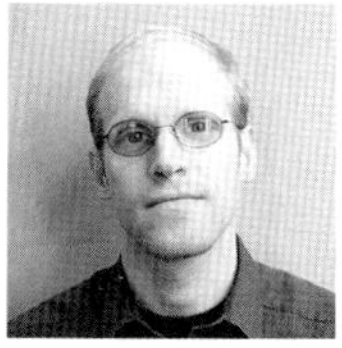
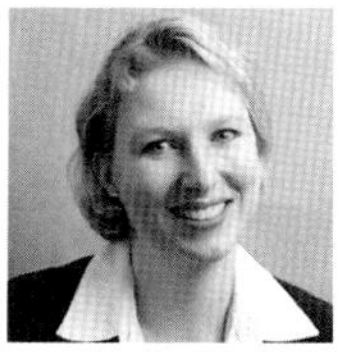
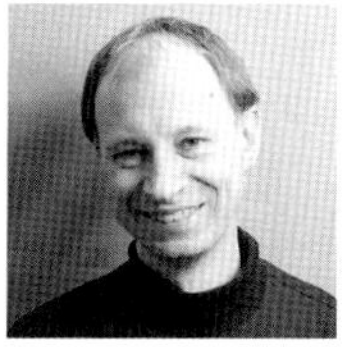
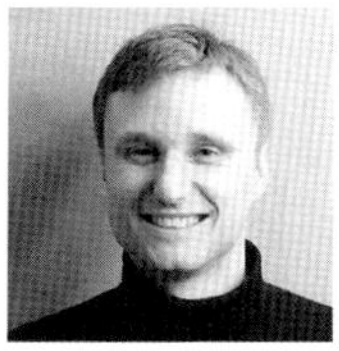
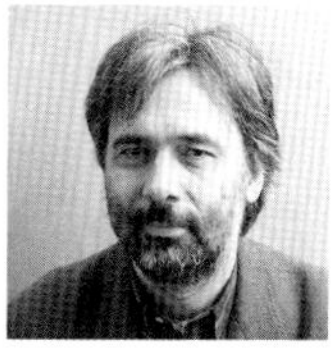
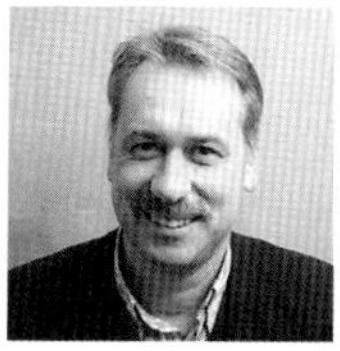
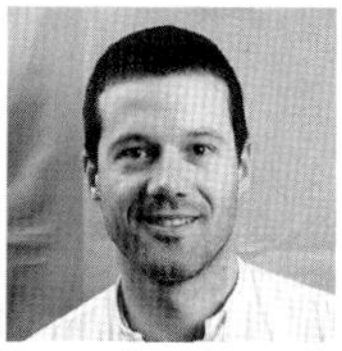
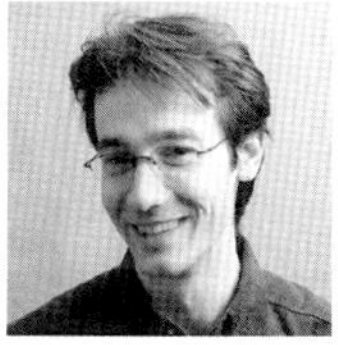
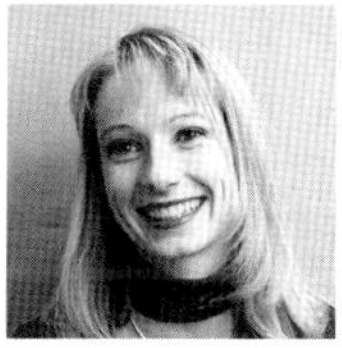
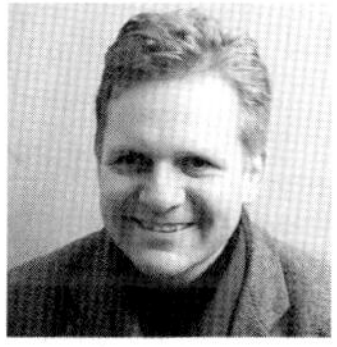
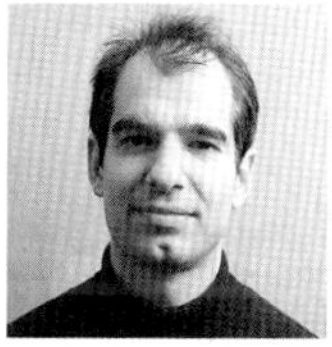
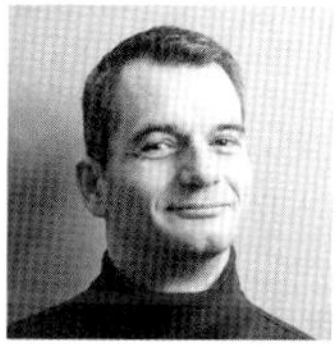
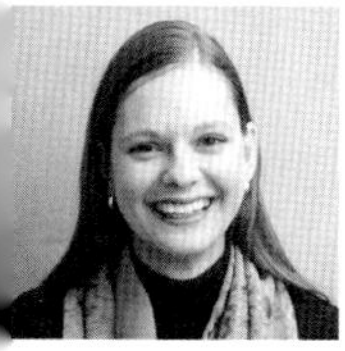
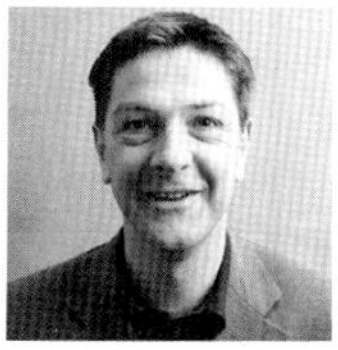

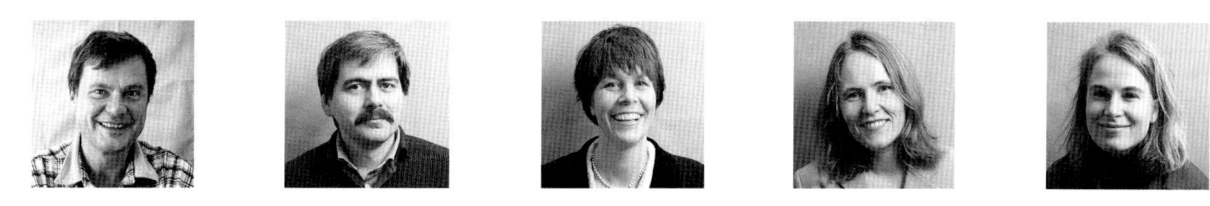

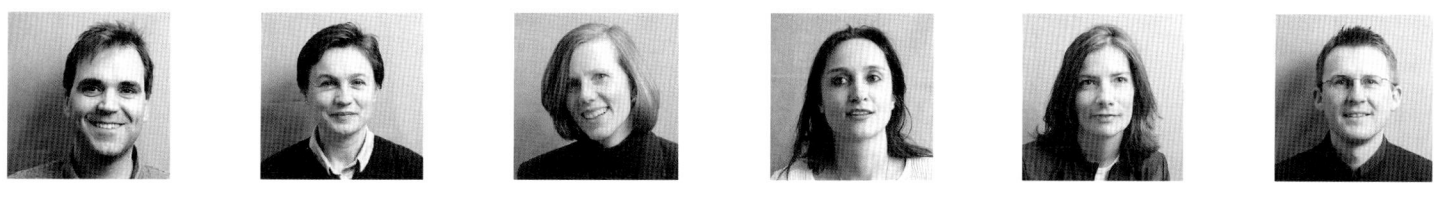

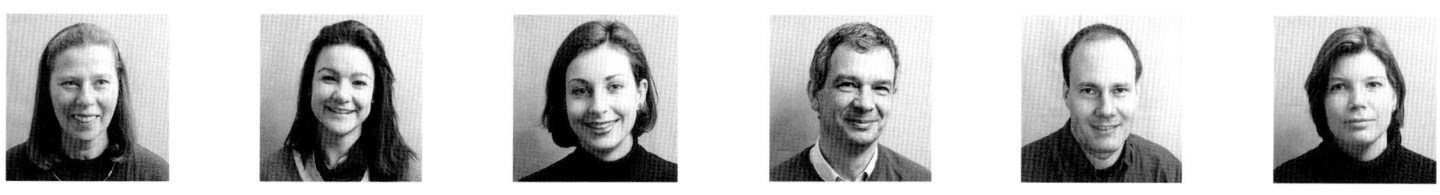

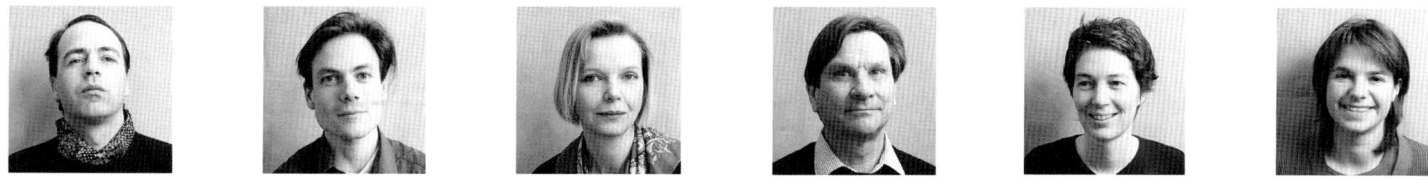

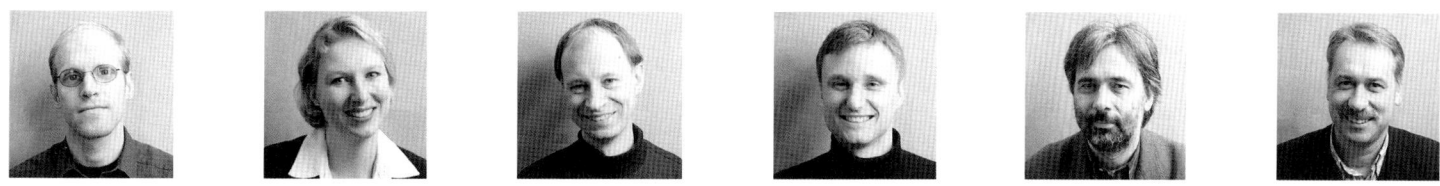

A CIP catalogue record for this book is available from the Library of Congress, Washington D.C., USA.

Deutsche Bibliothek Cataloging-in-Publication Data:
Koch + Partner <München>:
Koch + Partner : Architekten und Stadtplaner ; 1970 - 2000 / Übers. aus dem Dt. ins Engl. von Peter Green. - Basel ; Boston ; Berlin : Birkhäuser, 2000
ISBN 3-7643-6213-8

This work is subject to copyright. All rights are reserved, whether the whole or part of the material is concerned, specifically the rights of translation, reprinting, re-use of illustrations, recitation, broadcasting, reproduction on microfilms or in other ways, and storage in data bases.
For any kind of use, permission of the copyright owner must be obtained.

© 2000 Birkhäuser – Publishers for Architecture,
P.O. Box 133, CH-4010 Basel, Switzerland.
Printed on acid-free paper produced from chlorine-free pulp. TCF ∞

Printed in Germany
ISBN 3-7643-6213-8

9 8 7 6 5 4 3 2 1

Impressum

Konzeption und Redaktion / Concept and editing	Astrid Eggensberger, Koch + Partner
Einführung / Introduction	Wolfgang Jean Stock, München
Thematische Texte / Thematic listing texts	Norbert Koch
Projekttexte / Project texts	Koch + Partner
Beratung und Lektorat / Editing consultant	Johannes Determann, München
Übersetzung / Translation	Peter Green, München/London
Graphische Gestaltung und Satz / Design and typesetting	Designgruppe Flath & Frank, München
Reinzeichnungen / Drawings	Friederike Michalek, München

Fotonachweis / Photocredits

Fotograf / Photographers	Seite / page
Volker Barthold, Leipzig	64
Luftbild-Bertram, München-Haar	78, 115, 180
Can Cobanli, München	23, 38, 42, 83, 89, 171
Stadtverwaltung Dresden	87, 60
H. G. Esch, Schüco International KG, Bielefeld	102
Petra Flath, München	Titelseite, 20, 21, 31, 32, 33, 35, 37, 40, 44, 45, 46, 47, 52, 55, 63, 64, 66, 68, 69, 75, 90, 92, 94, 95, 97, 100, 102, 103, 104, 106, 107, 114, 116, 117, 119, 120, 122, 123, 124, 125, 171, 172, 173, 174, 175, 176, 184
Sabine Grudda, München	118
Florian Heine, München	172
Rolf Heselbarth, Dresden	58
Uschi Horz, München	30, 34, 36, 110, 170
Alex Kempkens	Titelseite, 138, 140, 142, 143, 144, 146, 147
Foto Klarner, Panitzsch bei Leipzig	Titelseite, 70, 71, 72, 74, 75, 76
Koch + Partner, München	37, 44, 45, 83, 102, 148, 172, 173, 177, 179, 181, 186, 188, 189
Landeshauptstadt München, Städtisches Vermessungsamt	48
Dieter Leistner, ARTUR, Köln	126, 127
Gottfried Lobmayr, Laufen	135
Photographiedepot Frank-Heinrich Müller, Leipzig	96, 97
Stefan Müller-Naumann, München	114, 118
Sigrid Neubert, München	81, 82, 177, 178
Klaus Uhlmann, München	78, 136, 176, 177, 178
vize, Prag	Titelseite, 14, 16, 22, 24, 26, 27, 46, 170
Günther und Eva von Voithenberg, München	18, 19, 130, 137, 178, 179, 180, 181, 182, 183
wettbewerbe aktuell, Verlagsgesellschaft, Freiburg	178, 179, 182
Hans-Joachim Wuthenow, Berlin	174

Die Autorschaft einiger Fotos war zu Redaktionsschluss noch ungeklärt. Verwendungs- und Veröffentlichungsrechte bleiben gewahrt.

At the time of going to press, it was not possible to determine the autorship of certain photos. Use and publication rights remain unaffected.